The Splendor of Azalea Garden

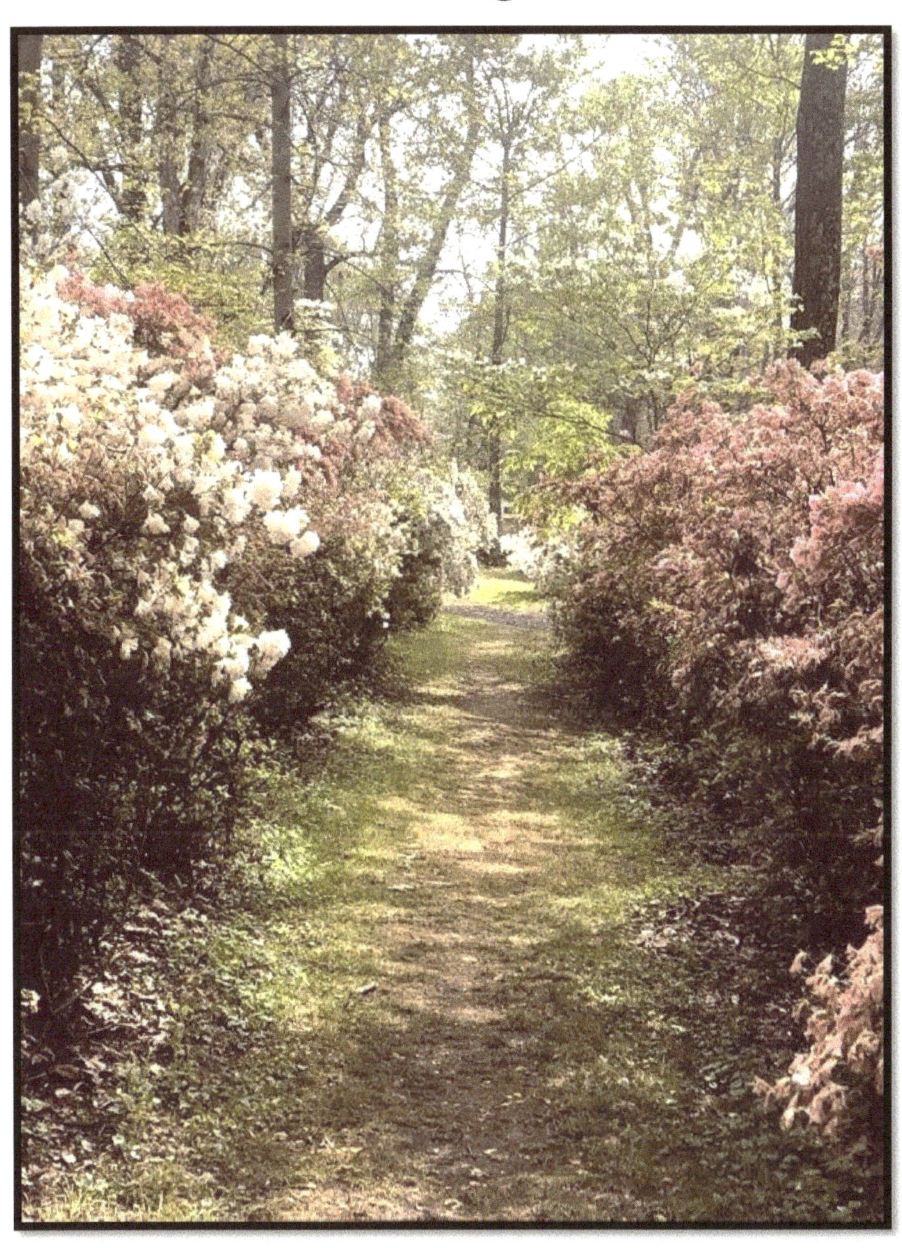

Wynette McKenzie

Publisher's Note: The photographs in this book were taken at Brighton Azalea Garden in Brookeville, Maryland.

.

All photographs were taken by Wynette McKenzie.

The Splendor of Azalea Garden© by Wynette McKenzie 2022

Photographs© by Wynette McKenzie

ISBN 978-1-941726-54-9

Five Little Angels Publishing.

All photographs by Wynette McKenzie.

Copyright 2022 by Five Little Angels, LLC.
Scenic Photography.

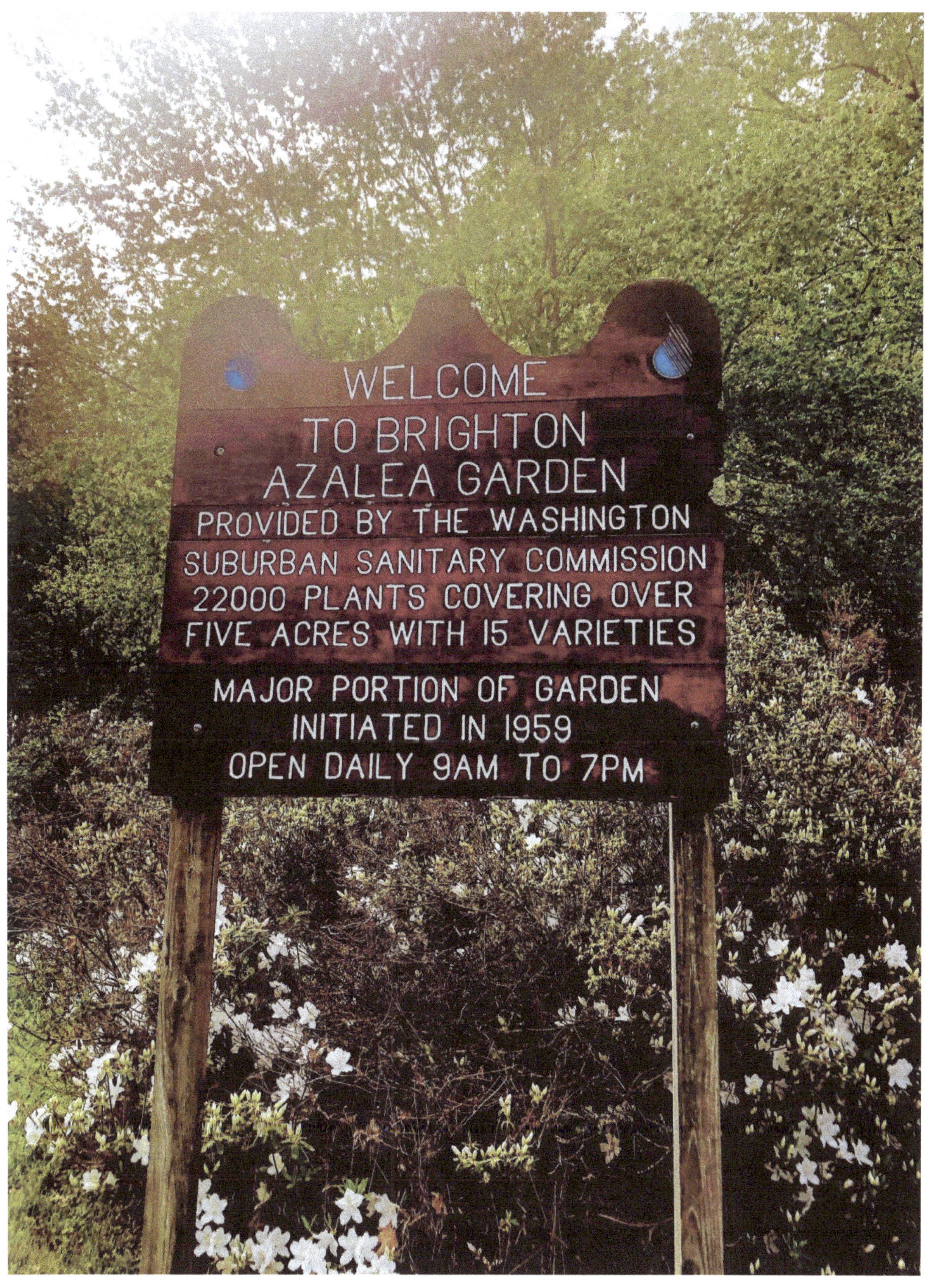

WELCOME
TO BRIGHTON
AZALEA GARDEN
PROVIDED BY THE WASHINGTON
SUBURBAN SANITARY COMMISSION
22000 PLANTS COVERING OVER
FIVE ACRES WITH 15 VARIETIES
MAJOR PORTION OF GARDEN
INITIATED IN 1959
OPEN DAILY 9AM TO 7PM

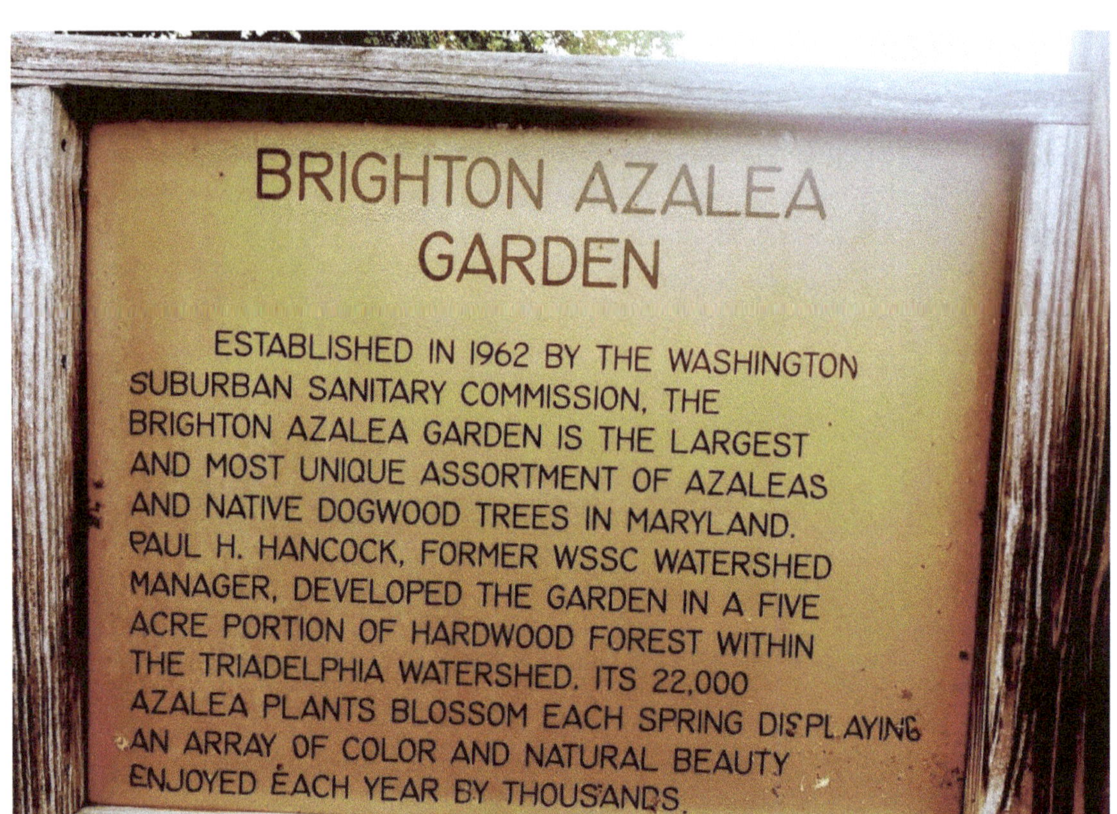

BRIGHTON AZALEA
GARDEN

ESTABLISHED IN 1962 BY THE WASHINGTON
SUBURBAN SANITARY COMMISSION, THE
BRIGHTON AZALEA GARDEN IS THE LARGEST
AND MOST UNIQUE ASSORTMENT OF AZALEAS
AND NATIVE DOGWOOD TREES IN MARYLAND.
PAUL H. HANCOCK, FORMER WSSC WATERSHED
MANAGER, DEVELOPED THE GARDEN IN A FIVE
ACRE PORTION OF HARDWOOD FOREST WITHIN
THE TRIADELPHIA WATERSHED. ITS 22,000
AZALEA PLANTS BLOSSOM EACH SPRING DISPLAYING
AN ARRAY OF COLOR AND NATURAL BEAUTY
ENJOYED EACH YEAR BY THOUSANDS.

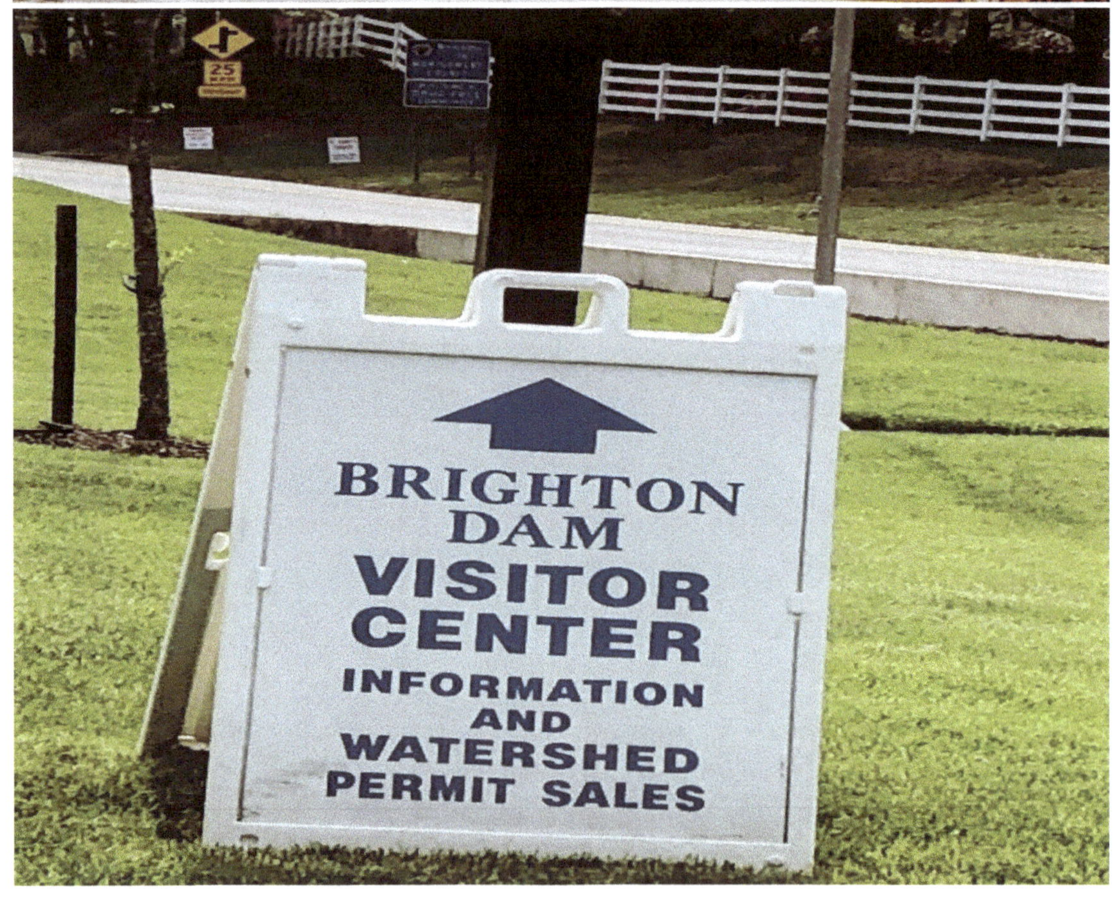

BRIGHTON
DAM
VISITOR
CENTER
INFORMATION
AND
WATERSHED
PERMIT SALES

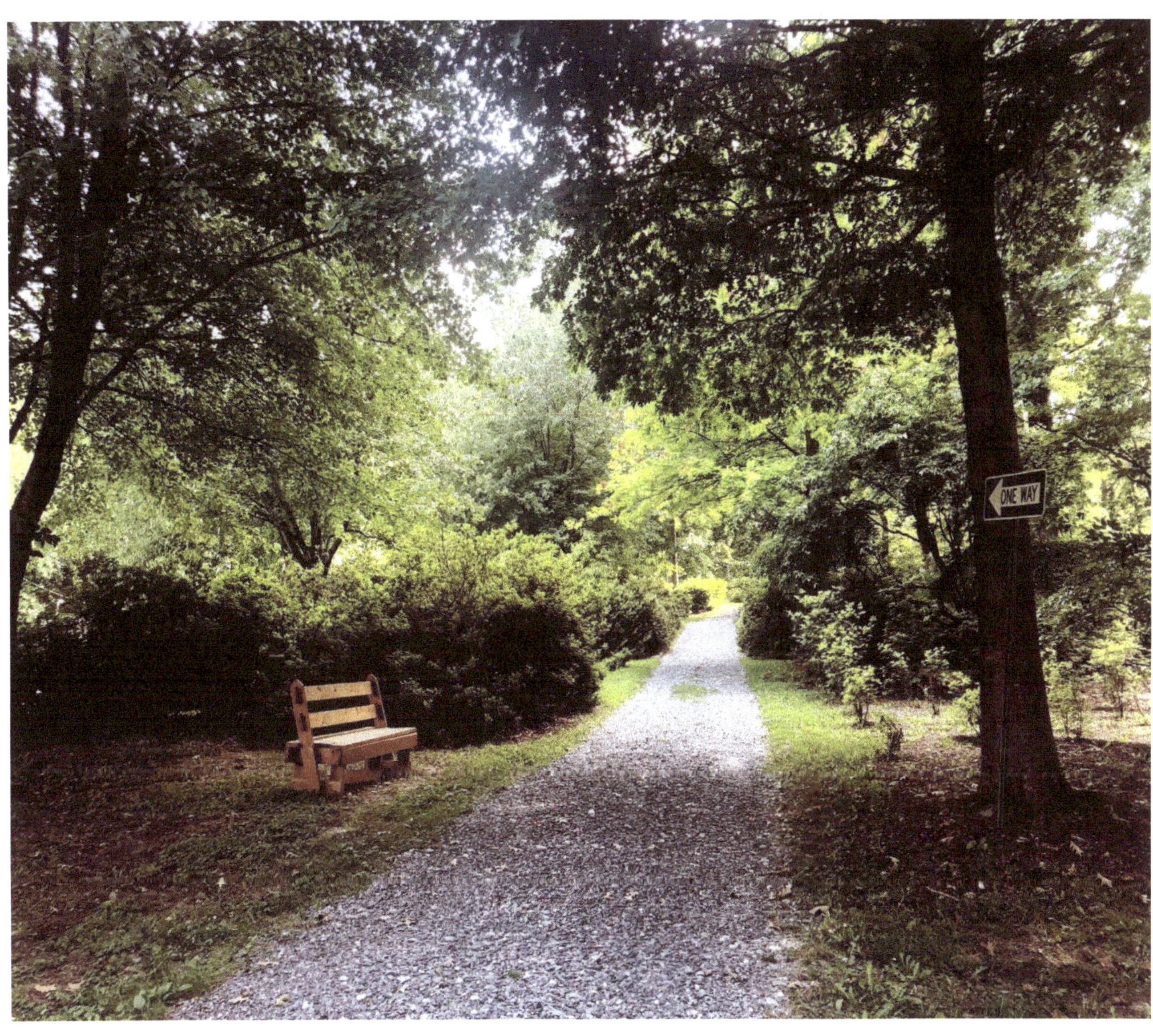
ONE WAY

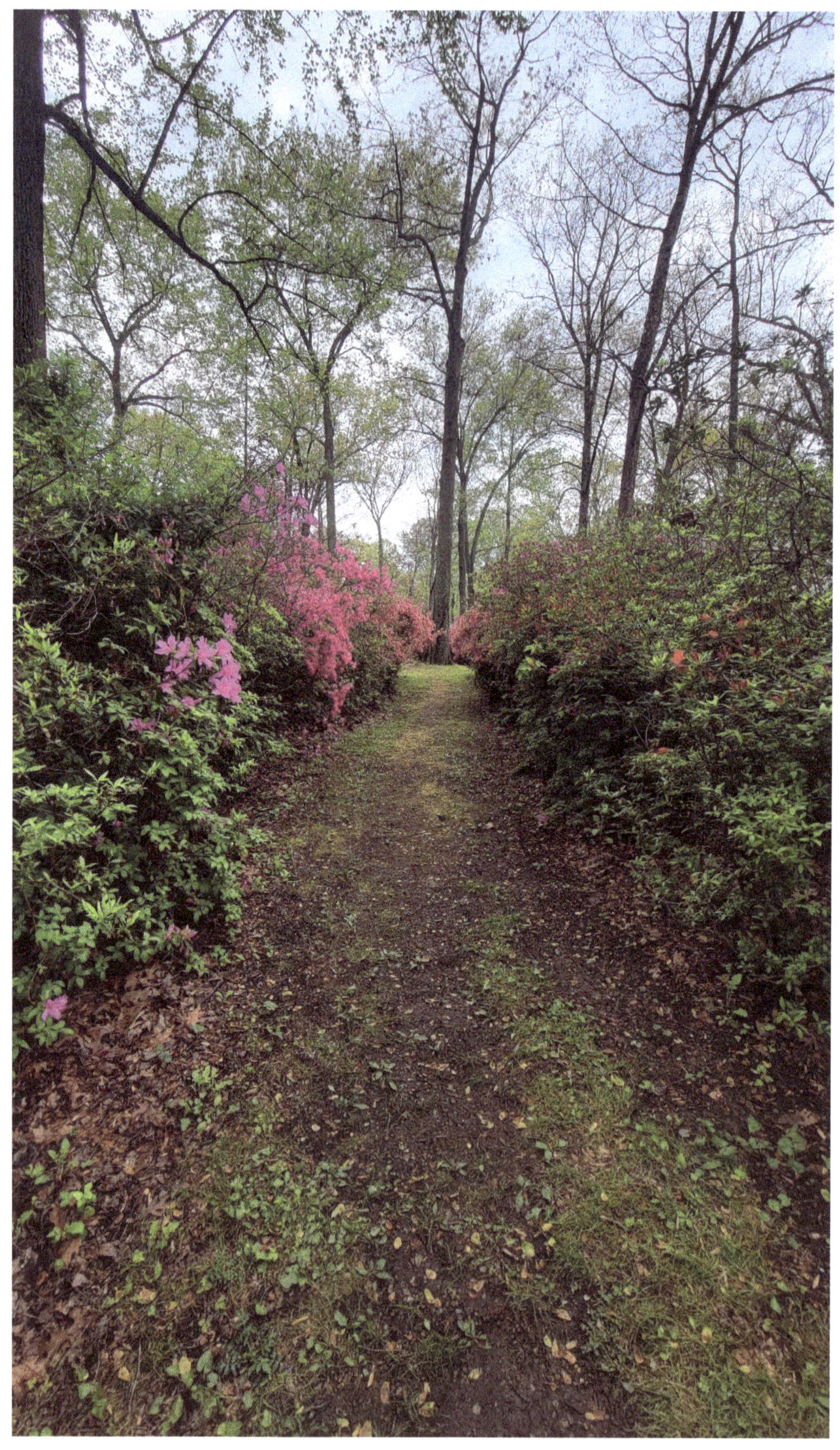

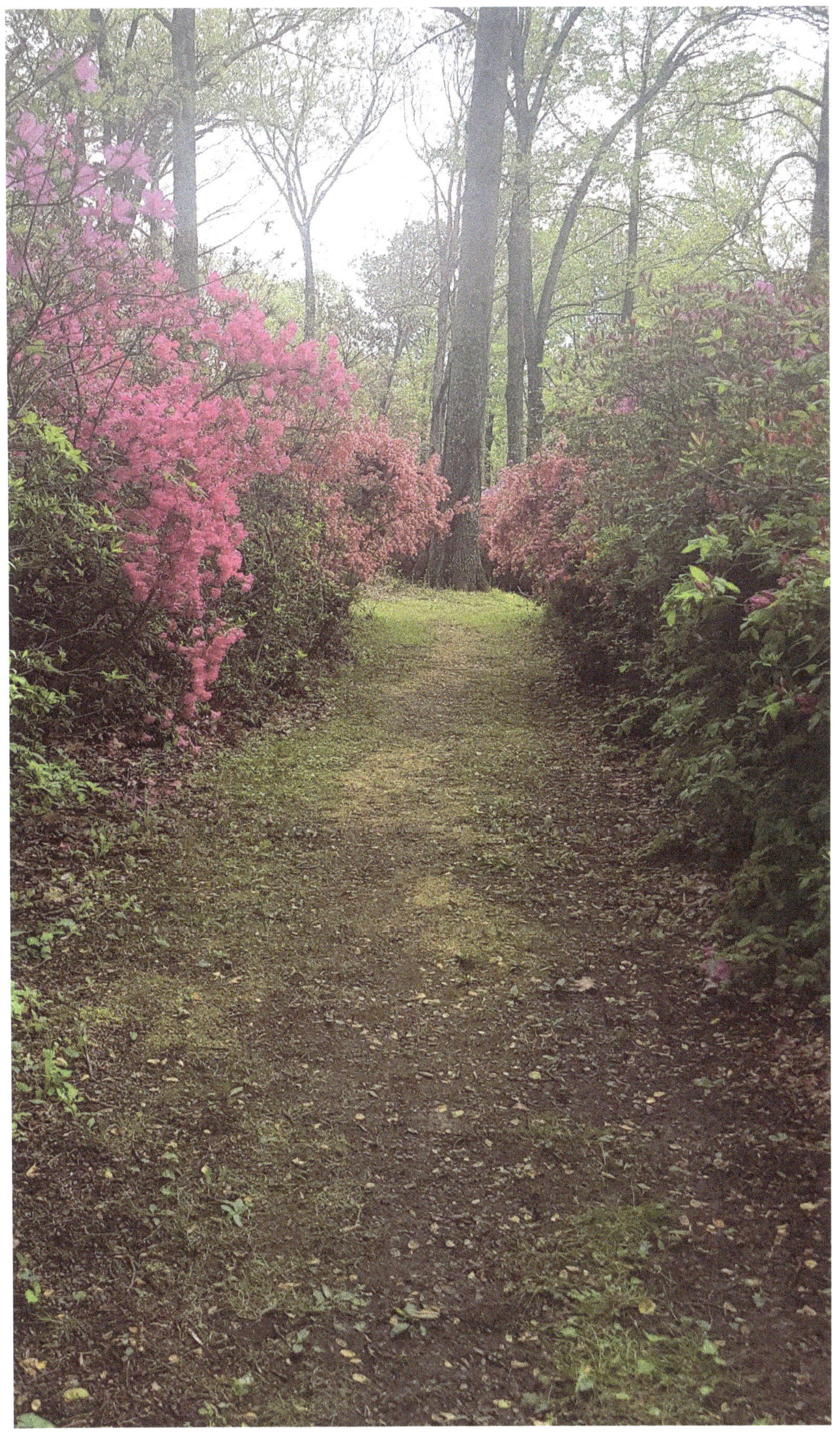

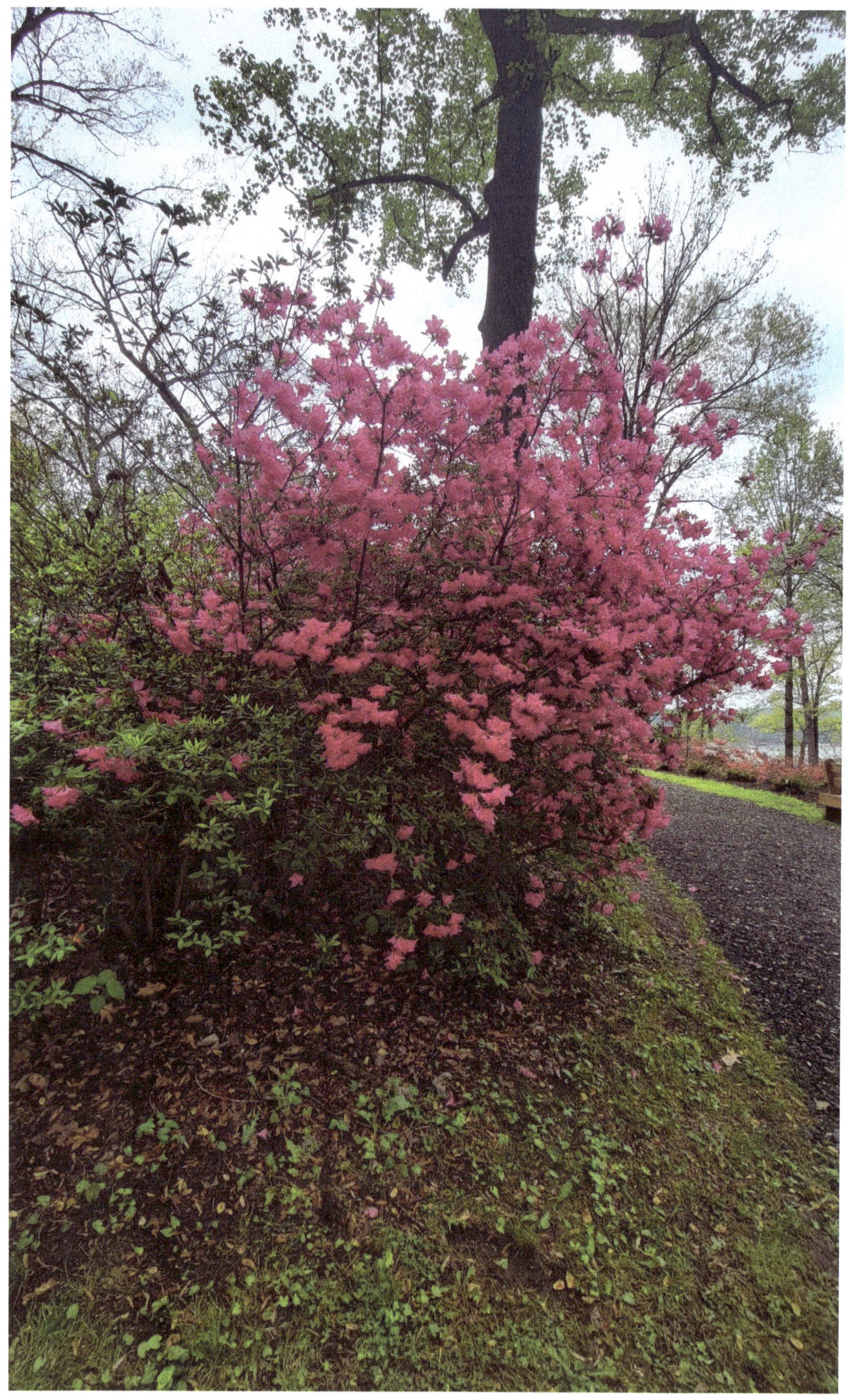

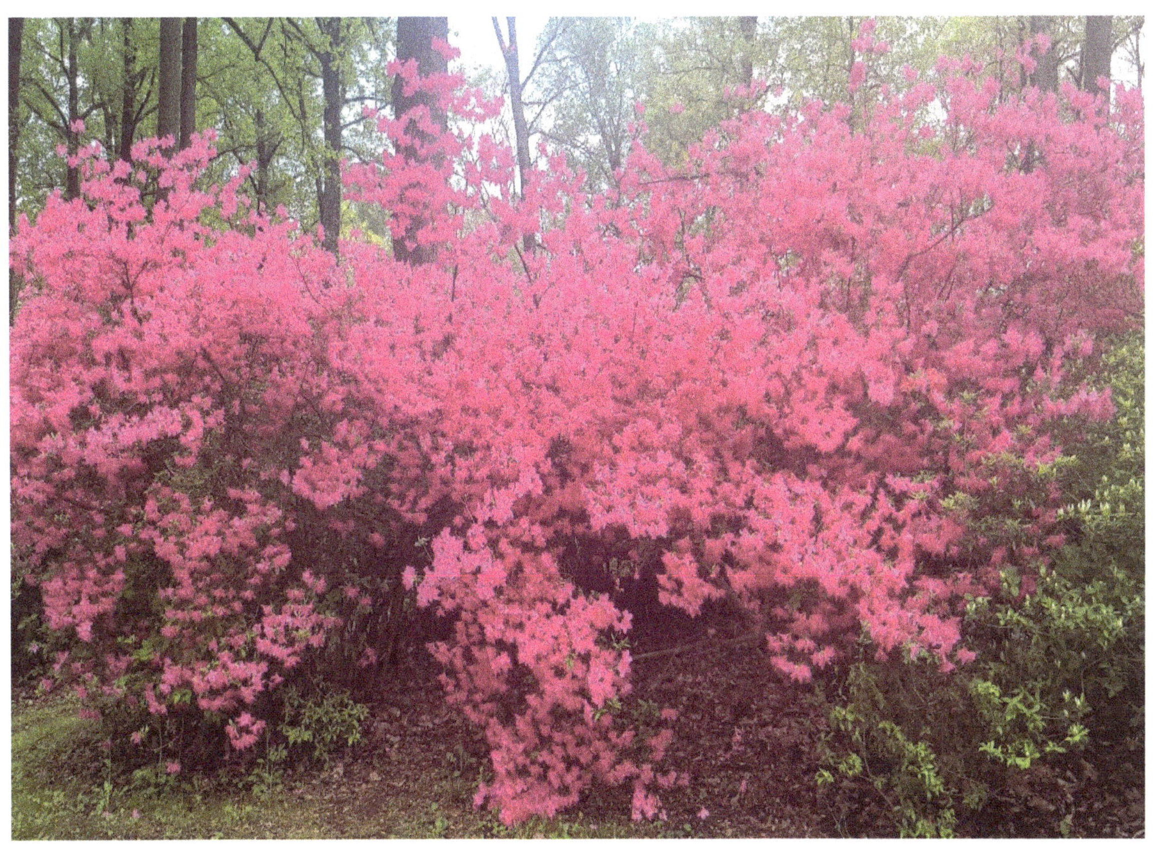

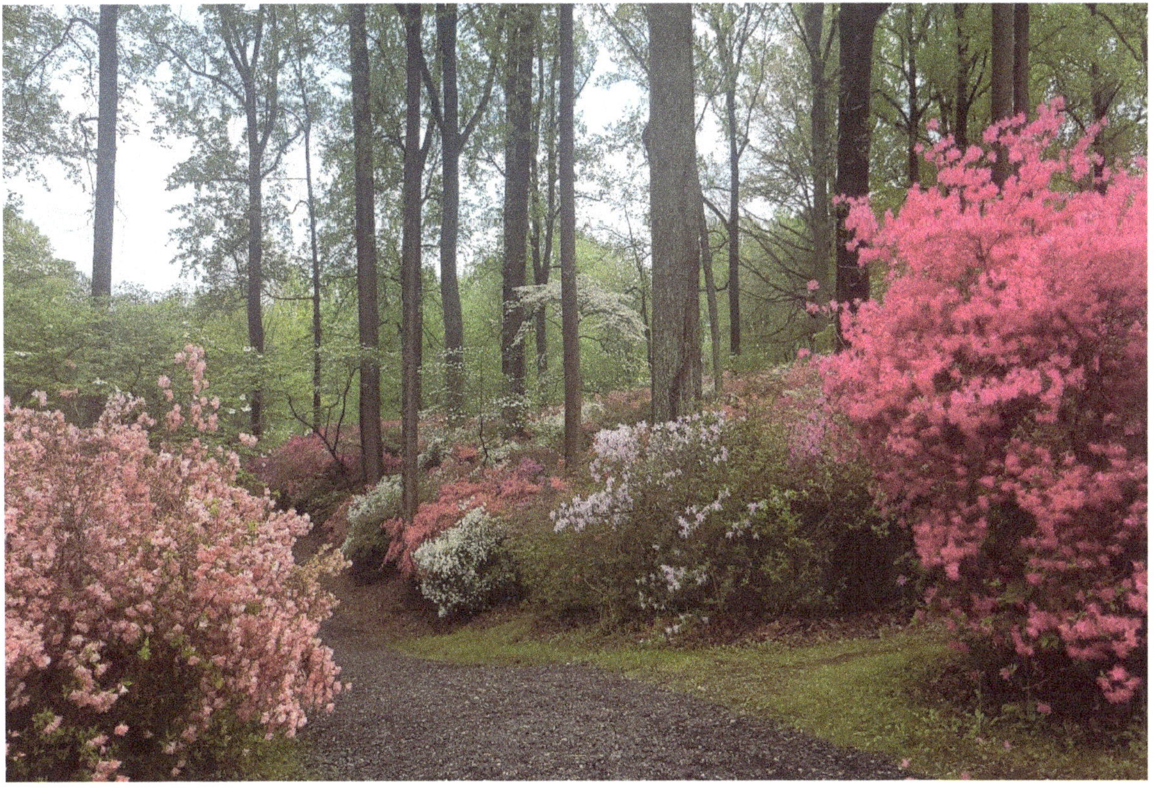

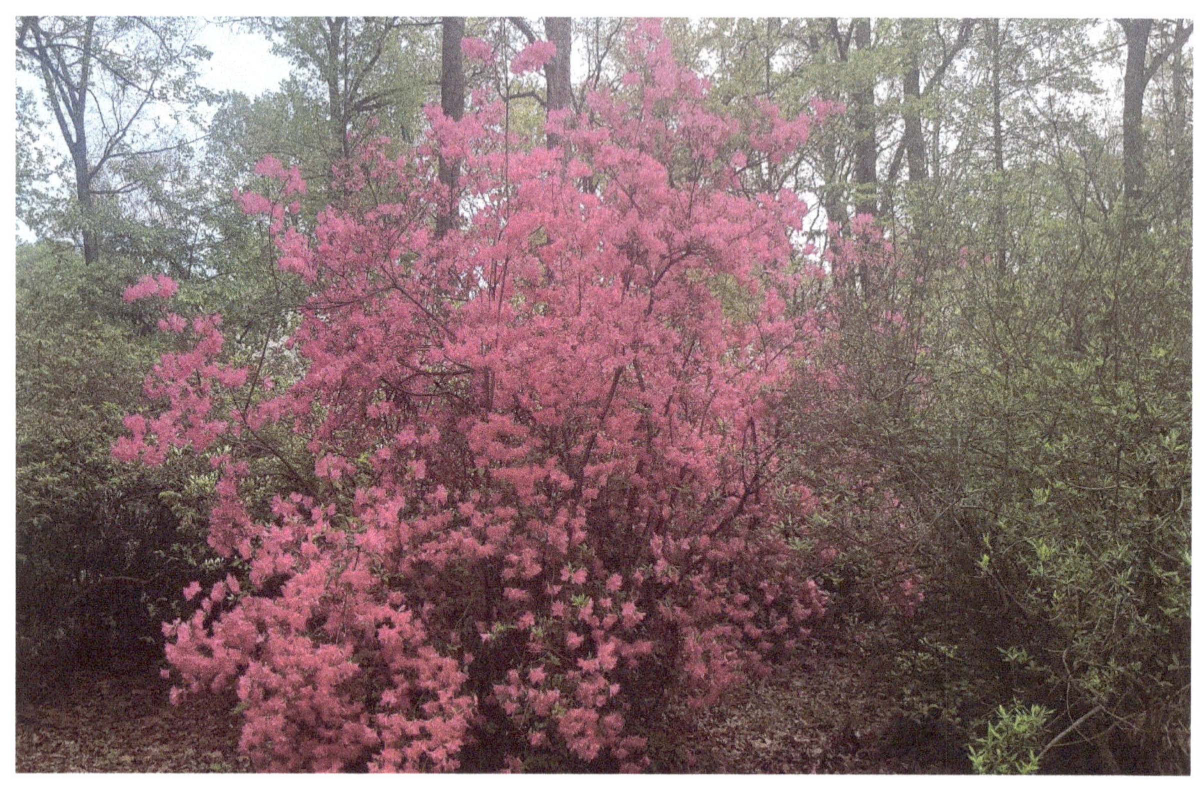

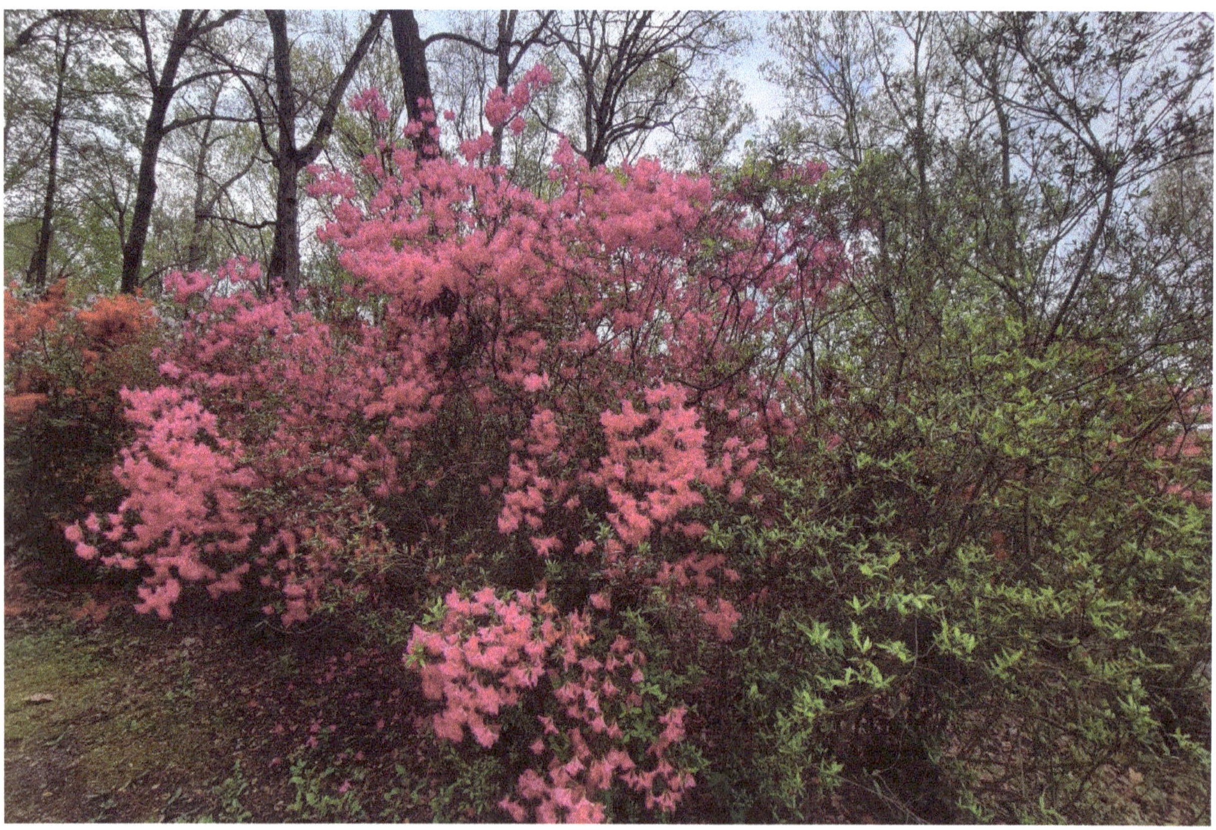

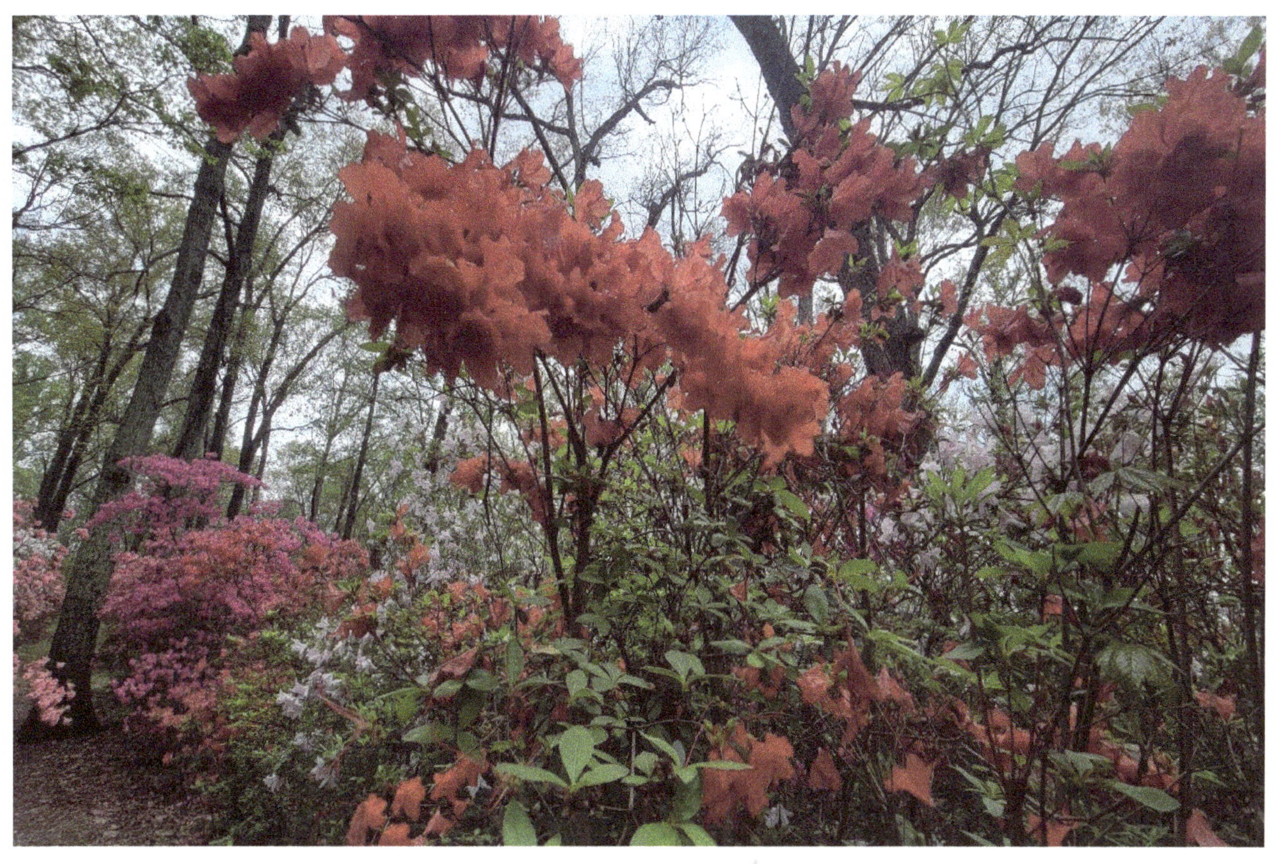

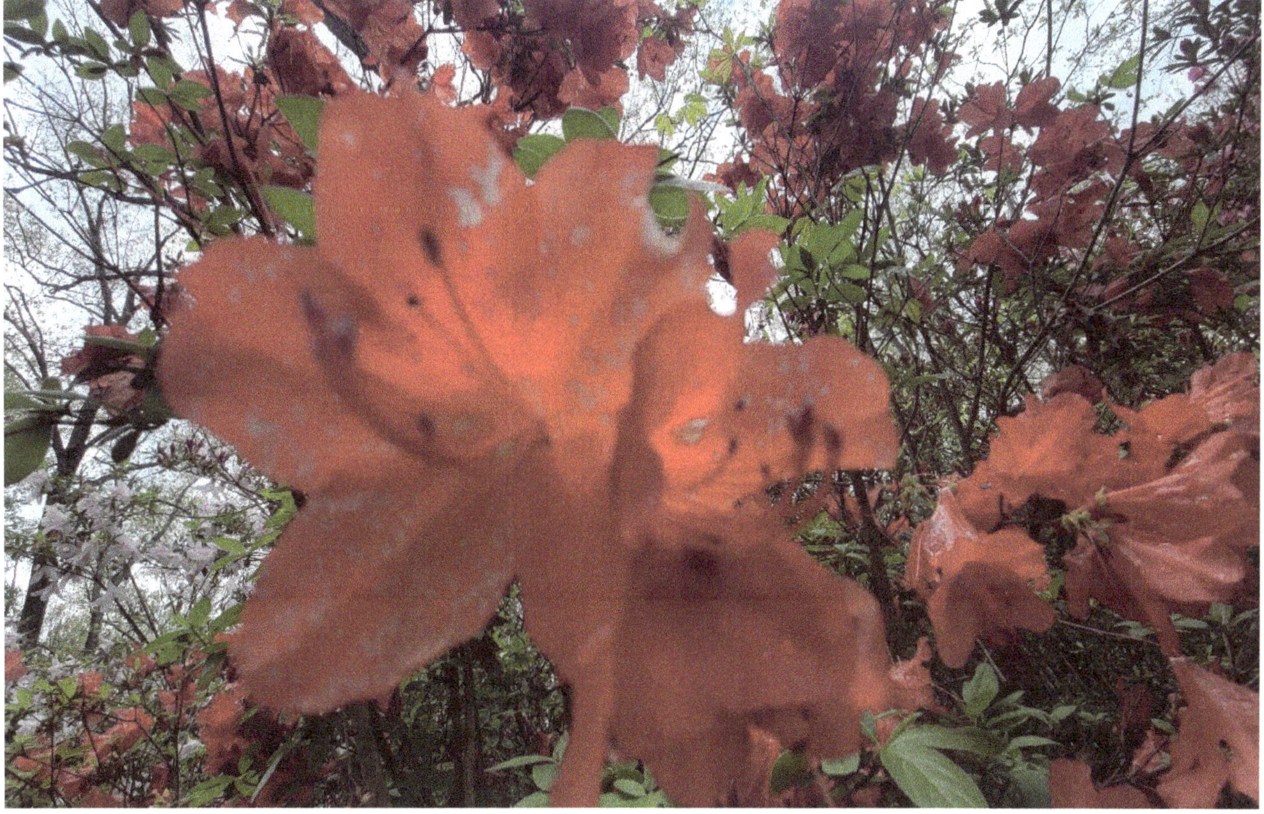

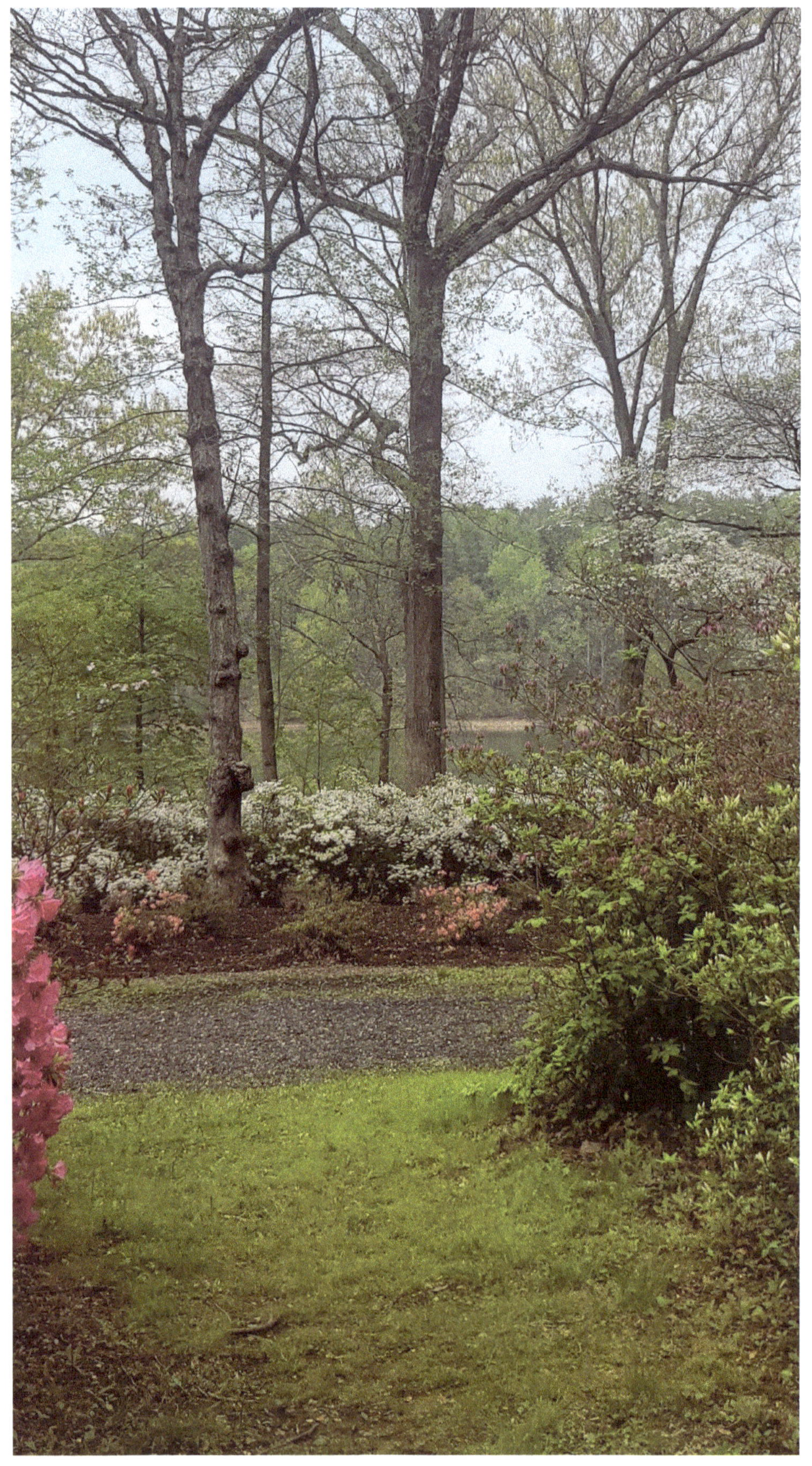

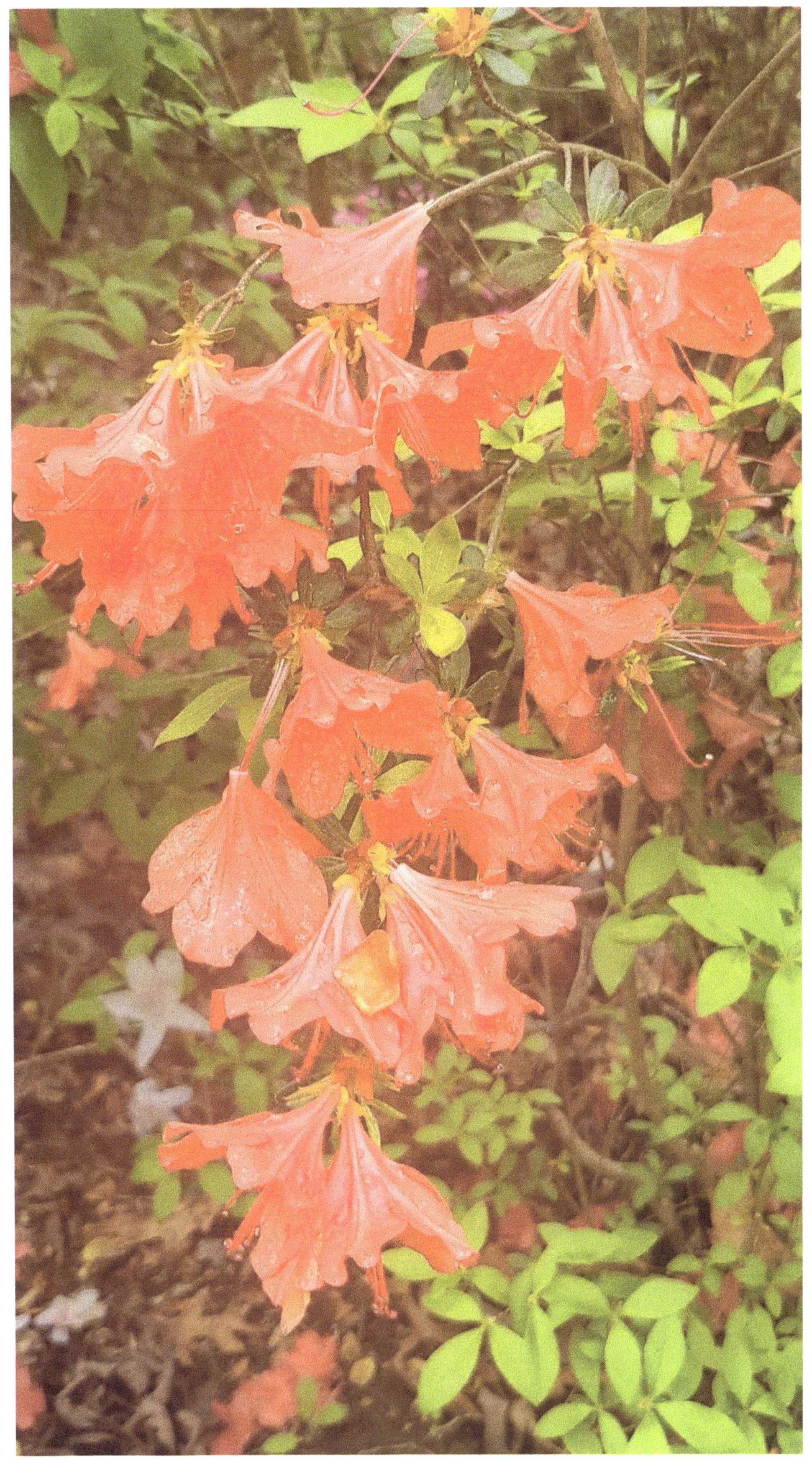

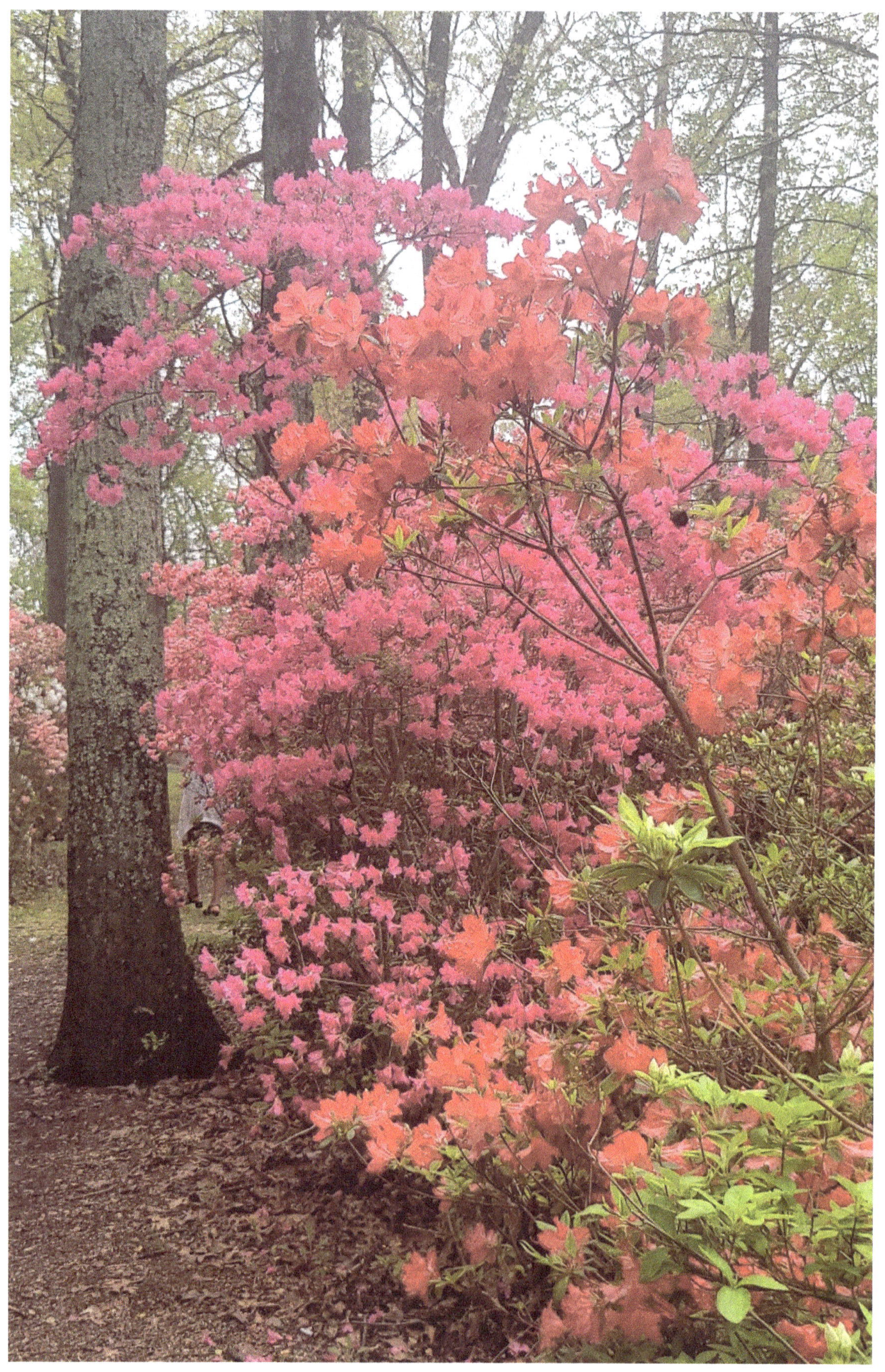

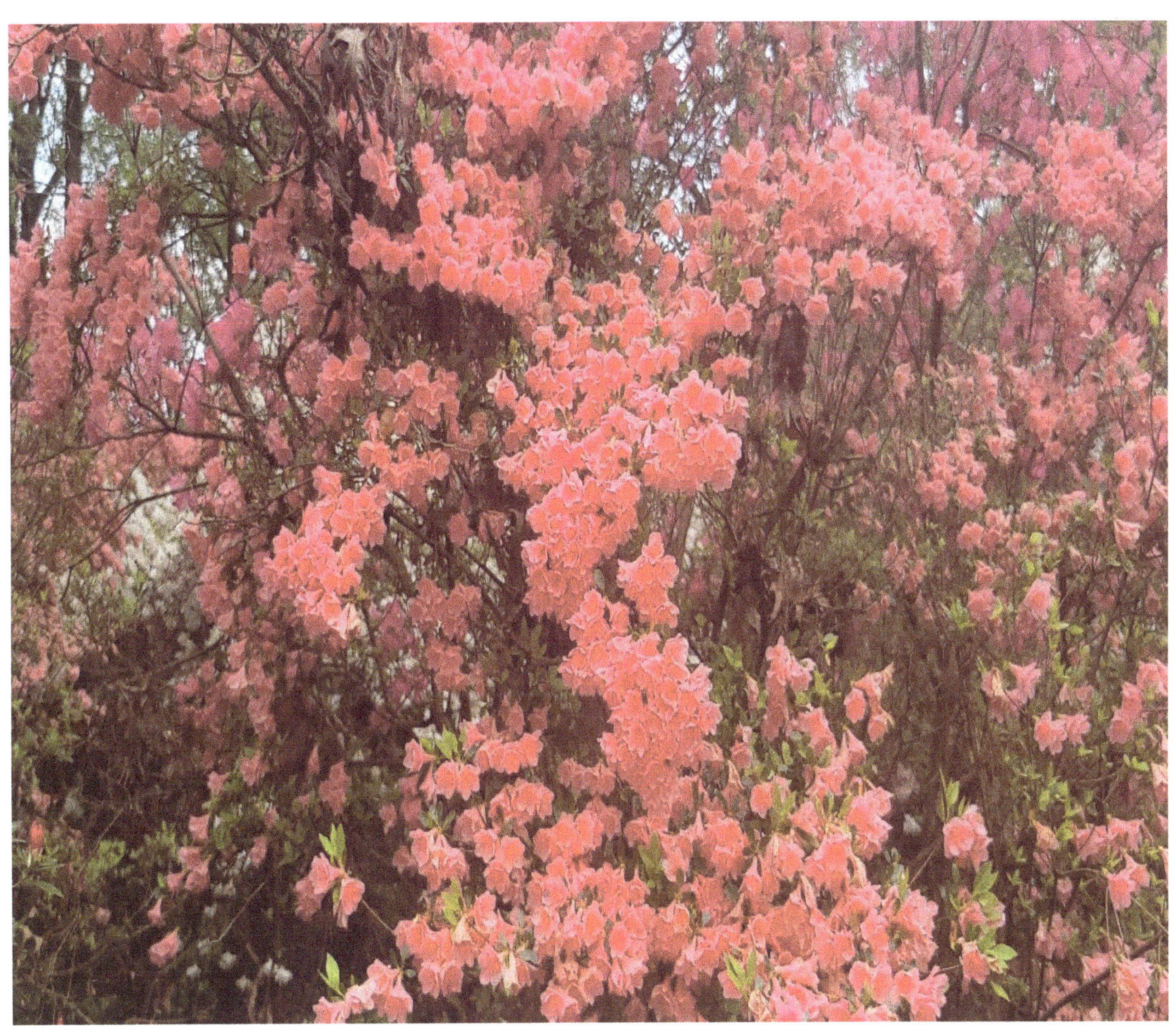

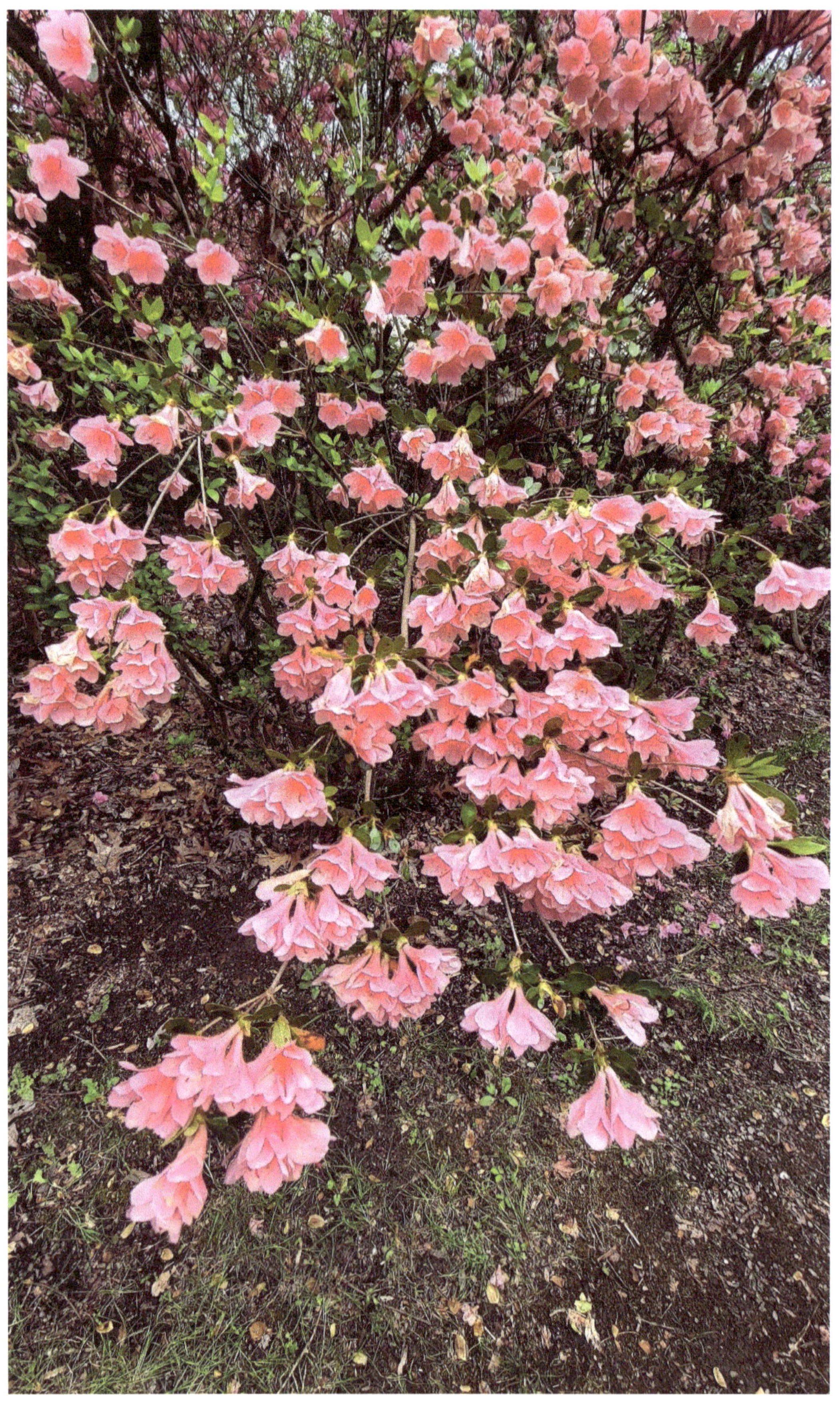

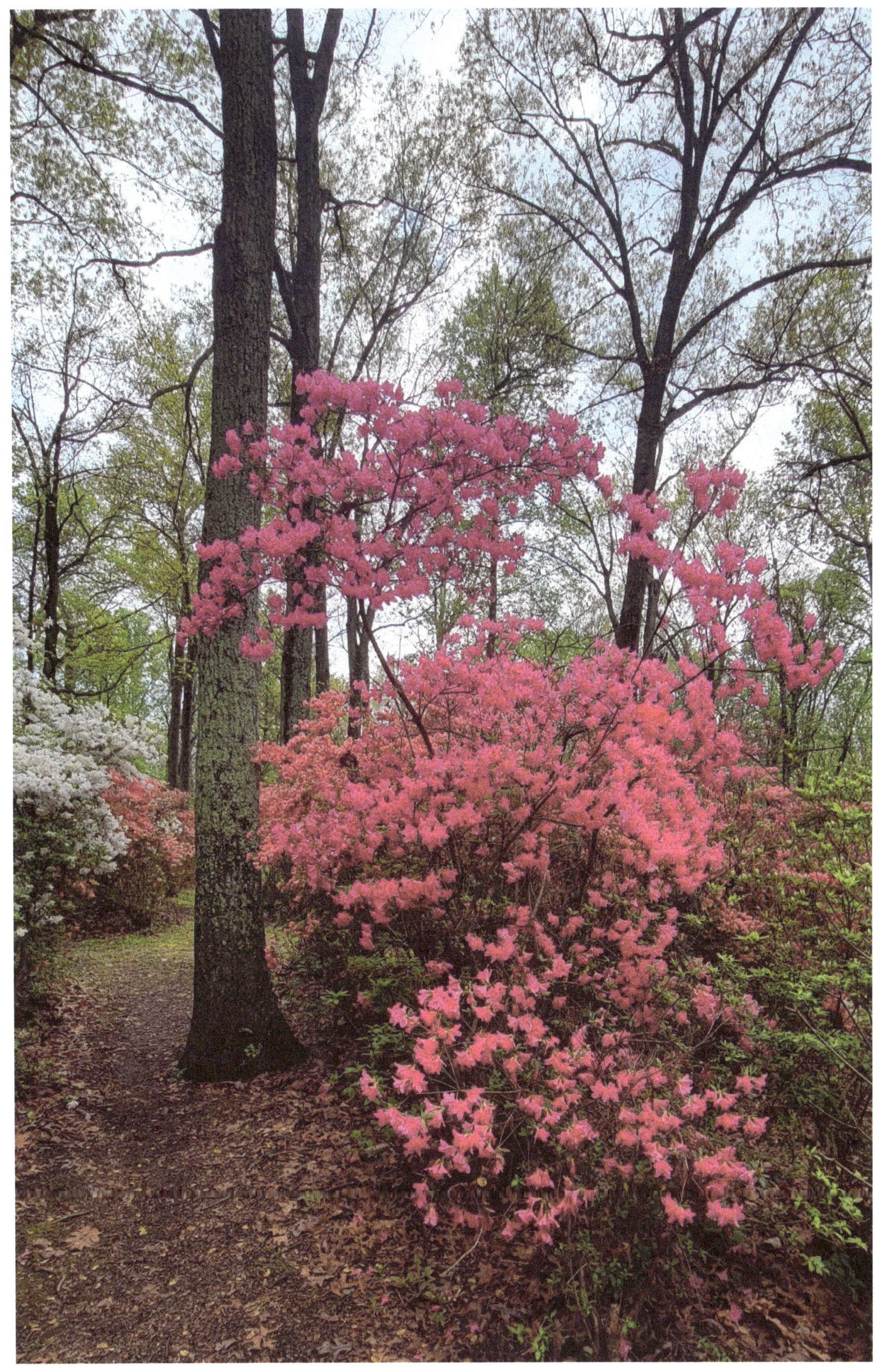

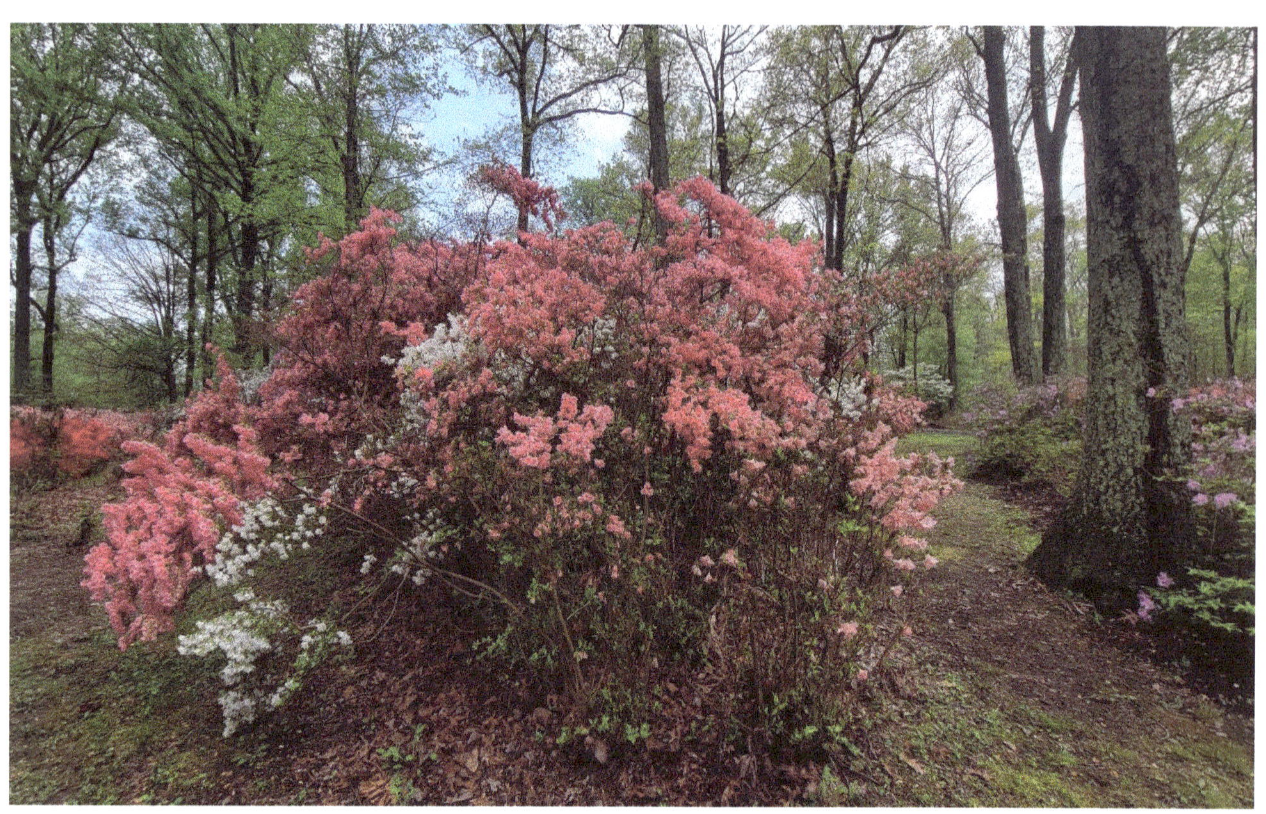

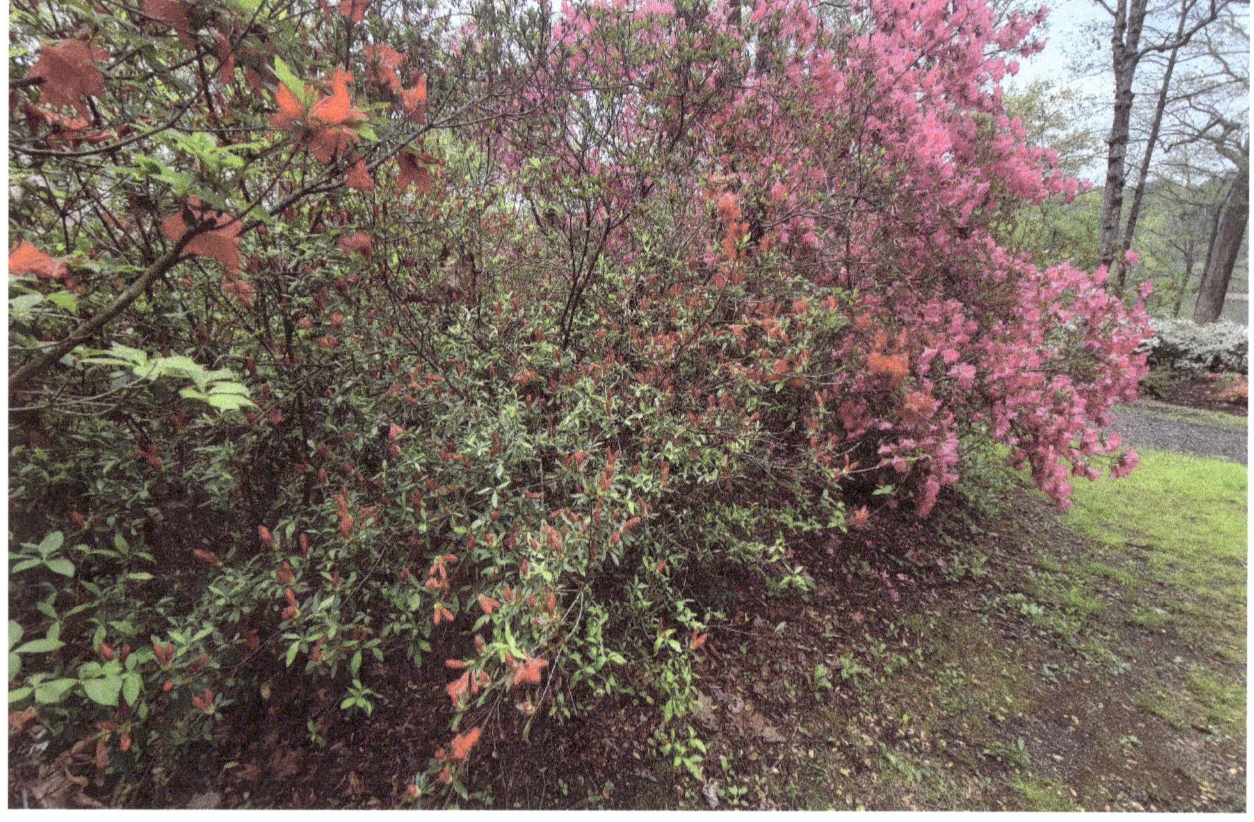

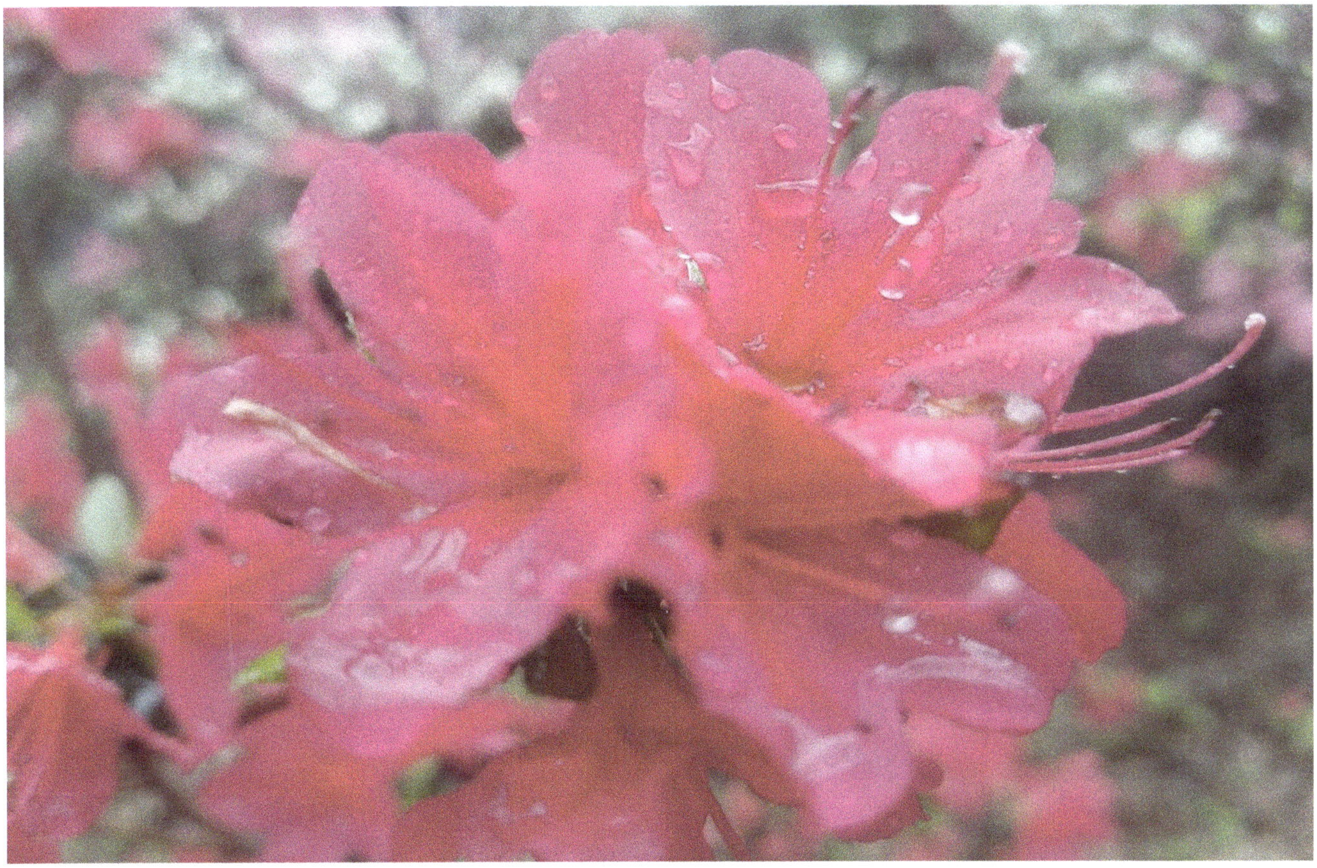

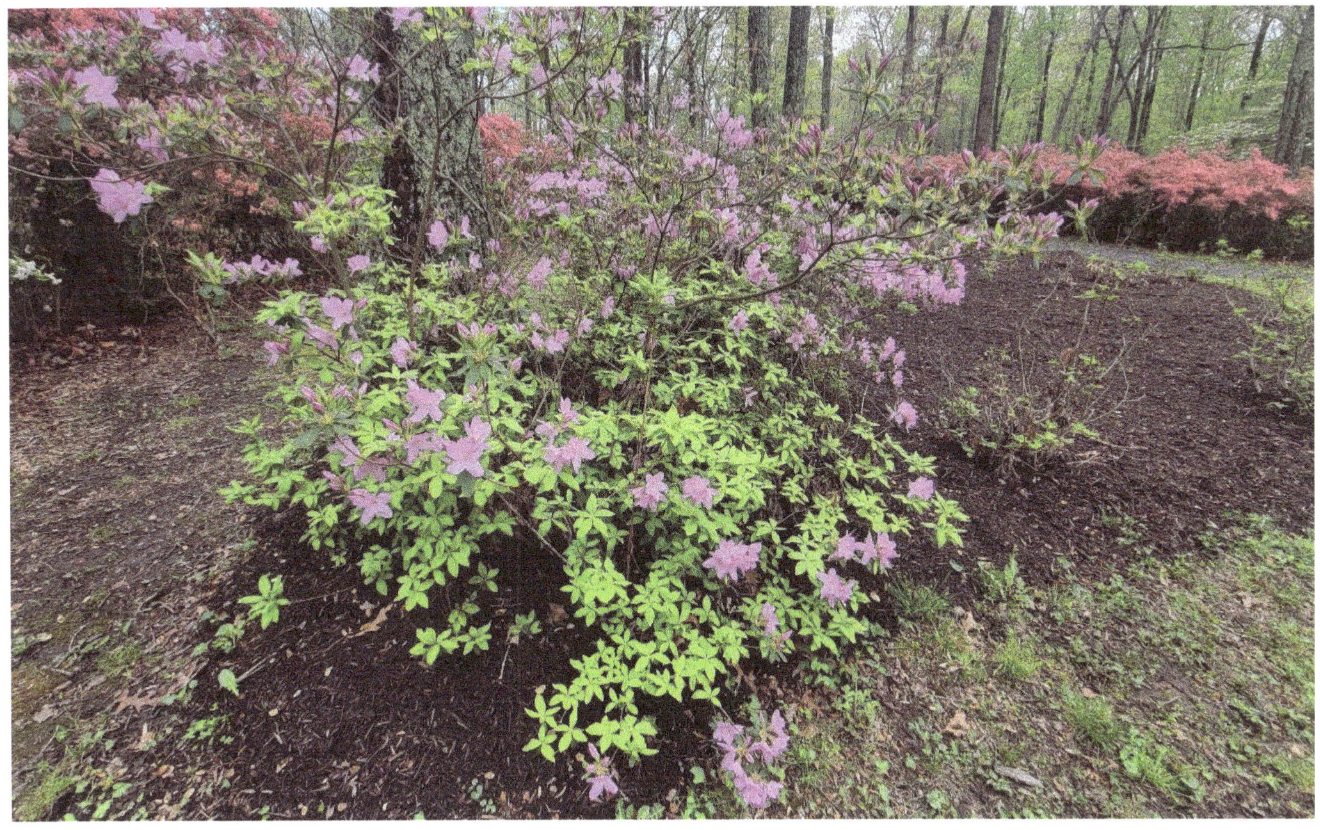

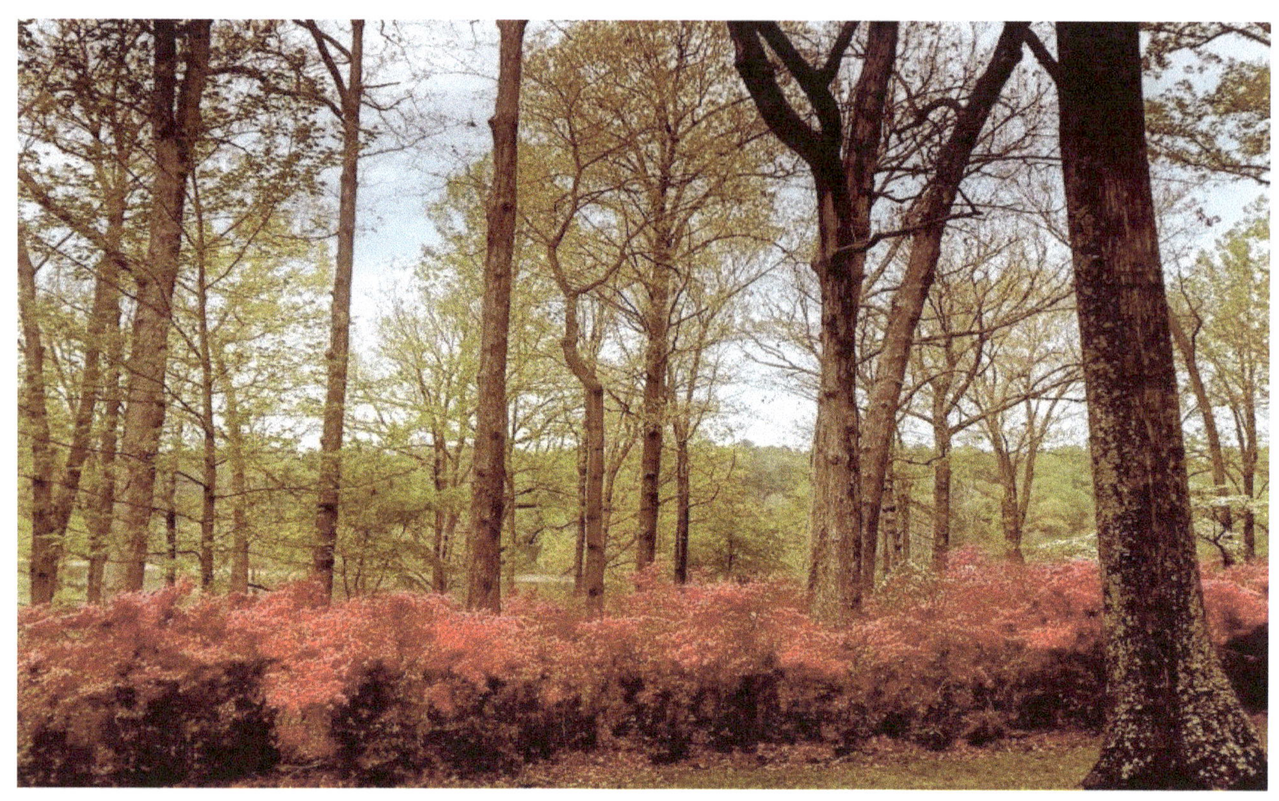

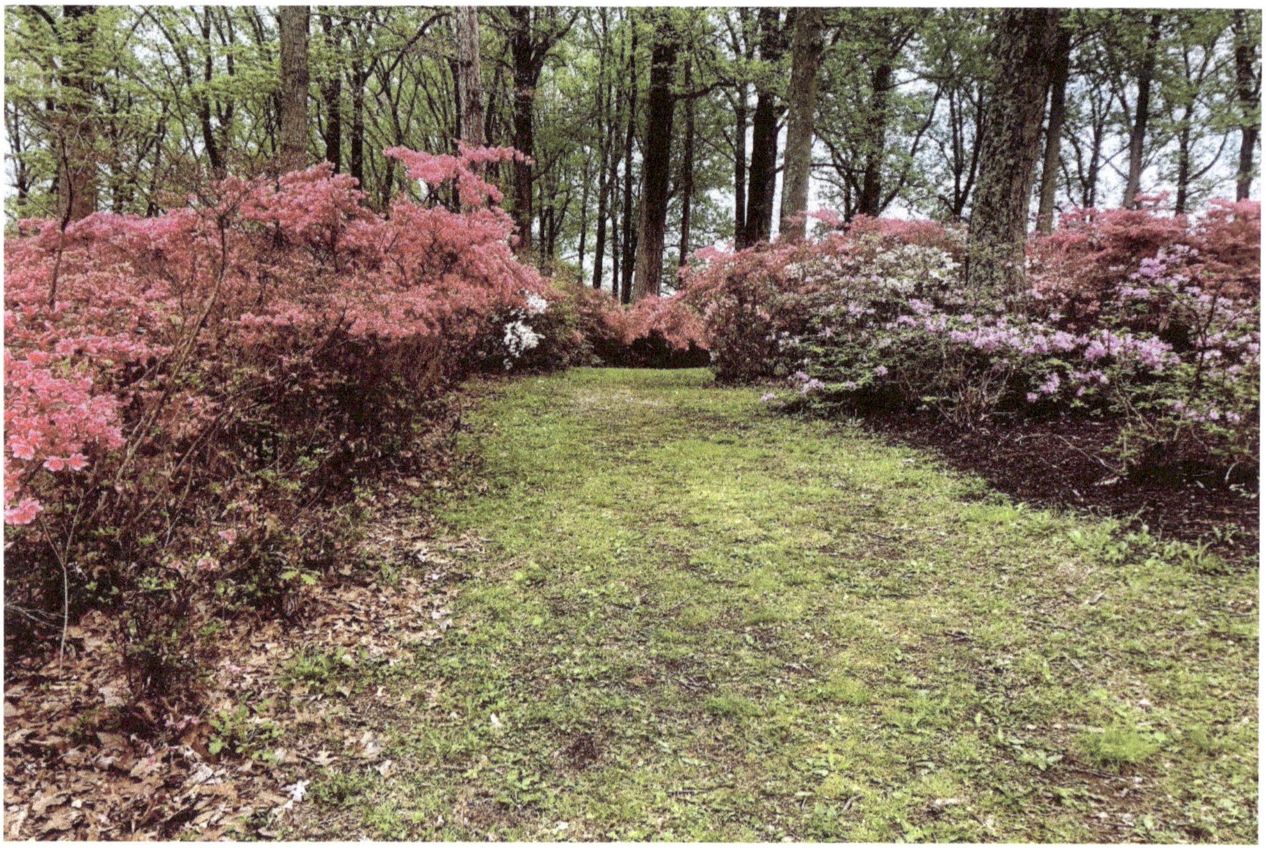

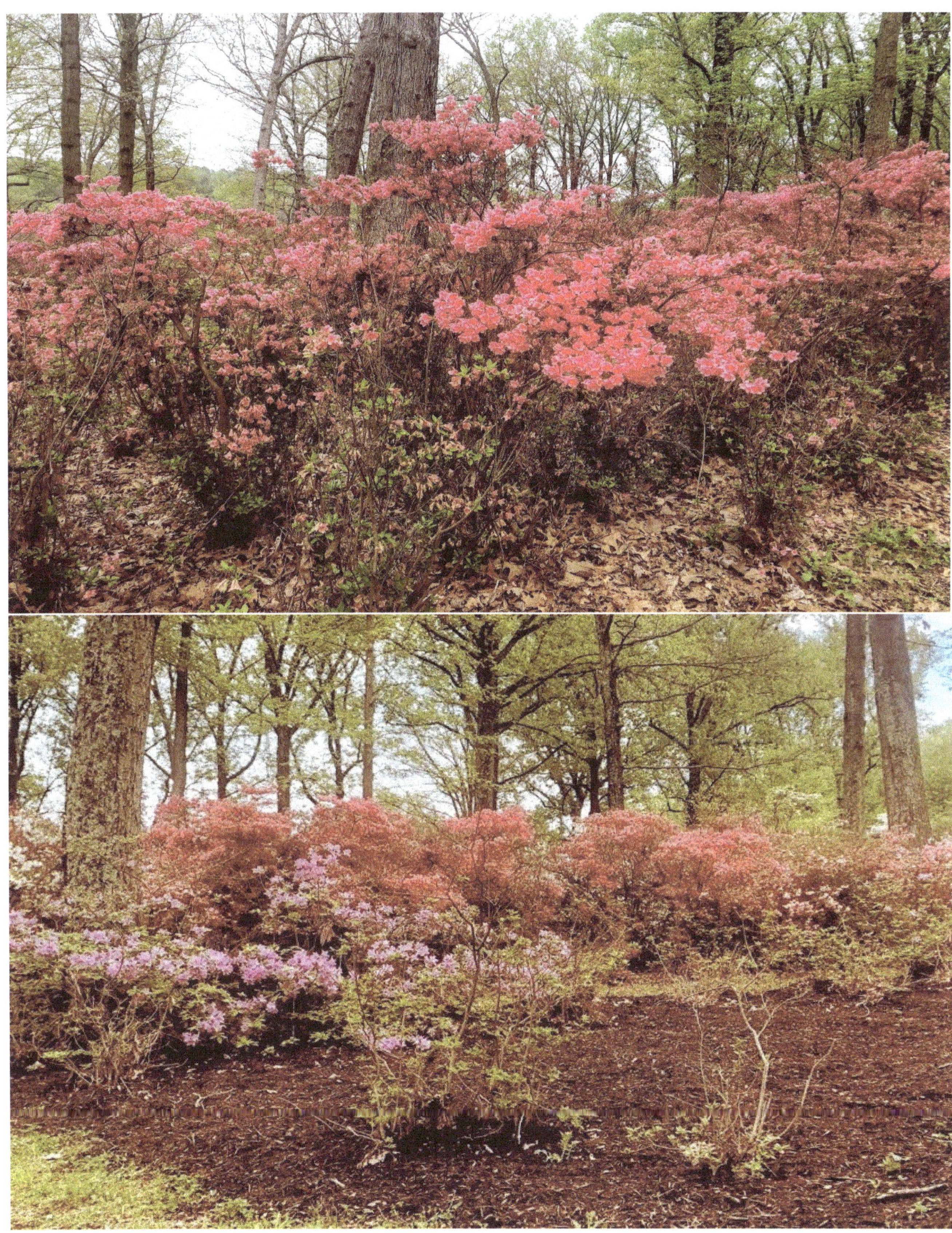

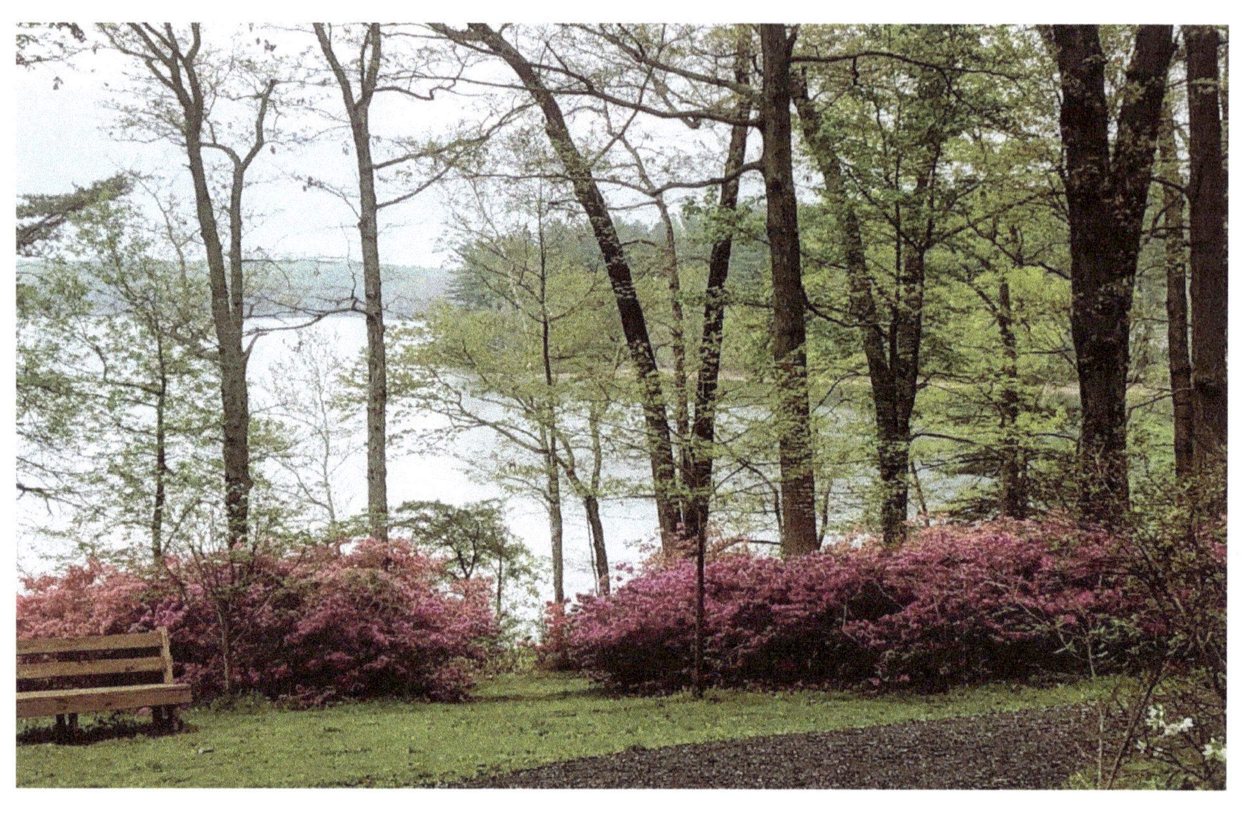

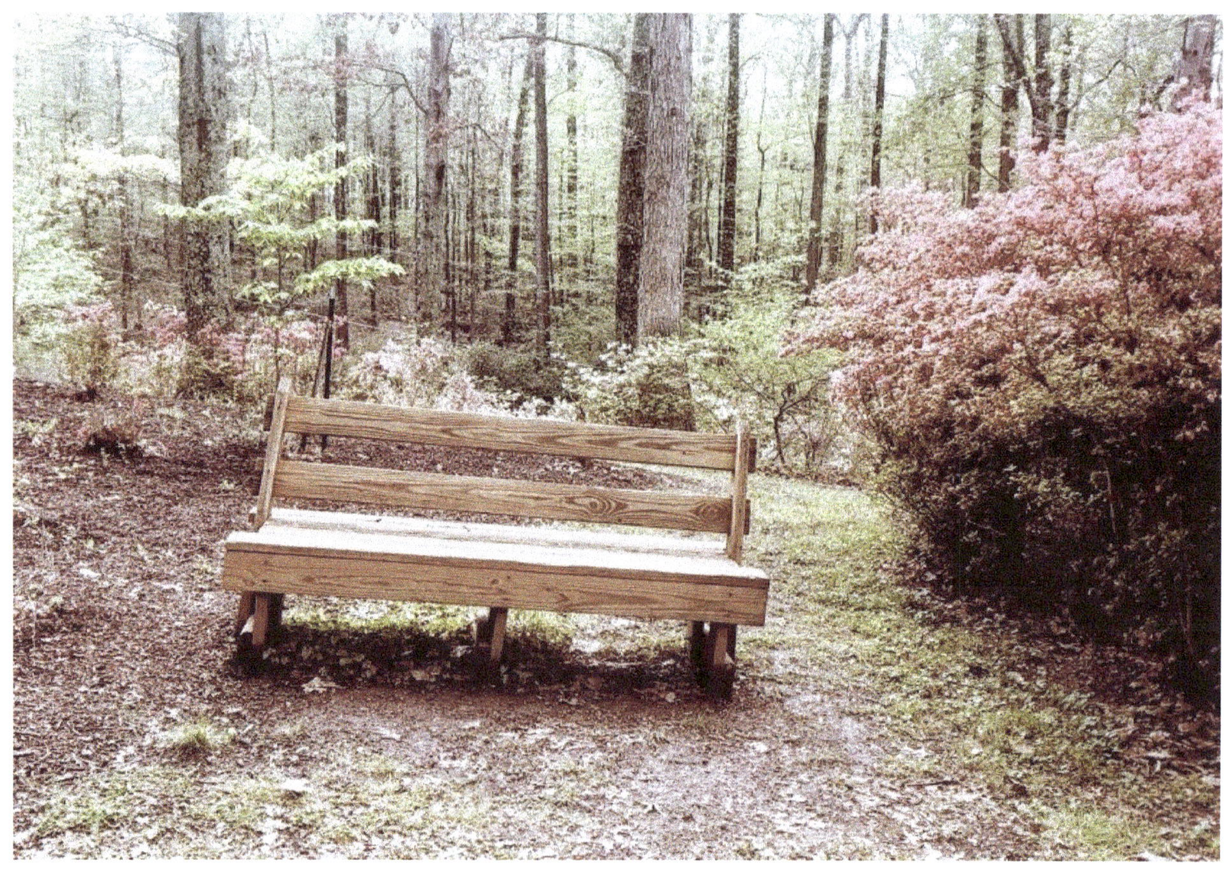

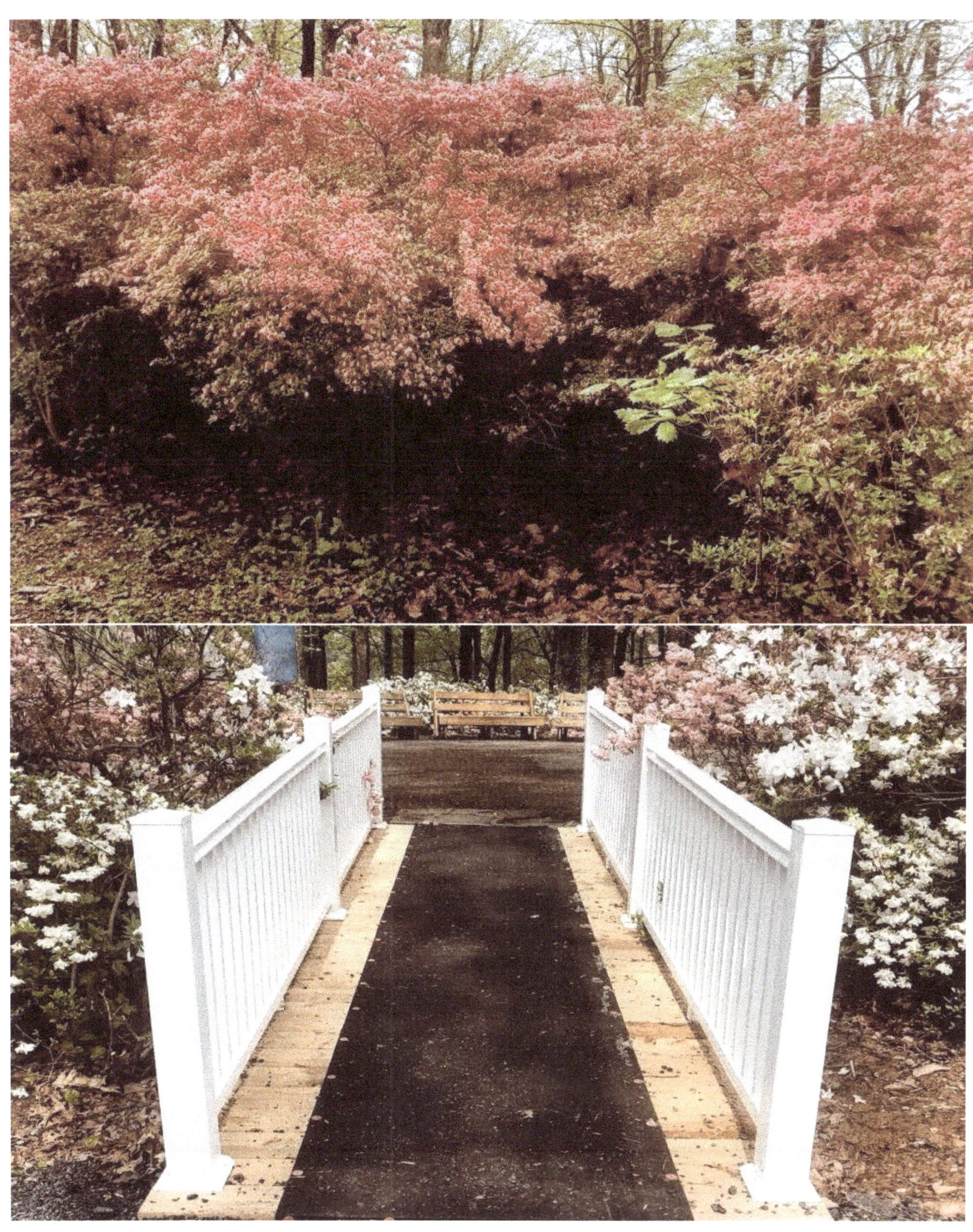

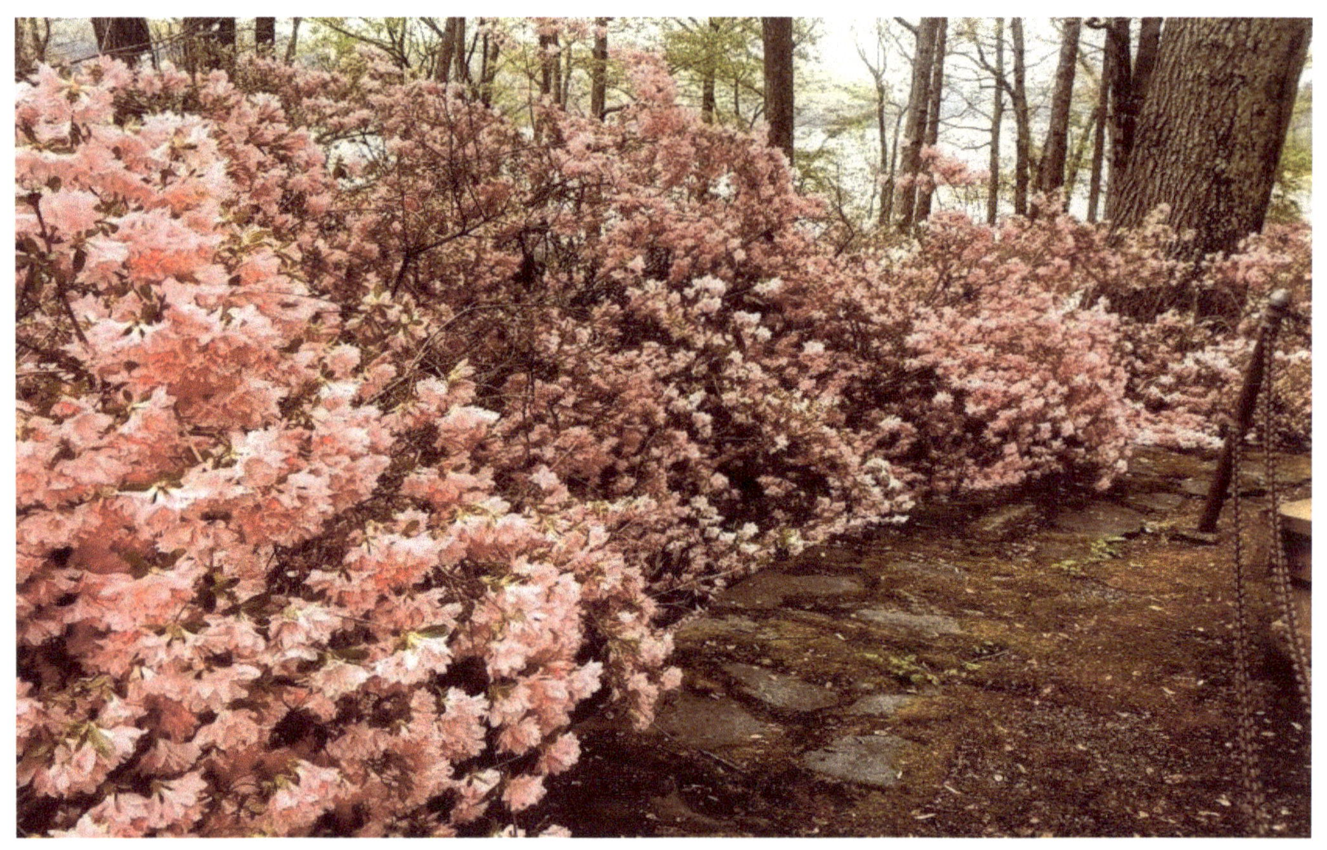

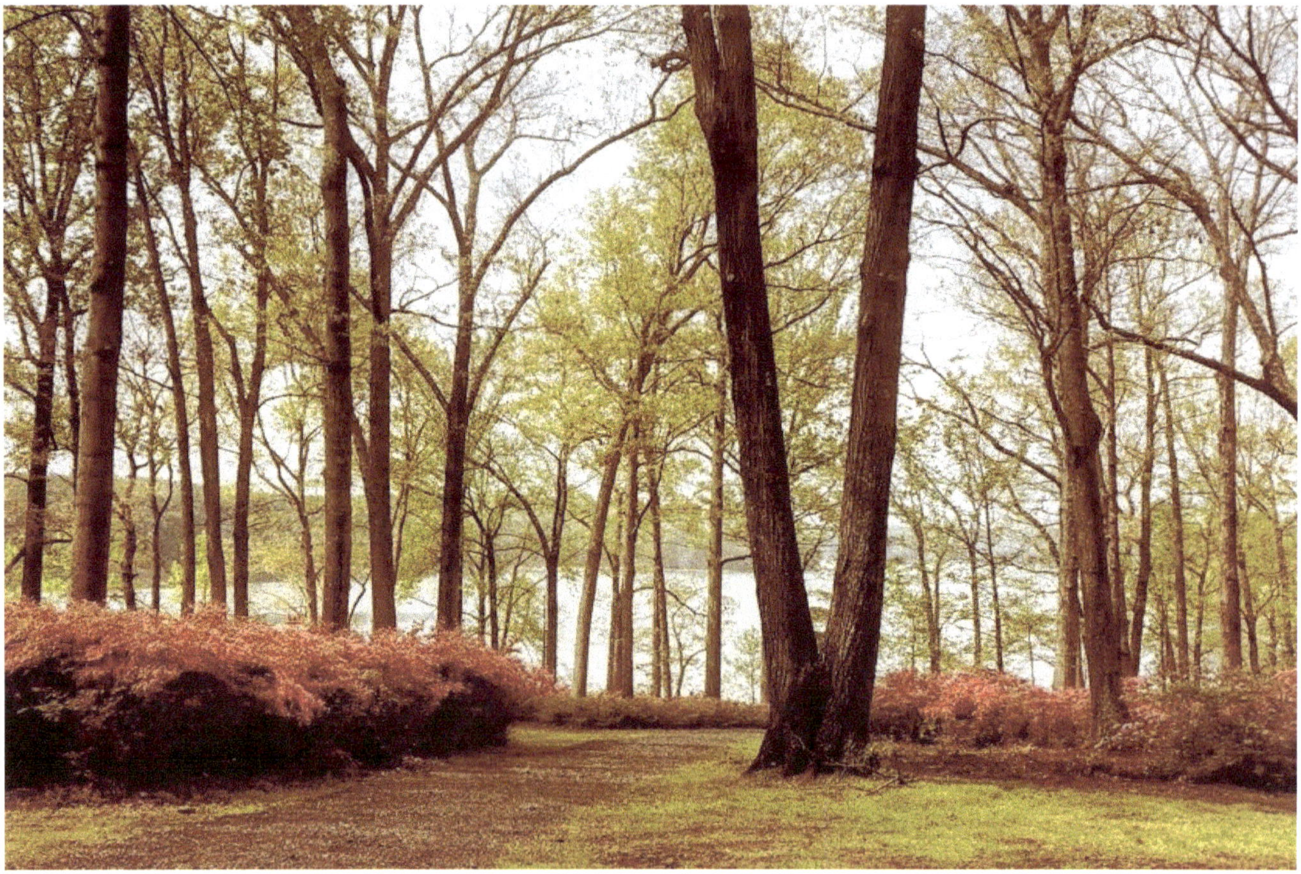

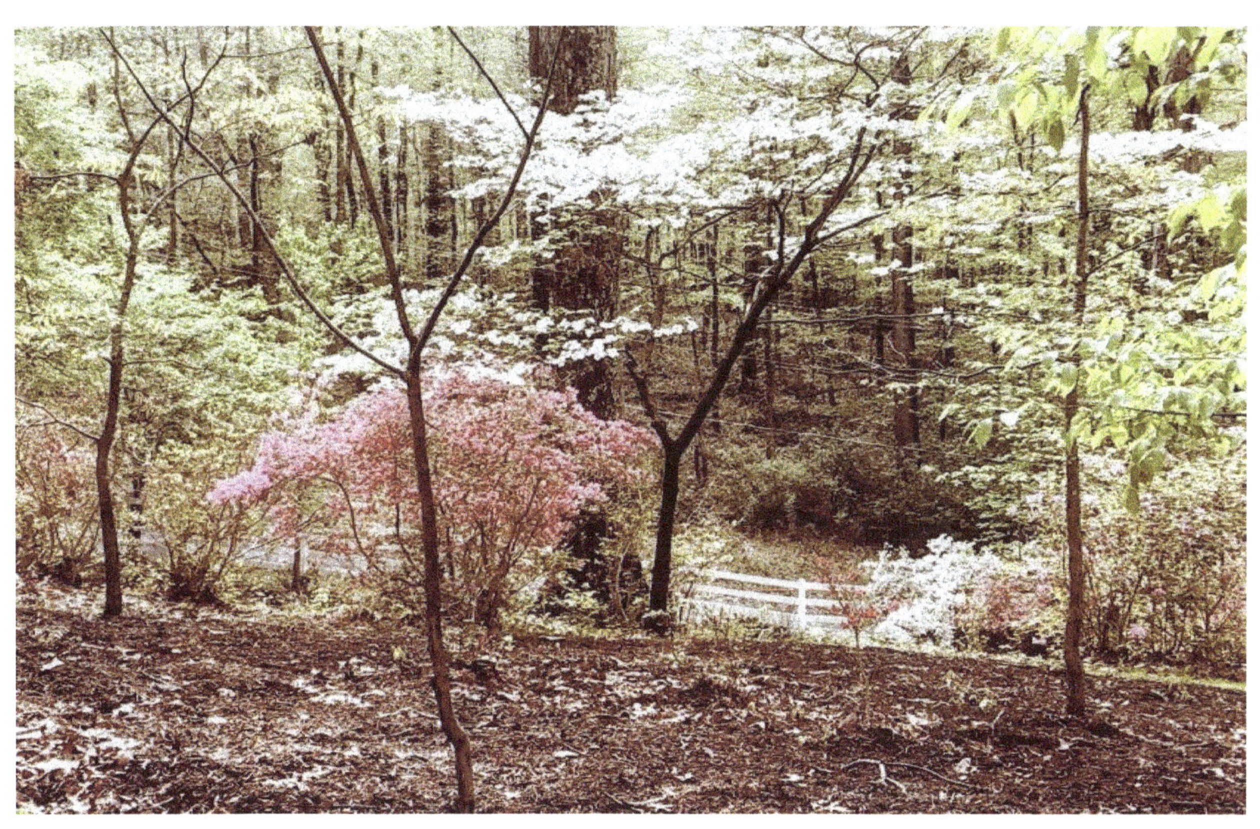

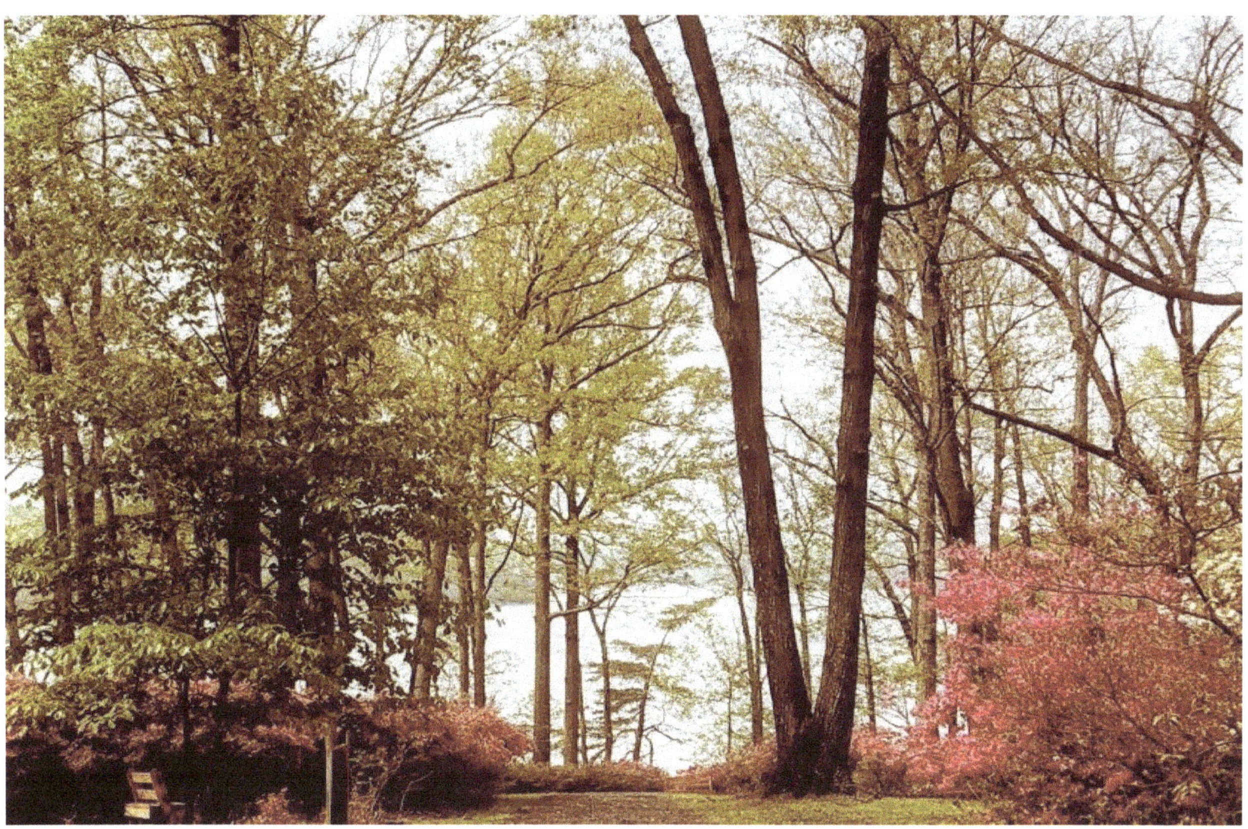

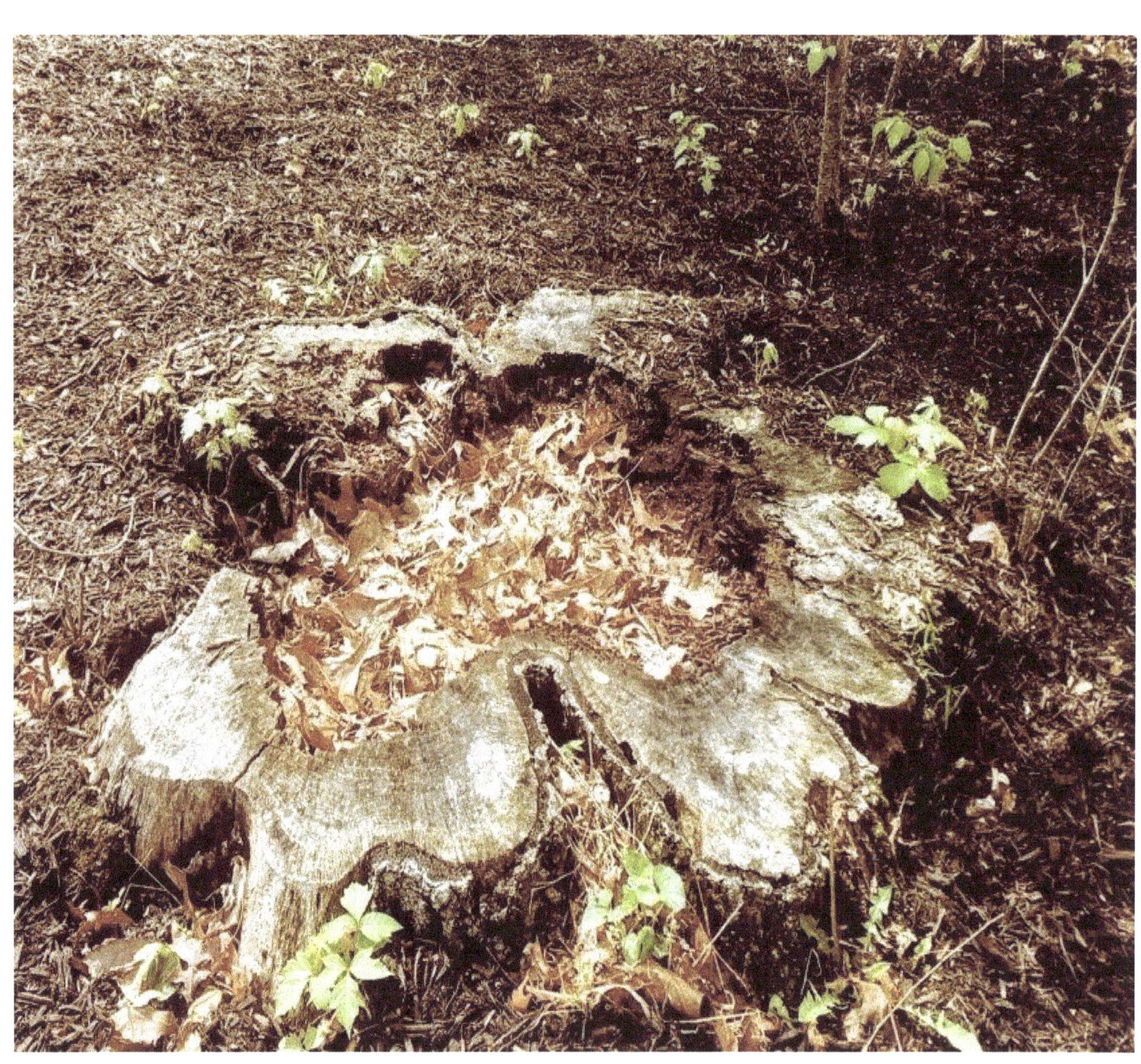

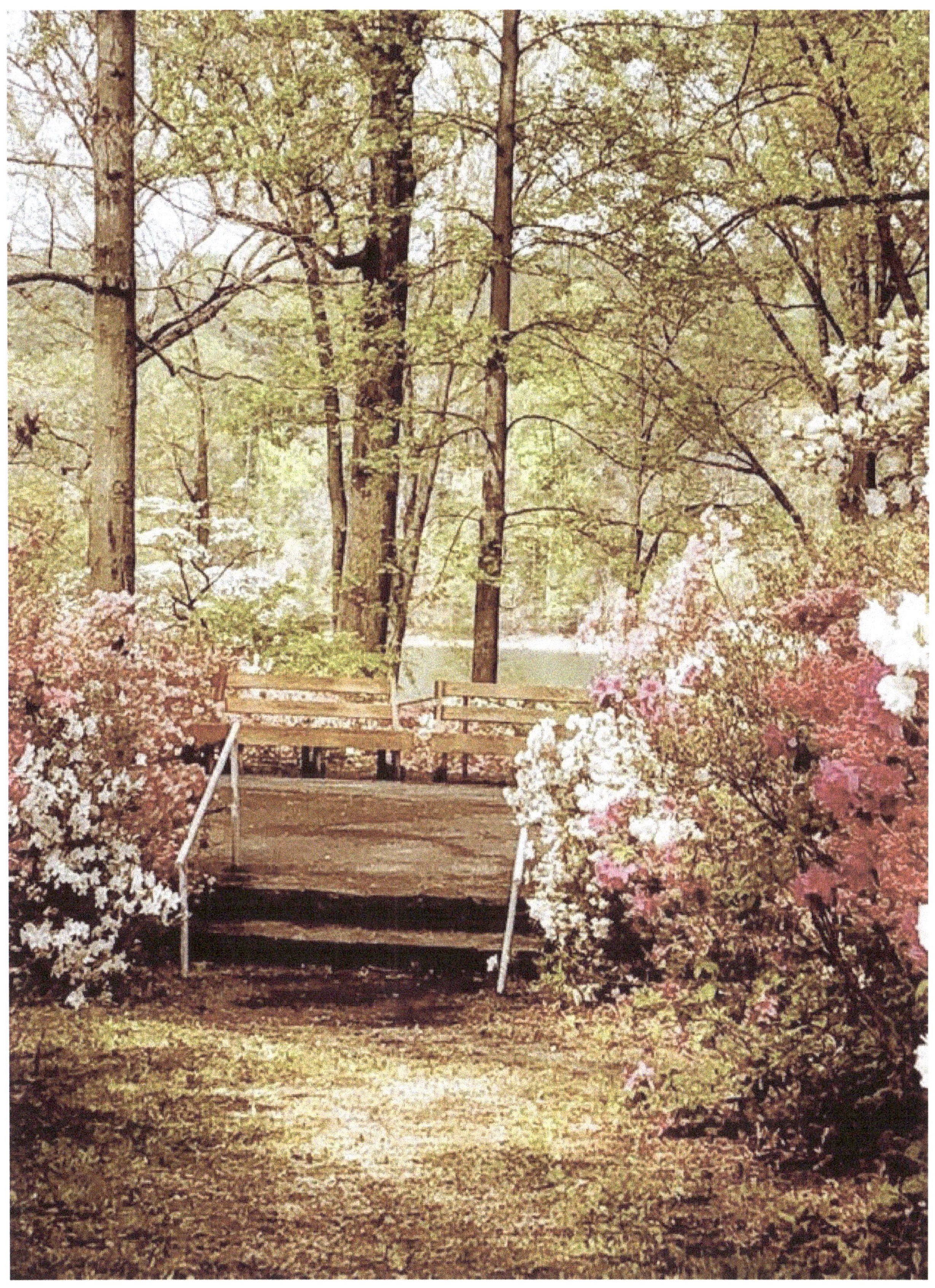

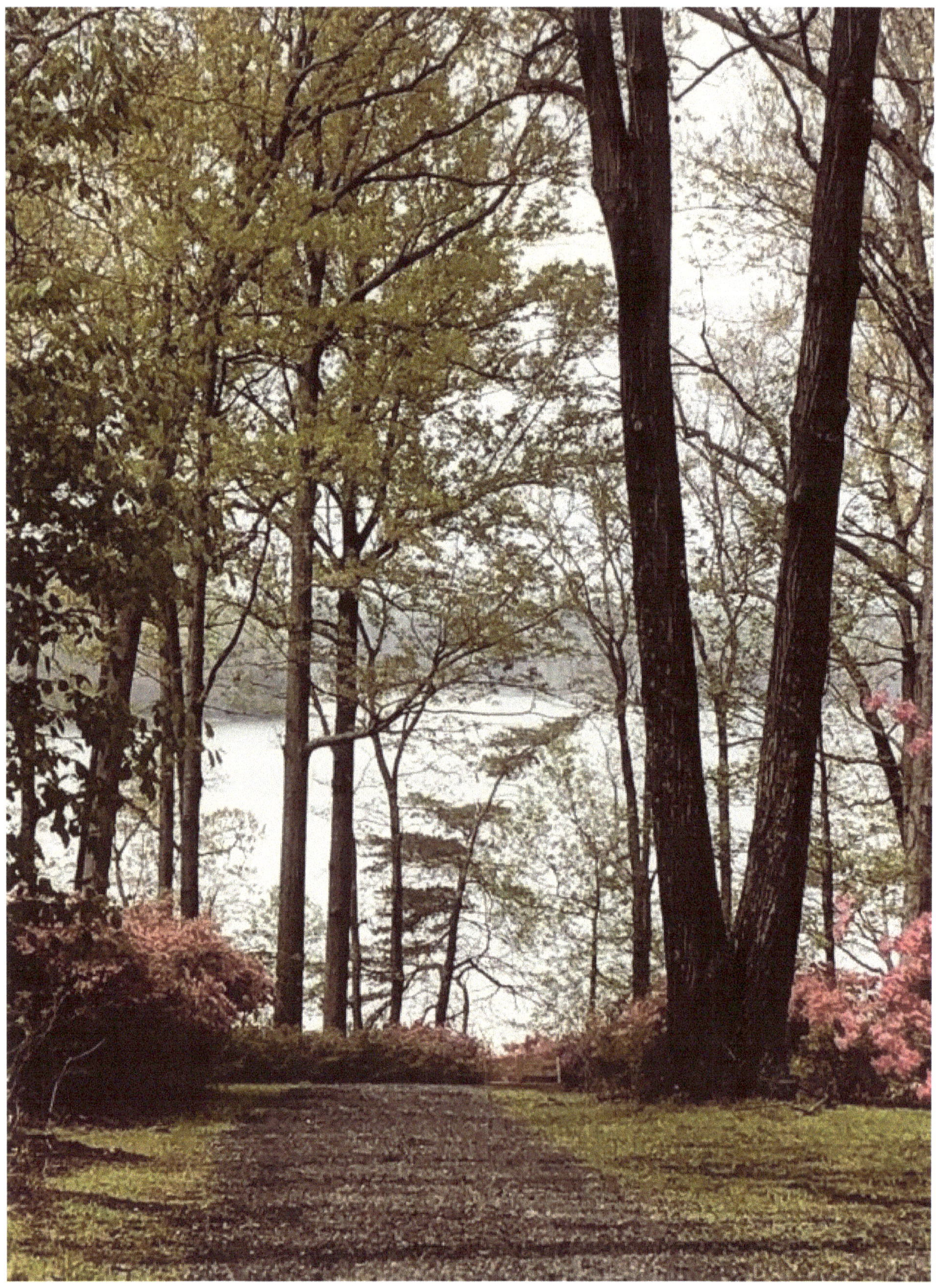

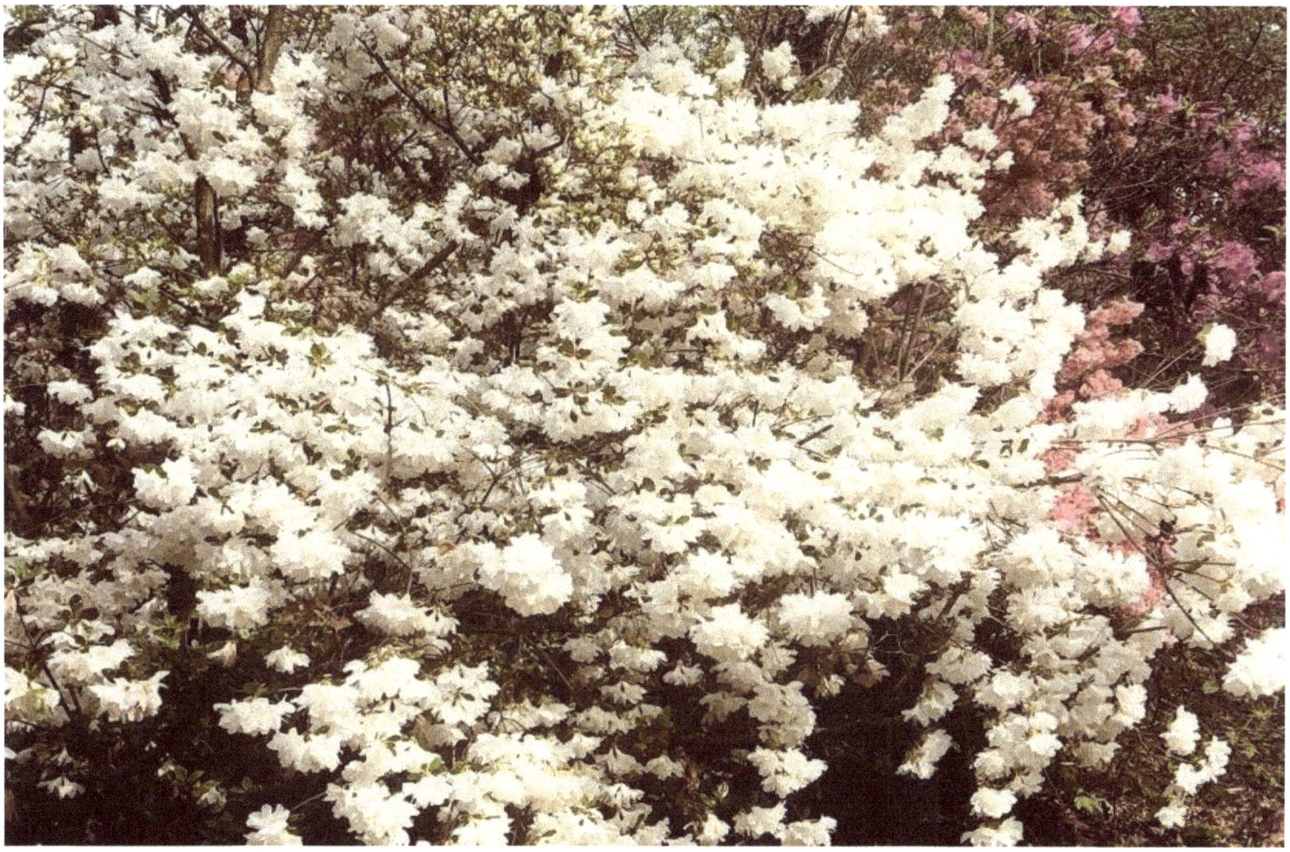

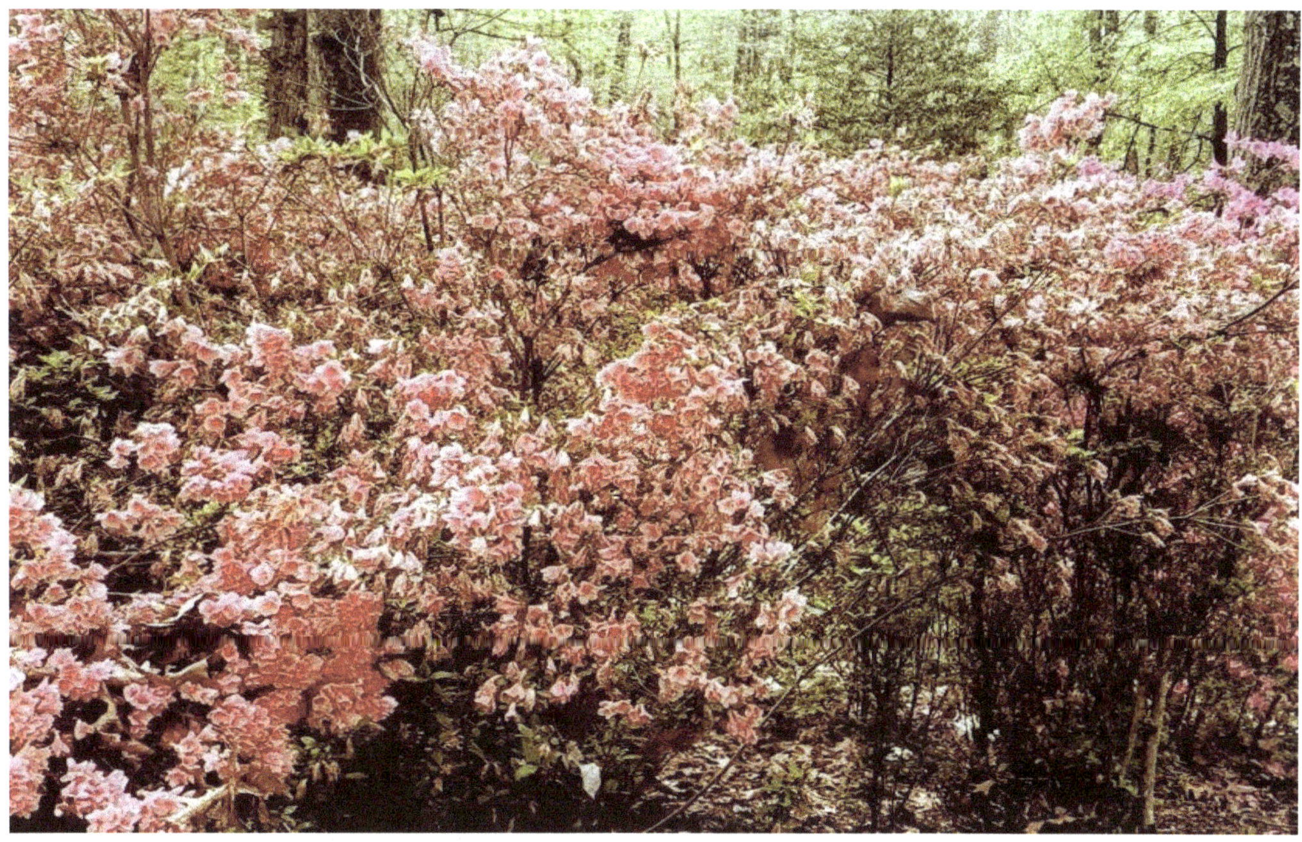

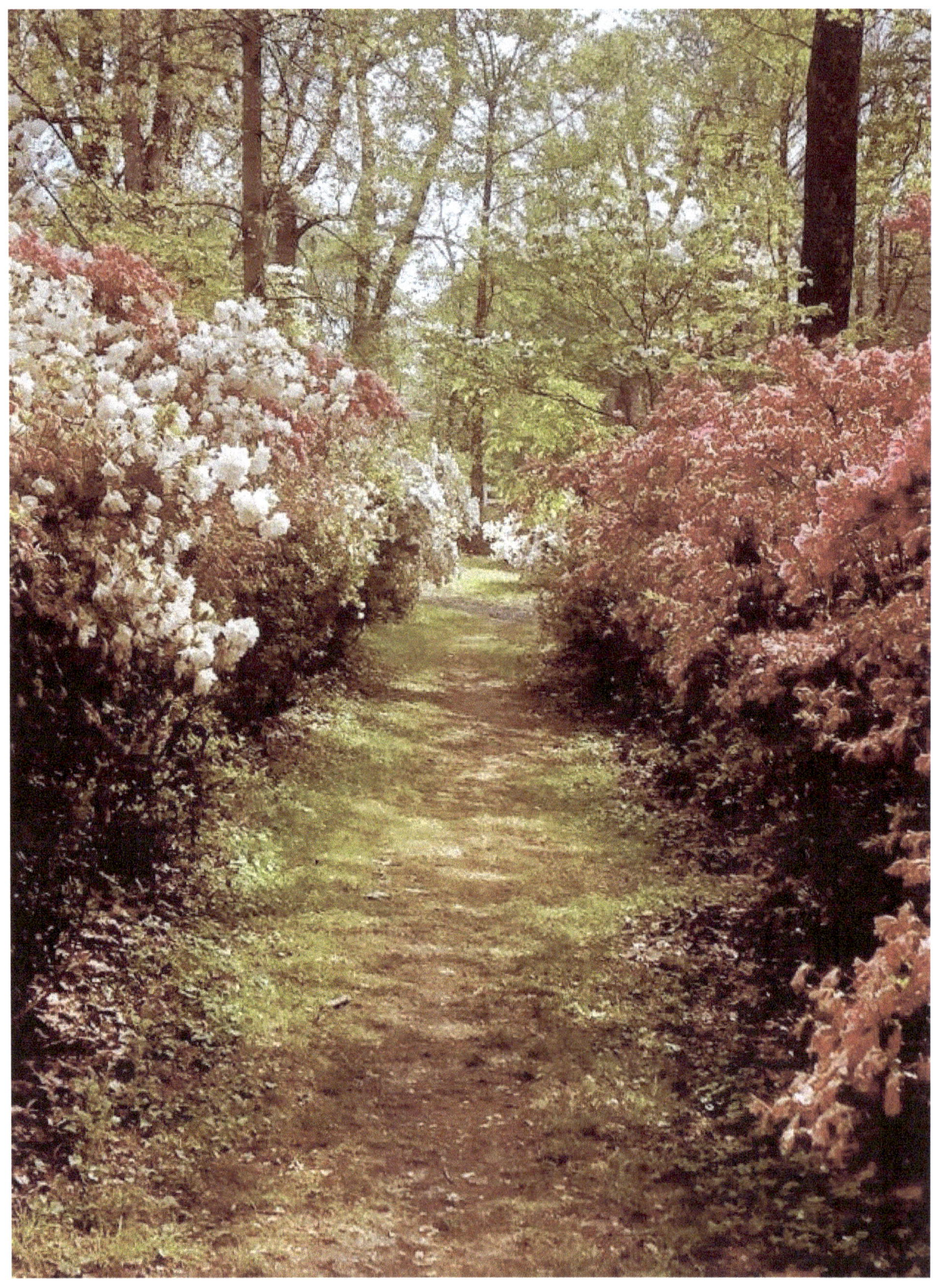

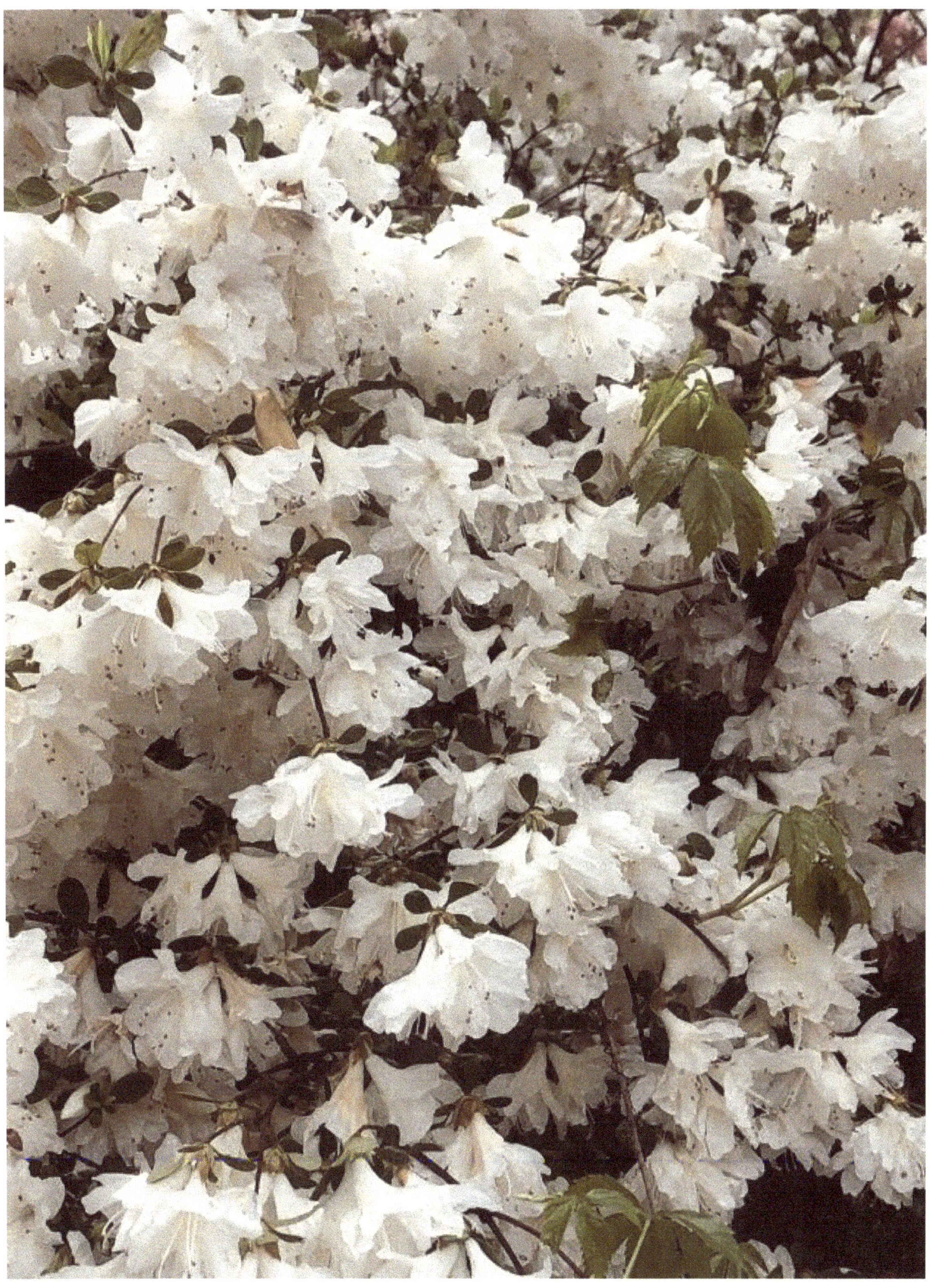

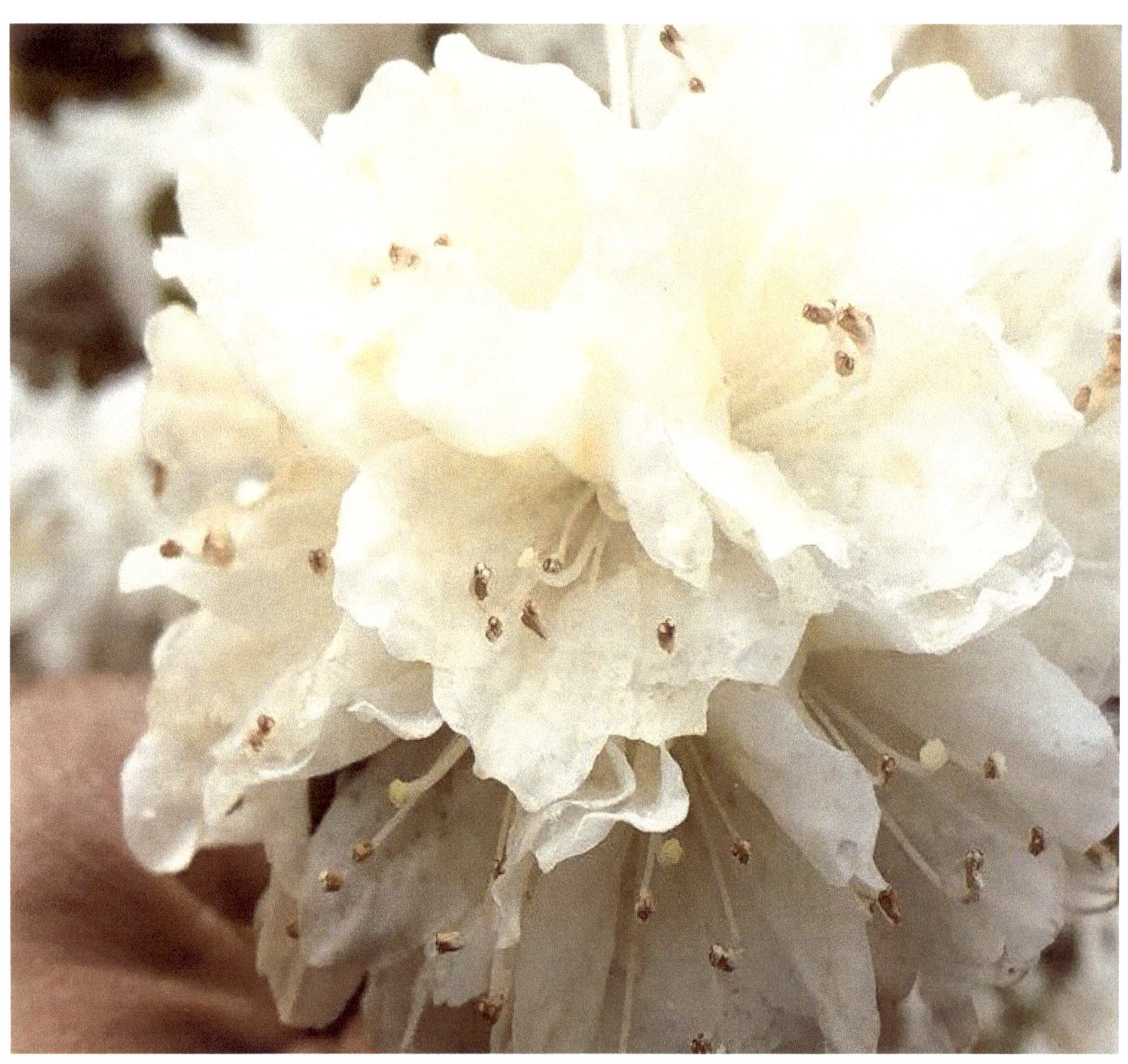

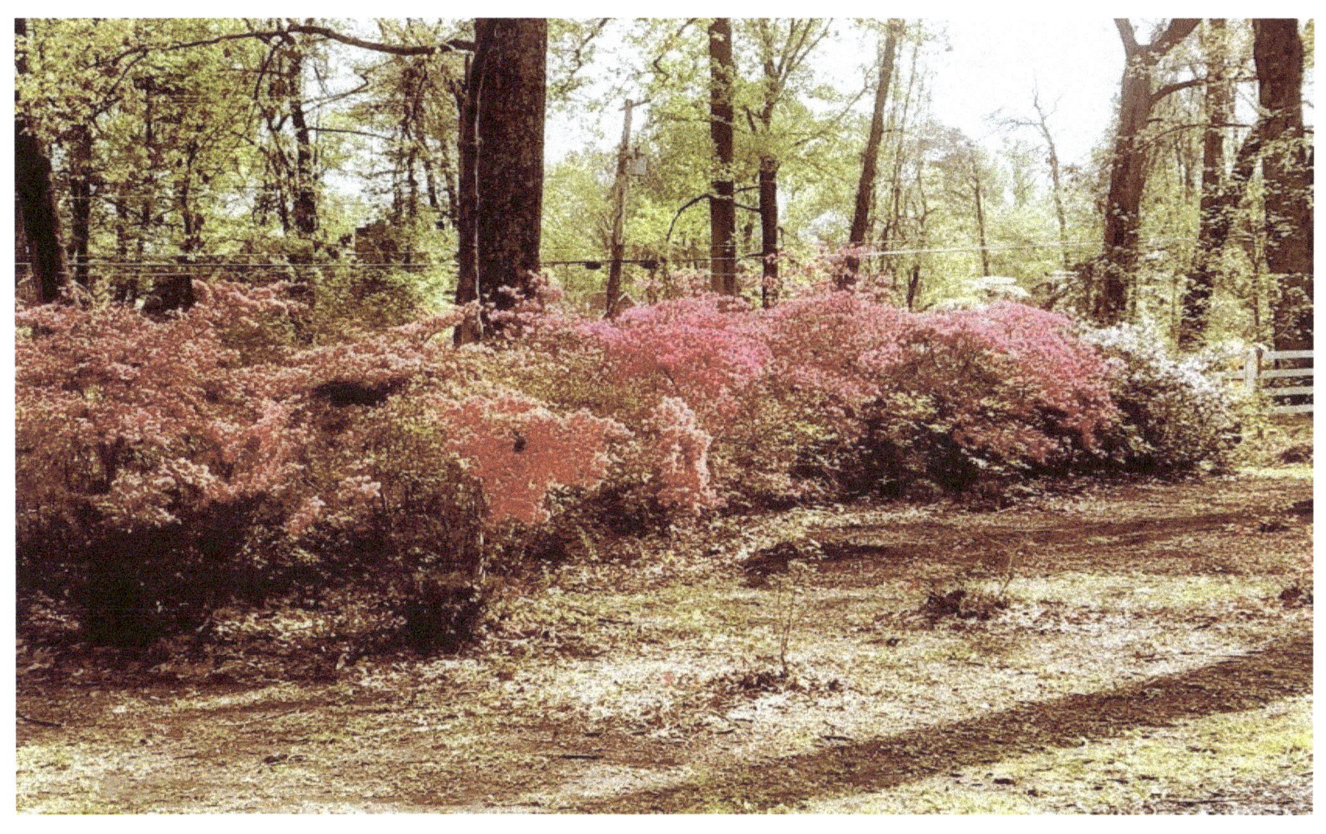

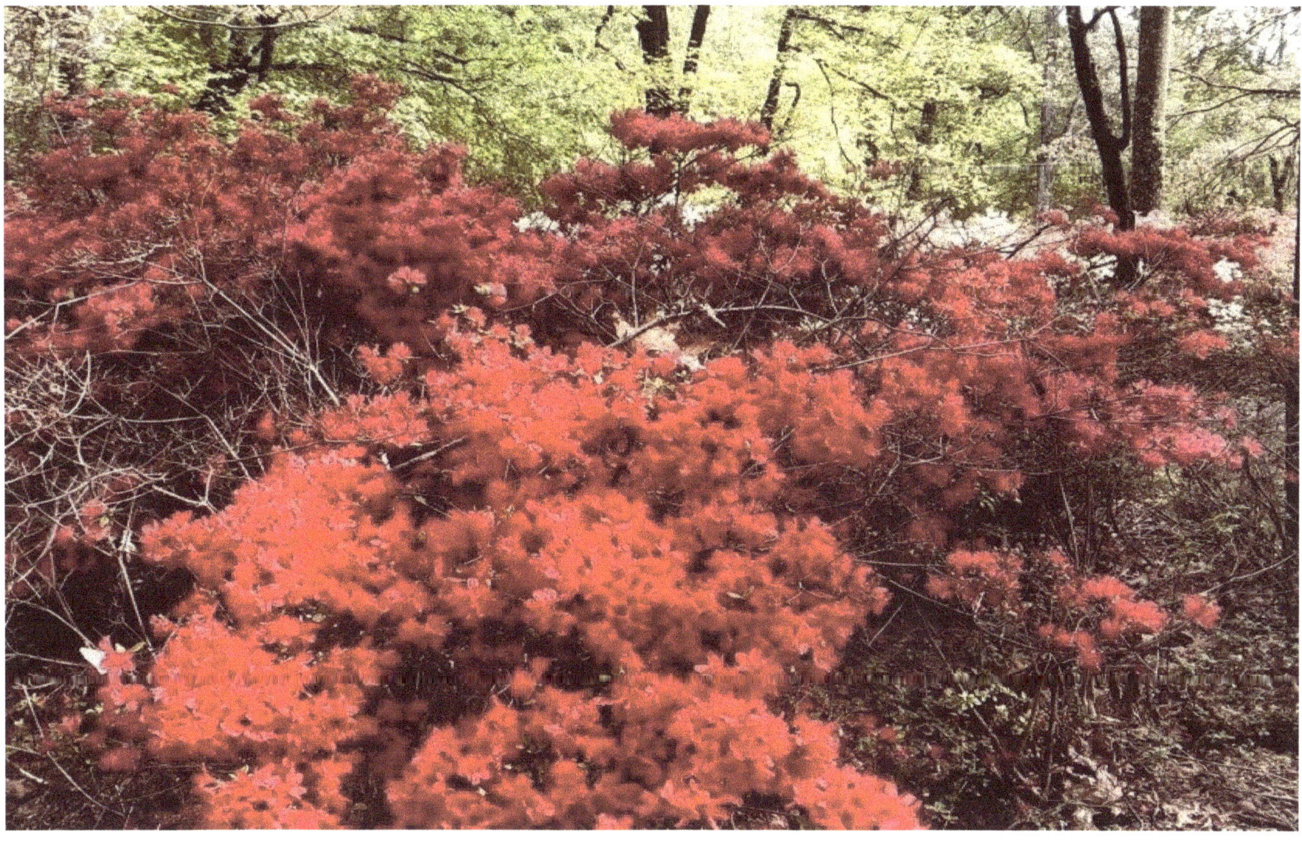

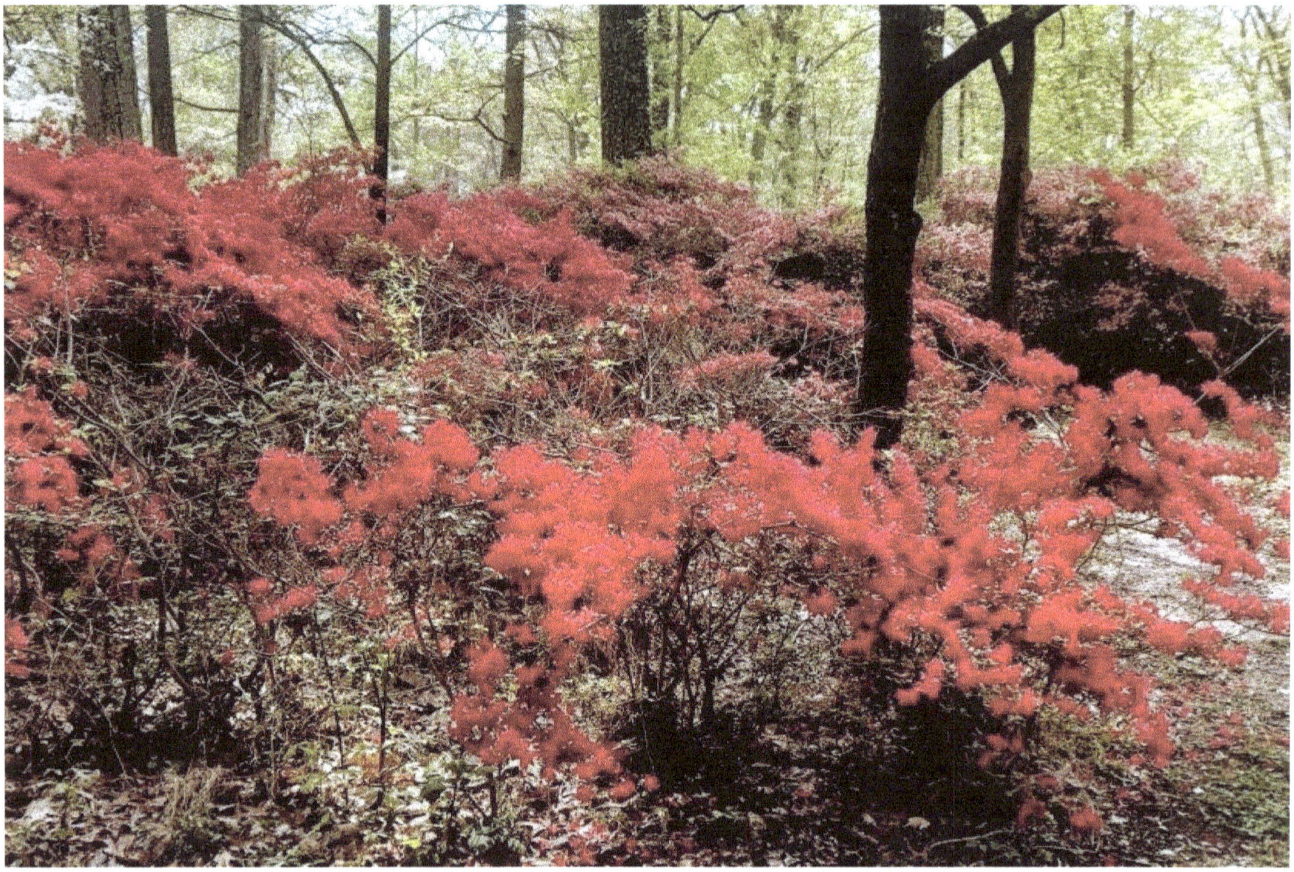

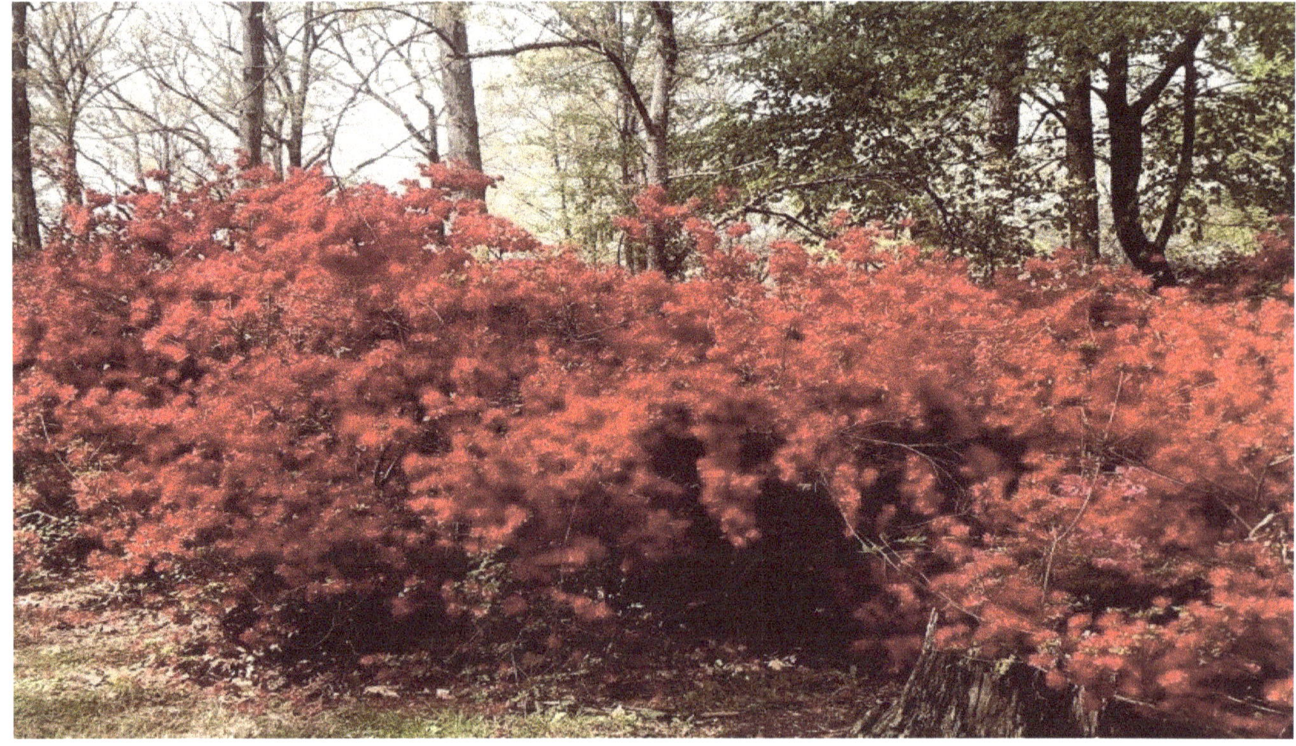

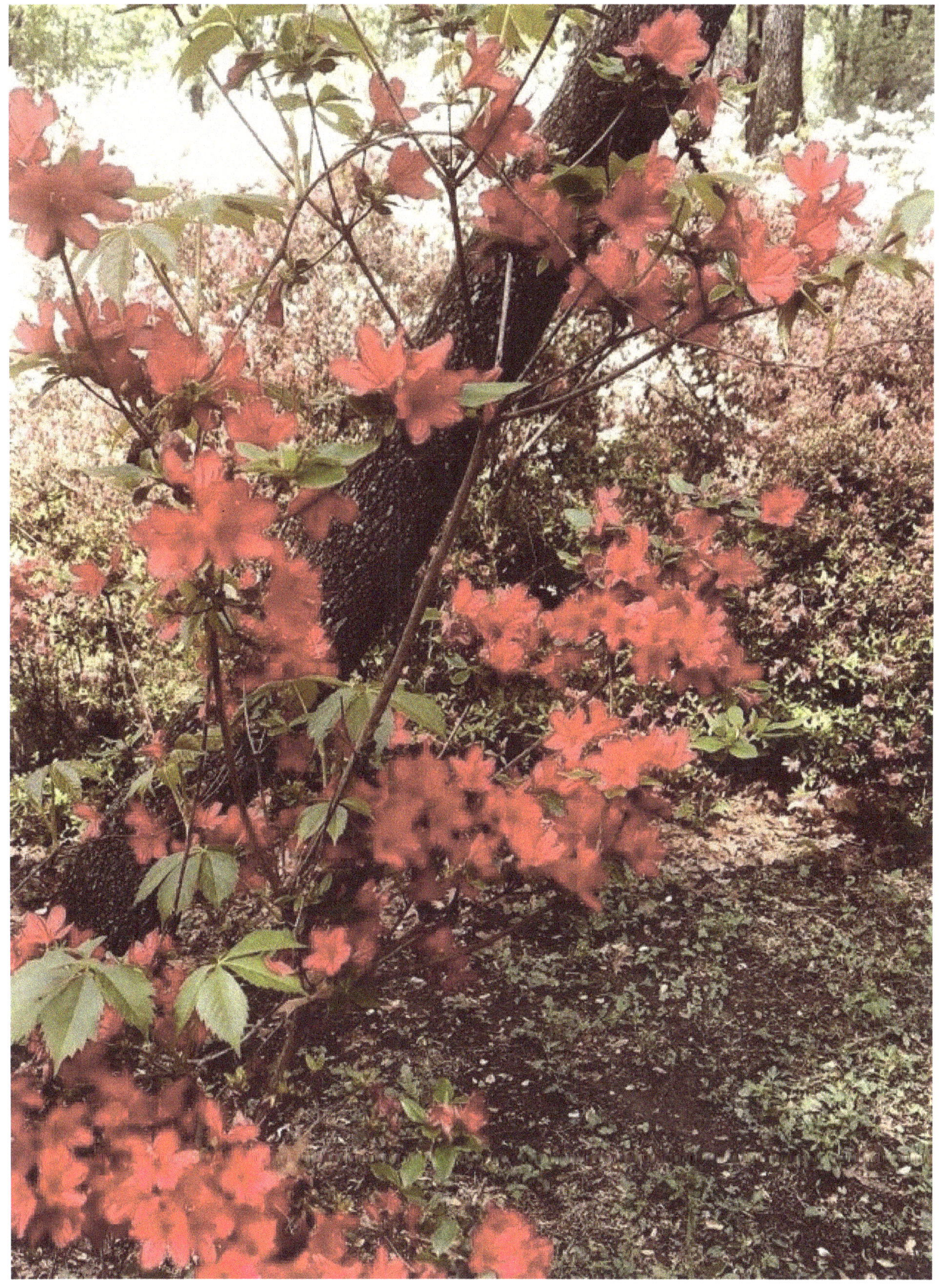

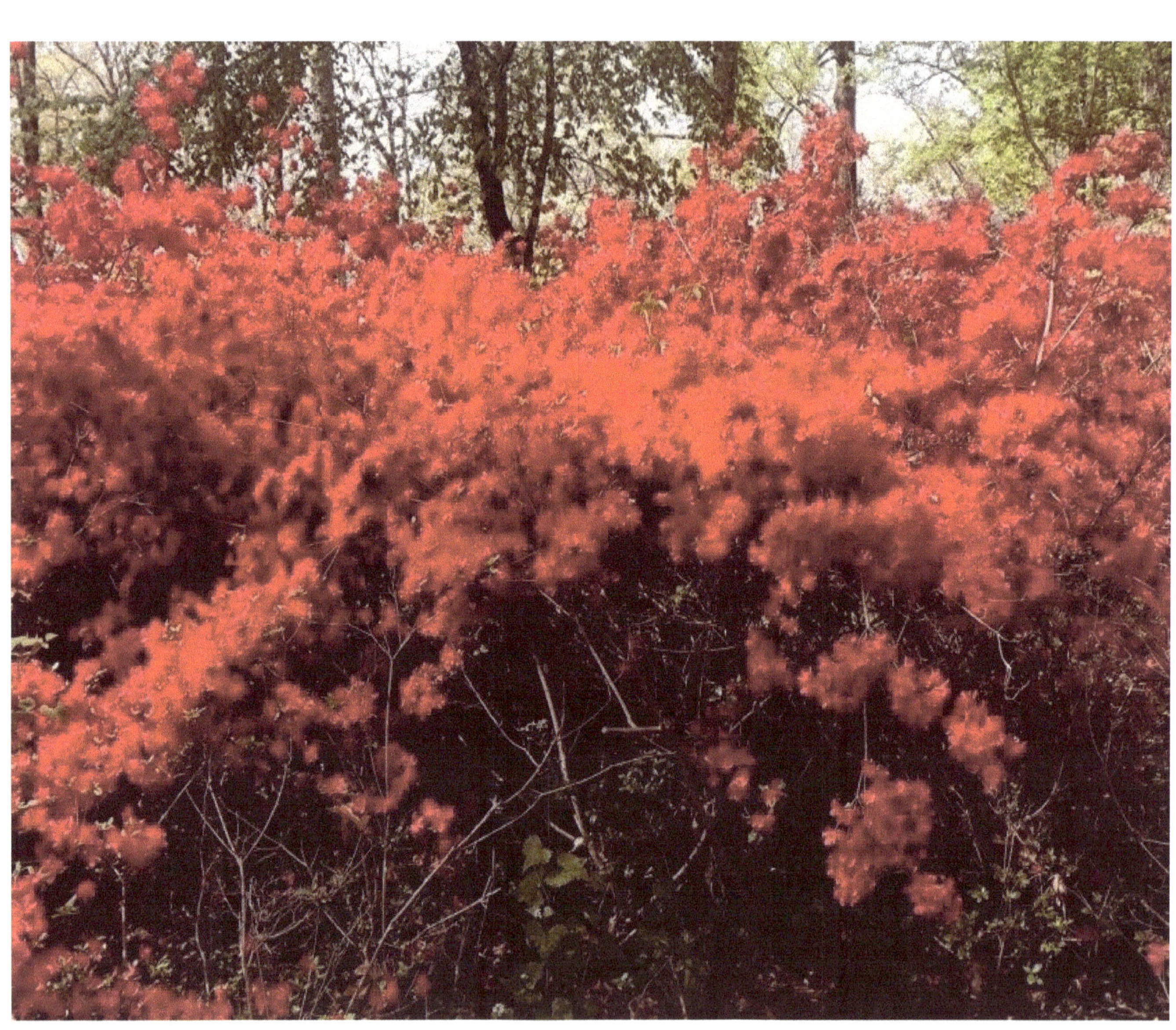

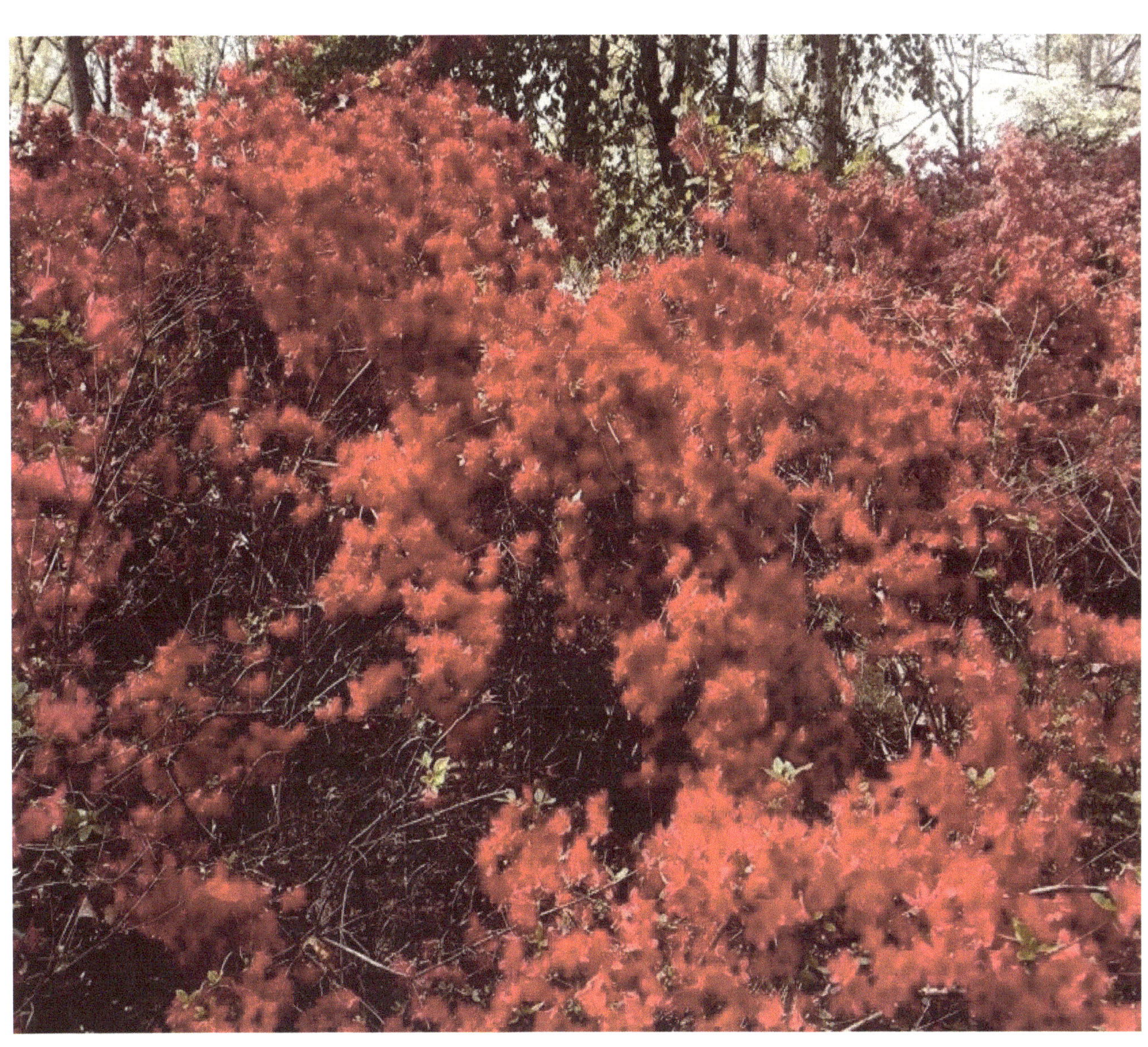

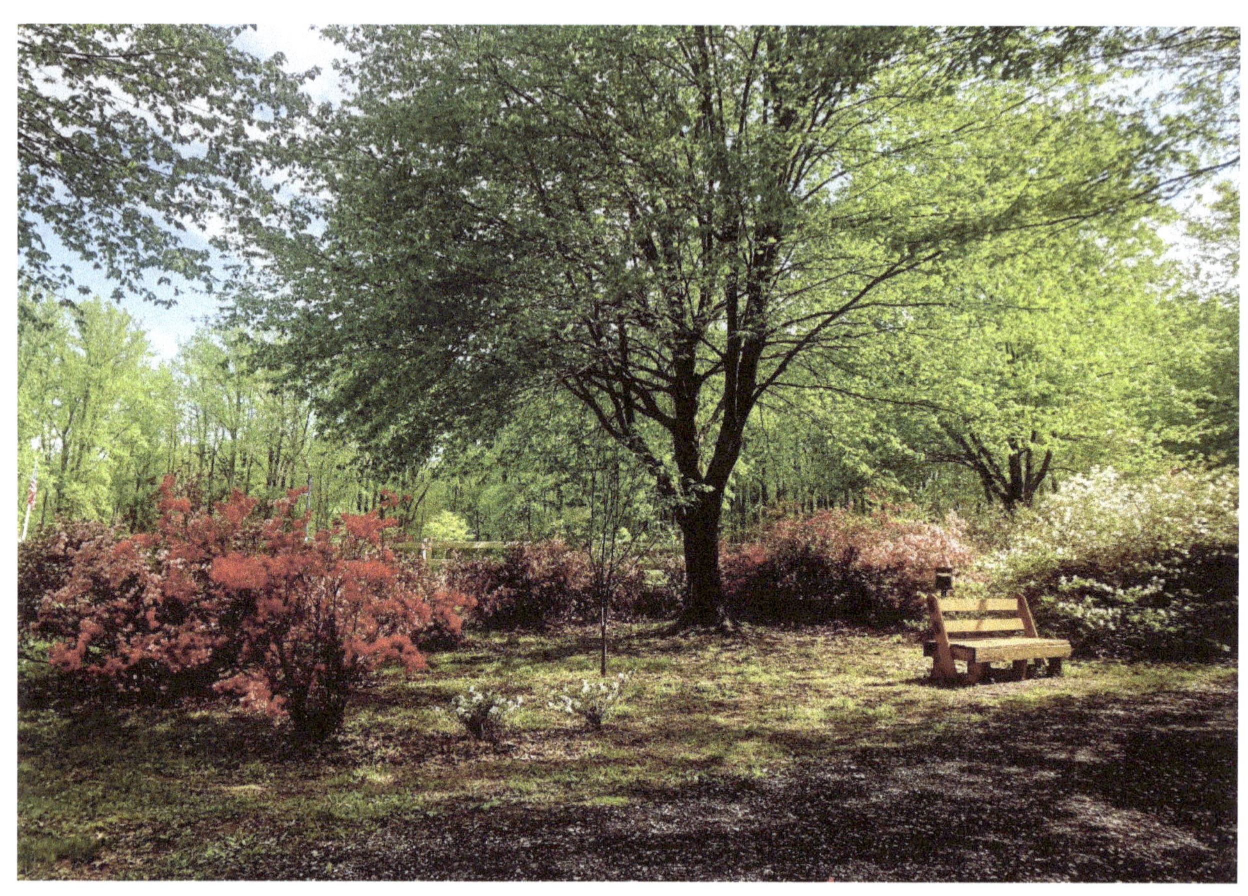

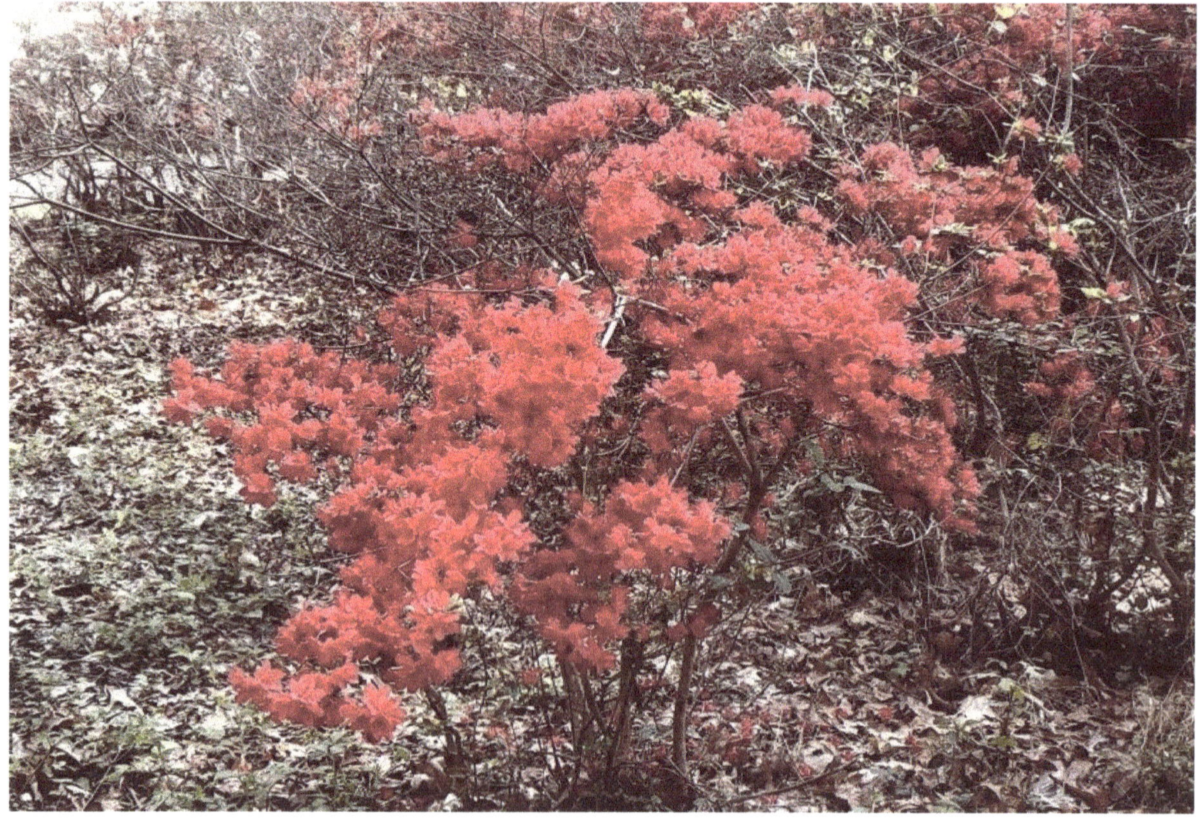

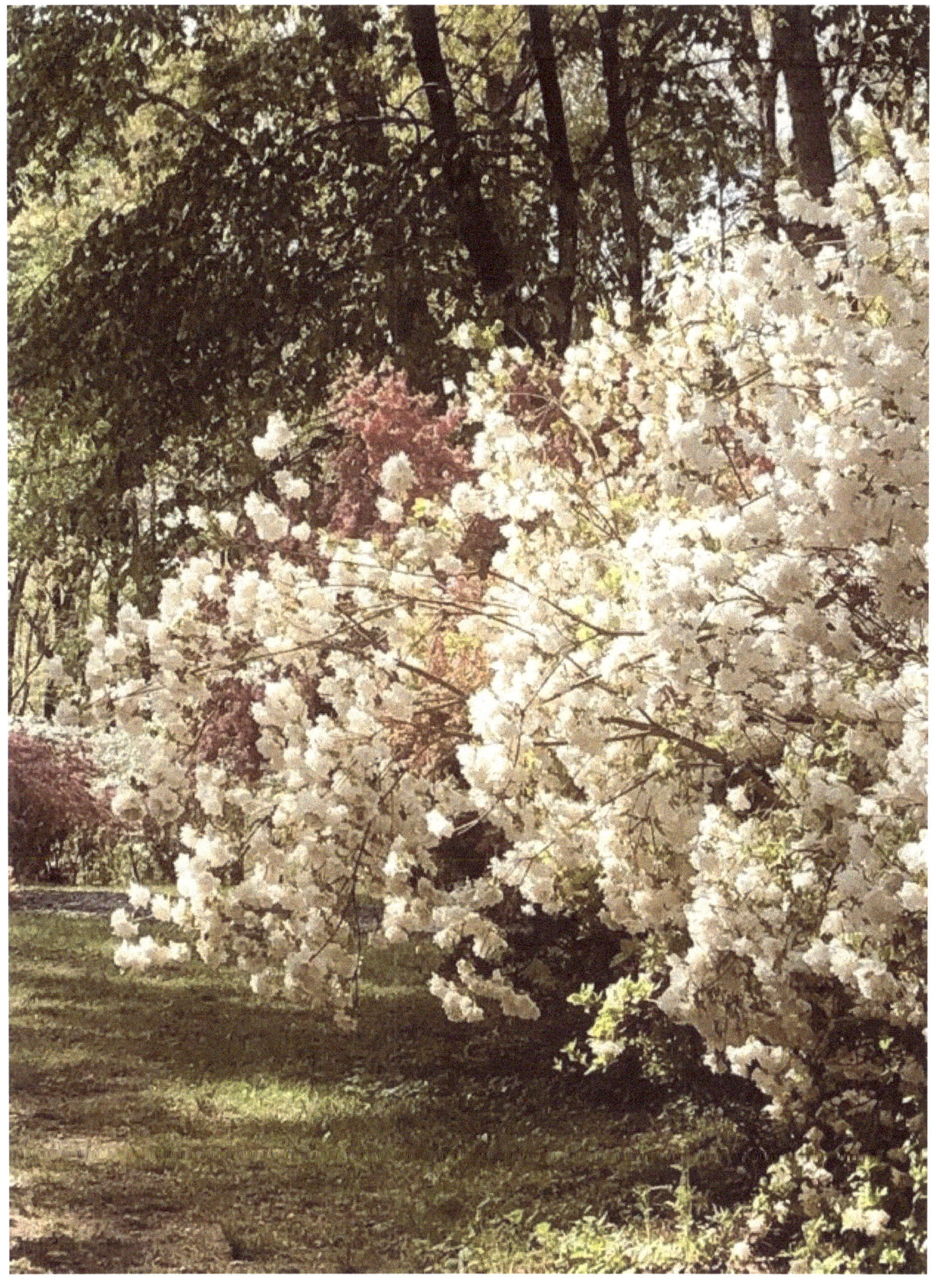

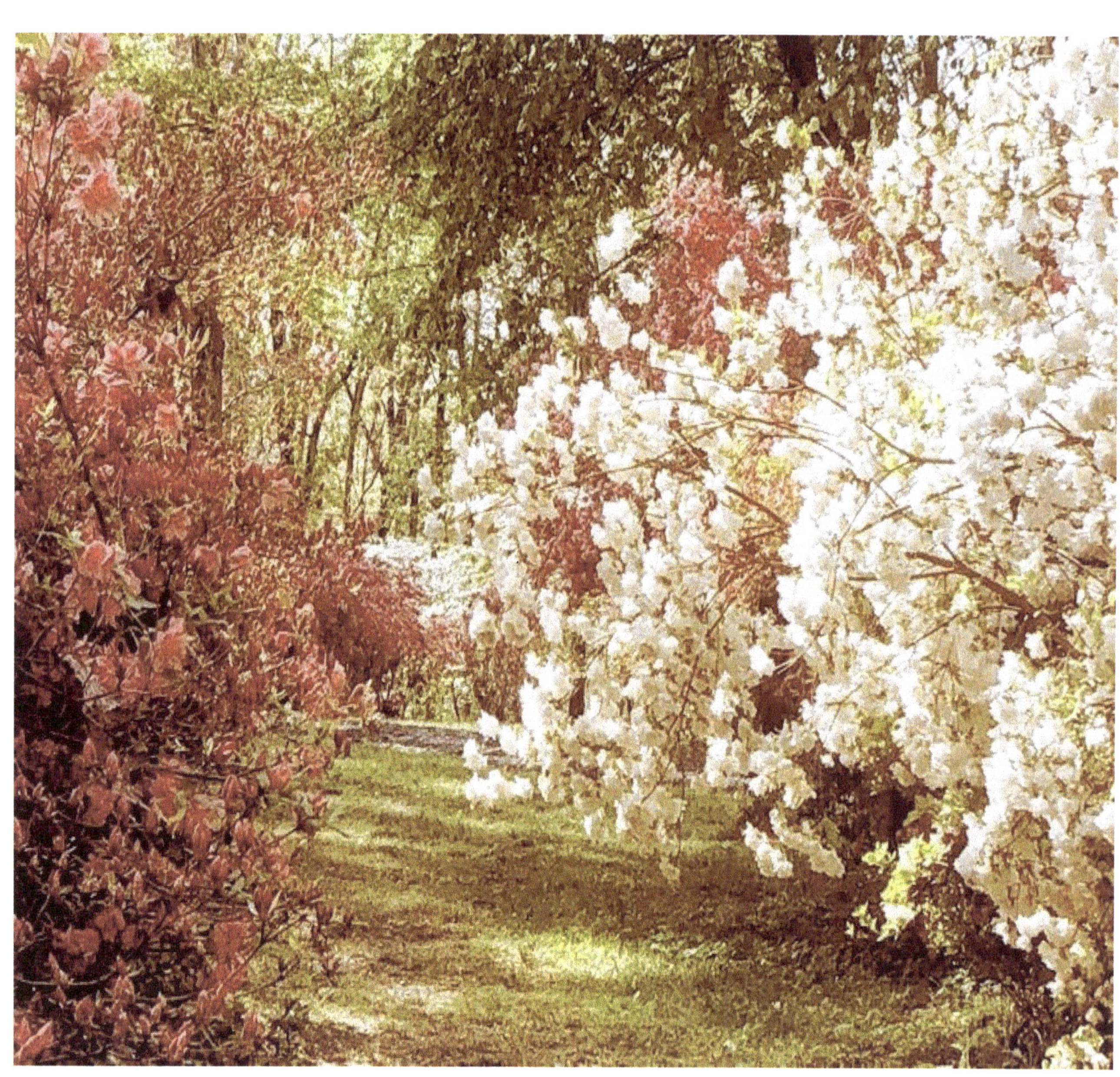

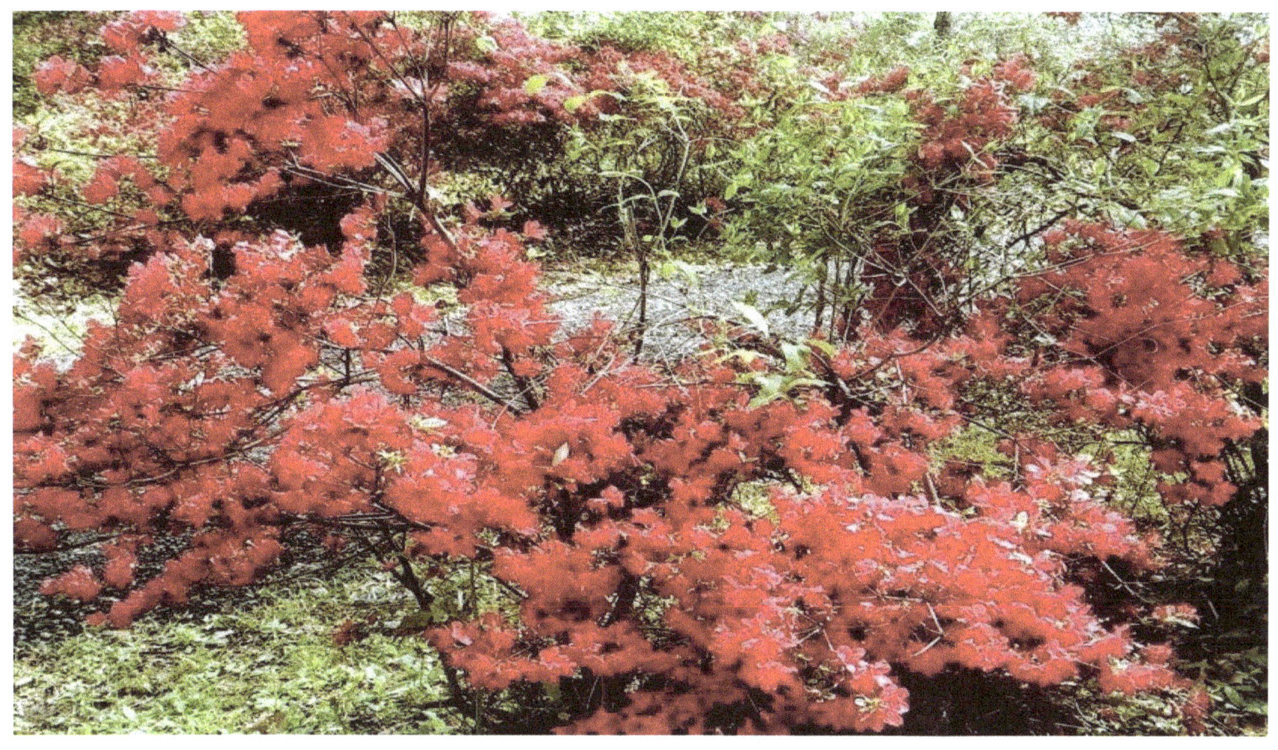

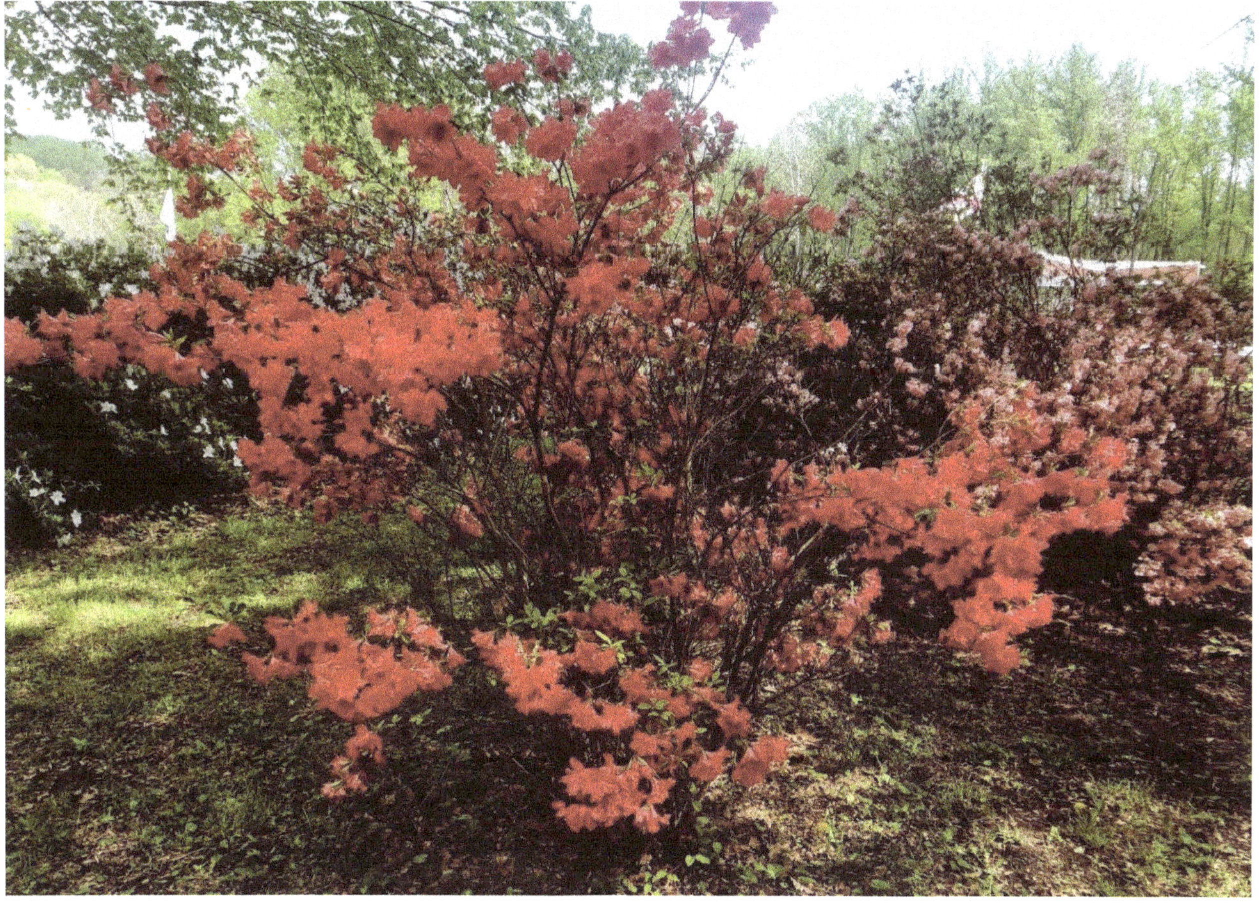

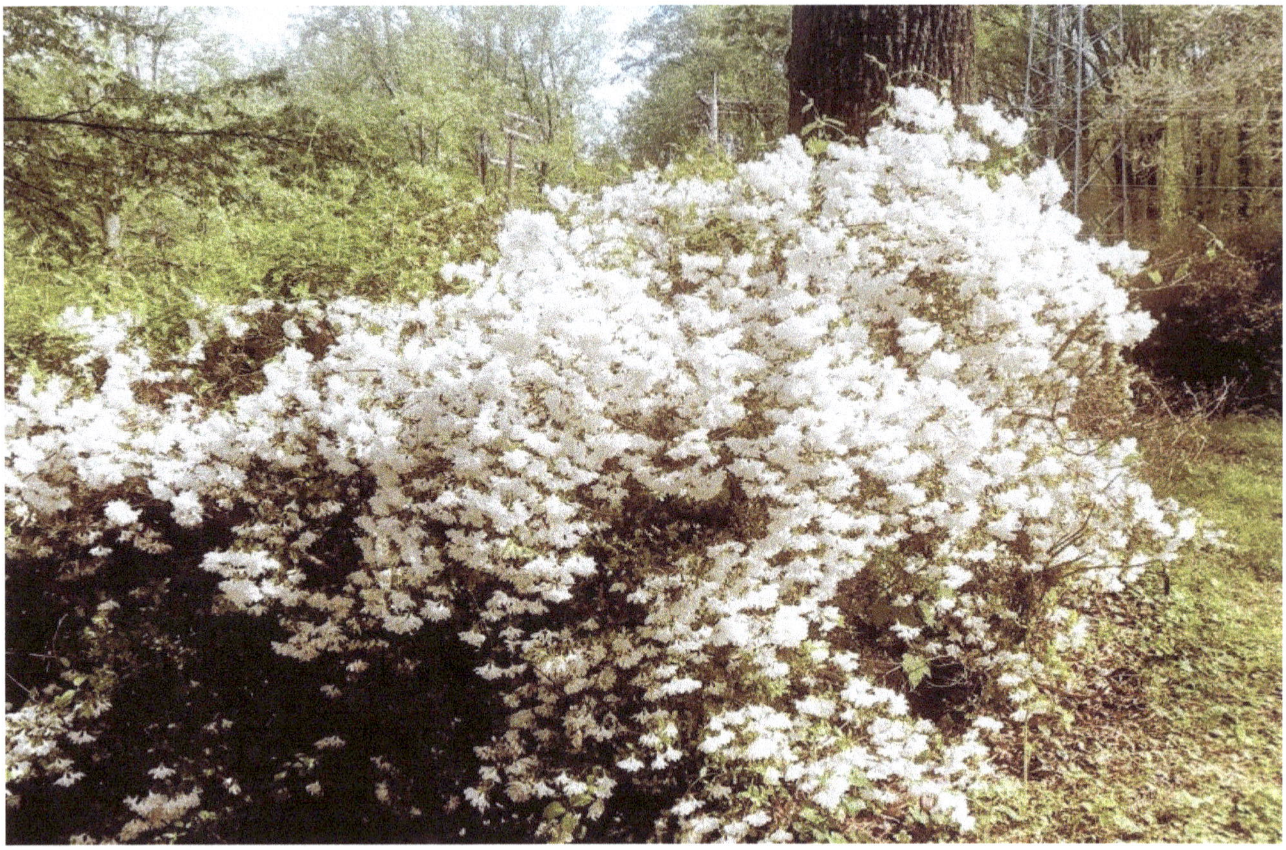

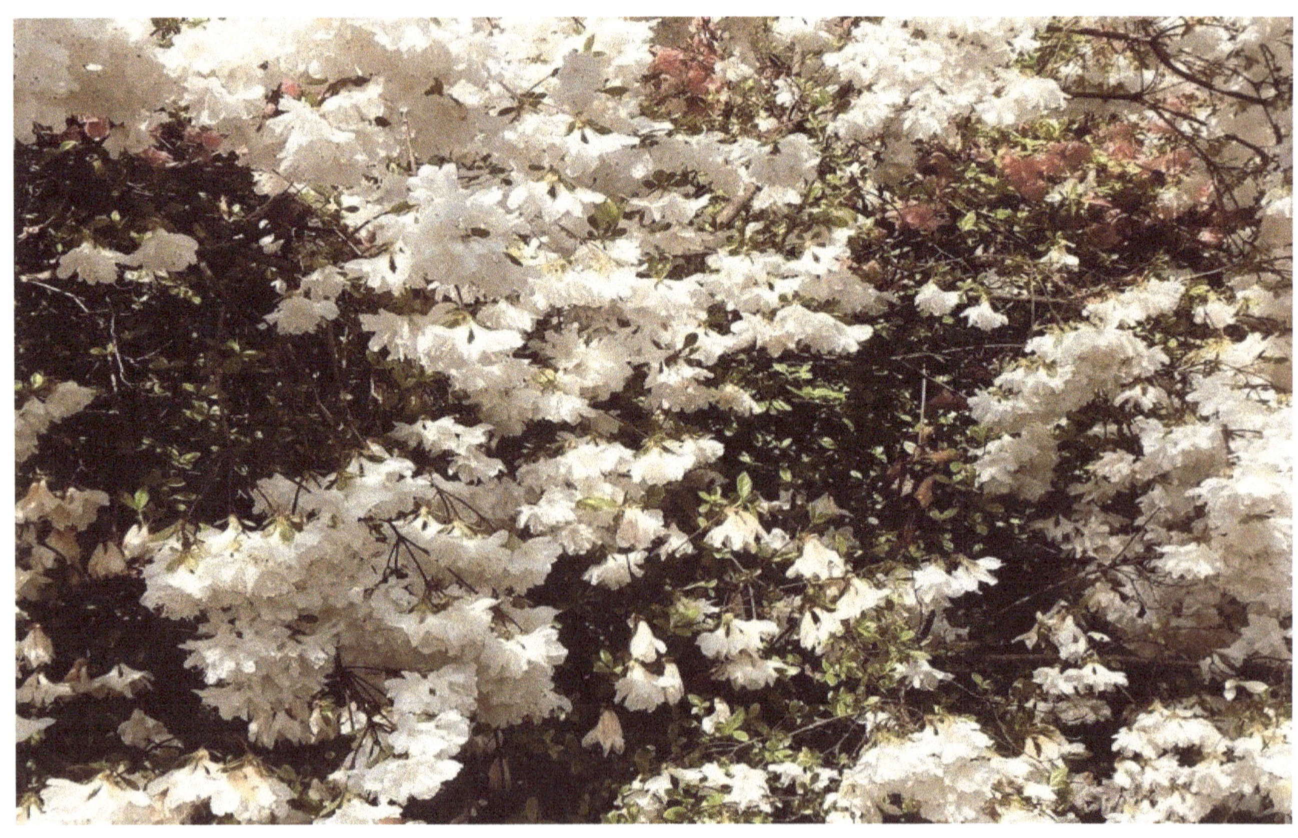

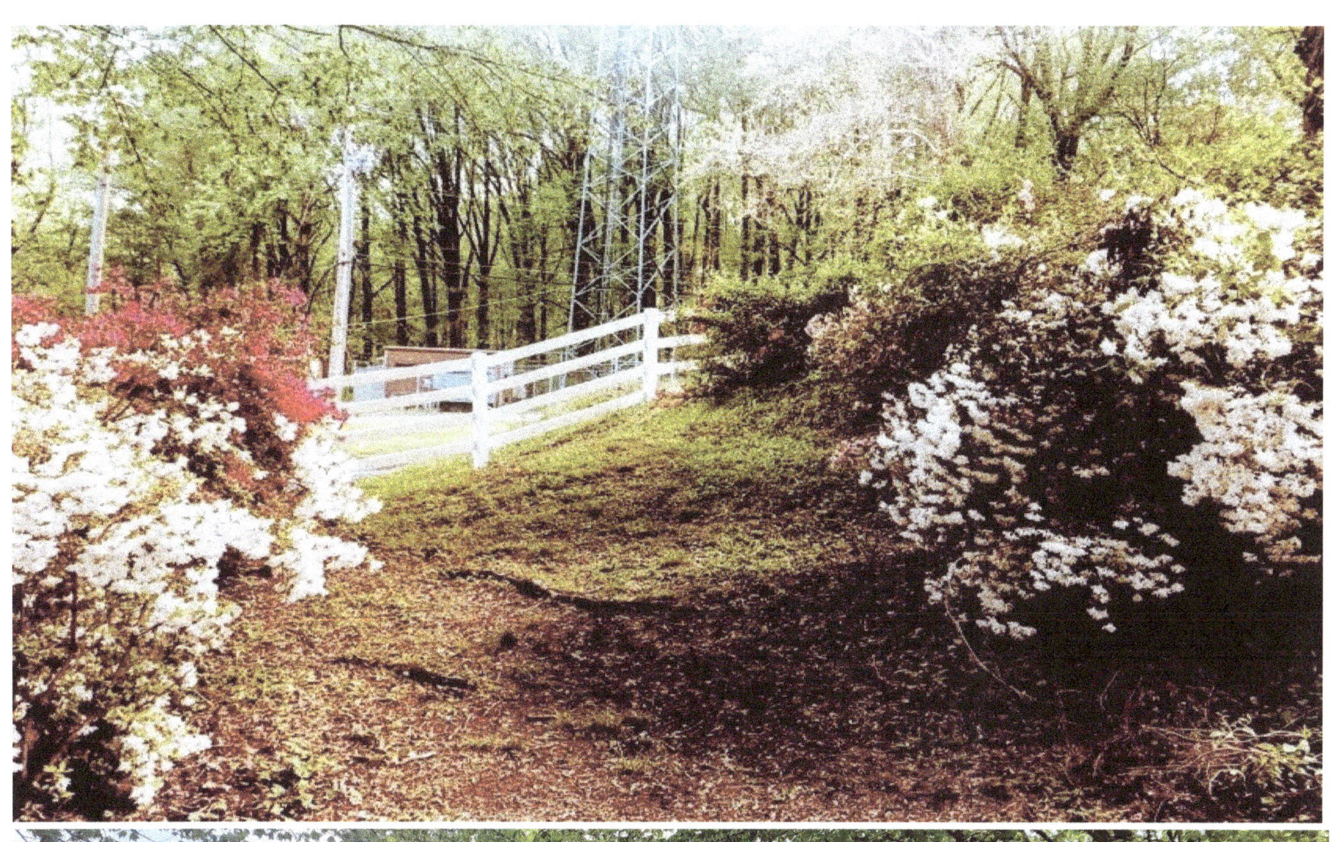

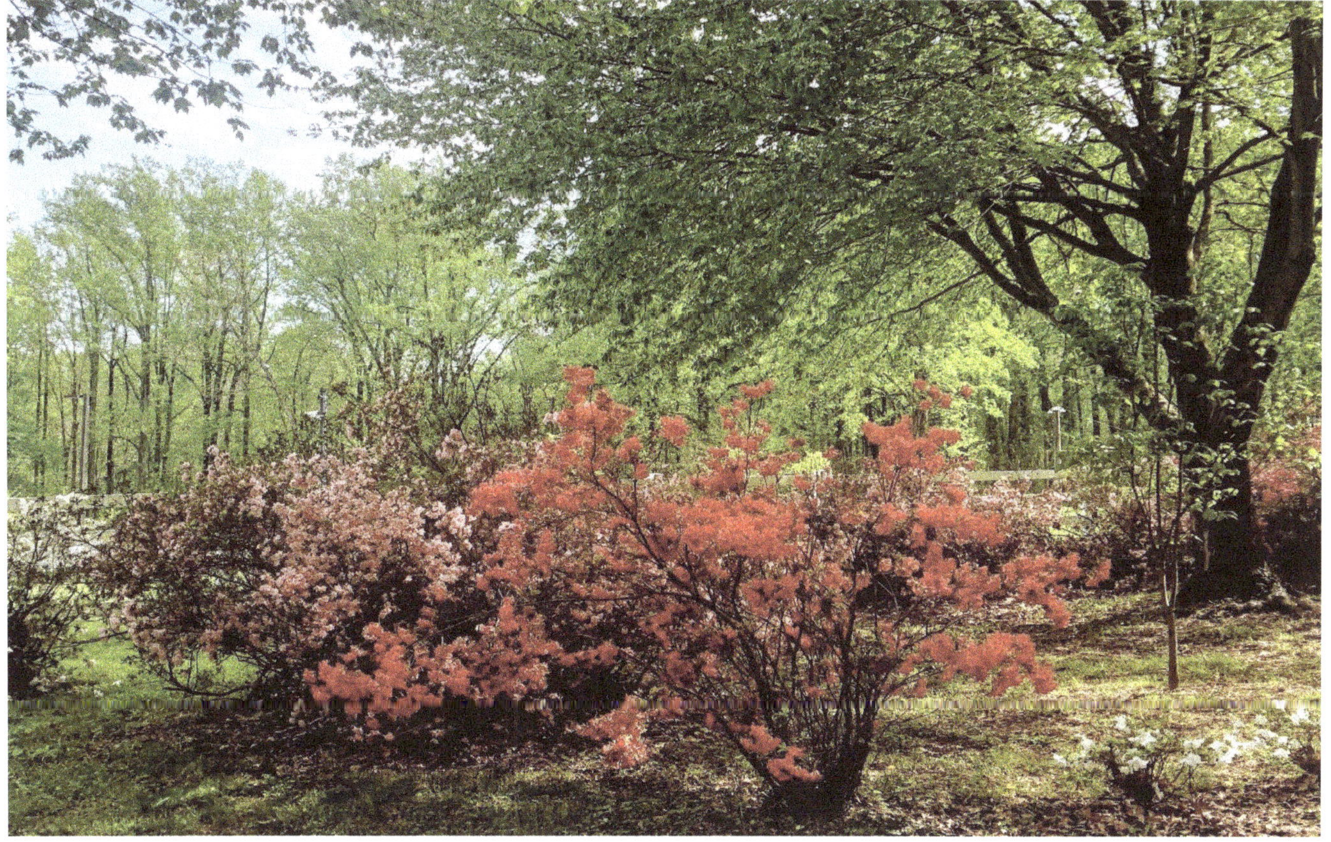

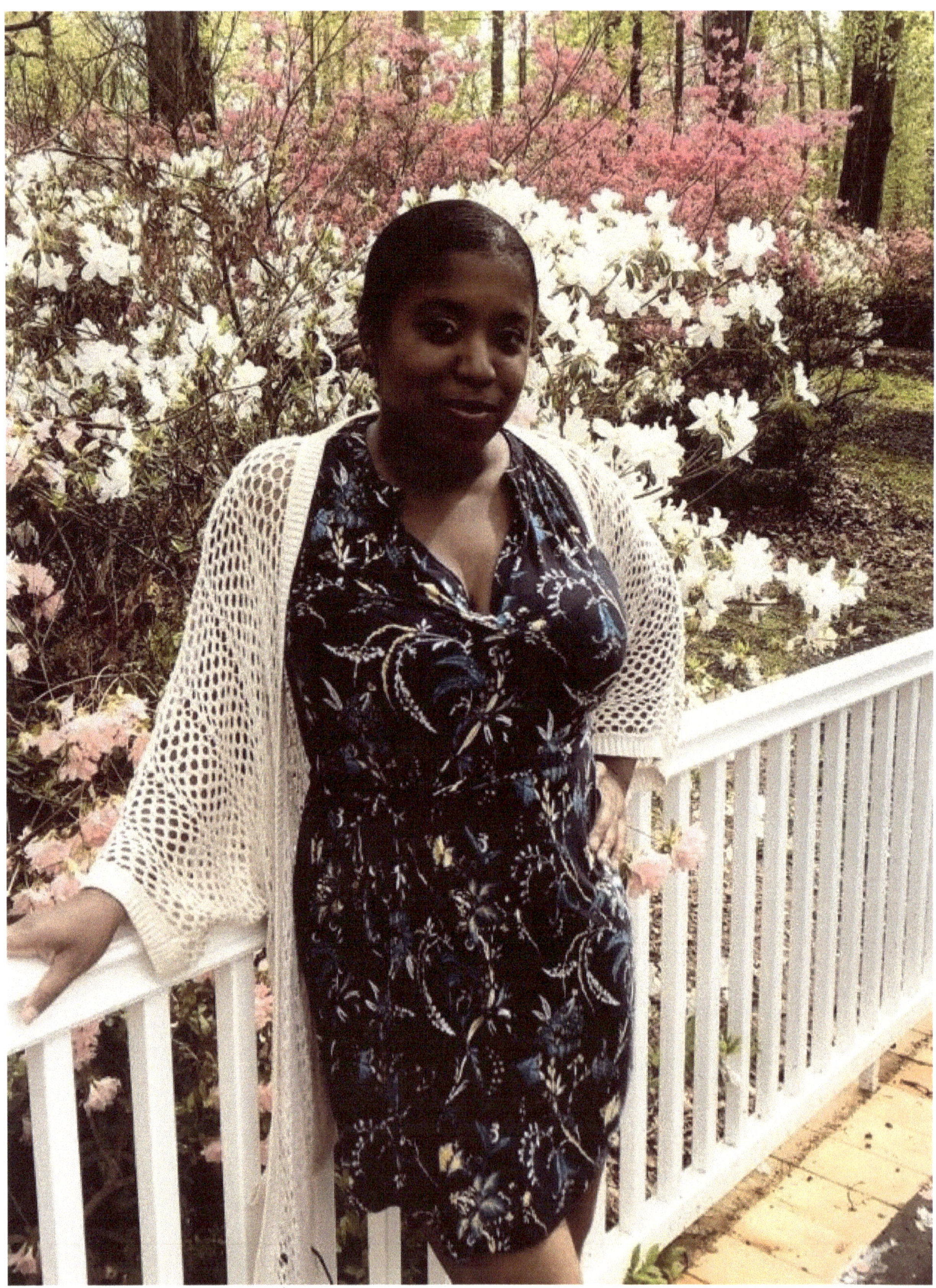

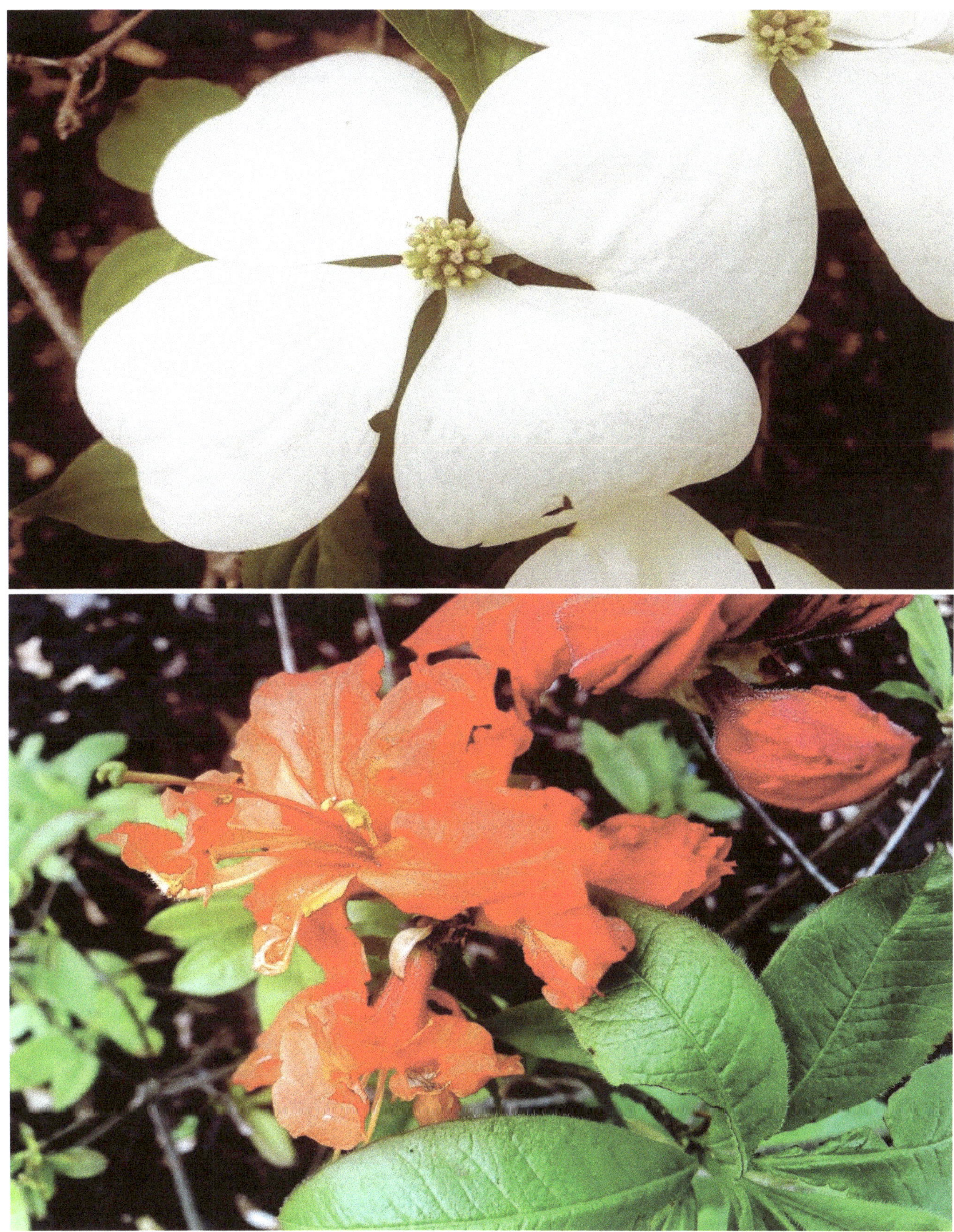

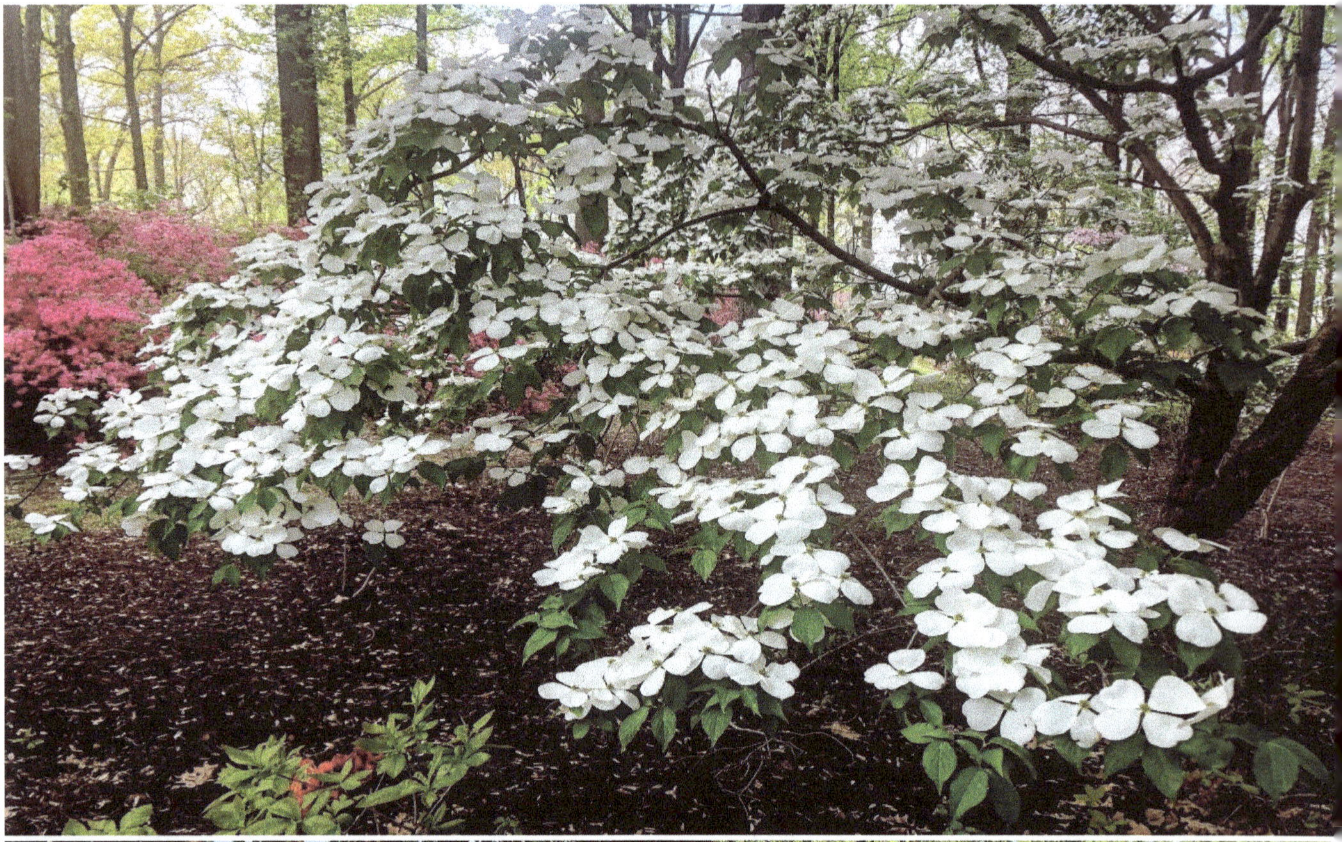

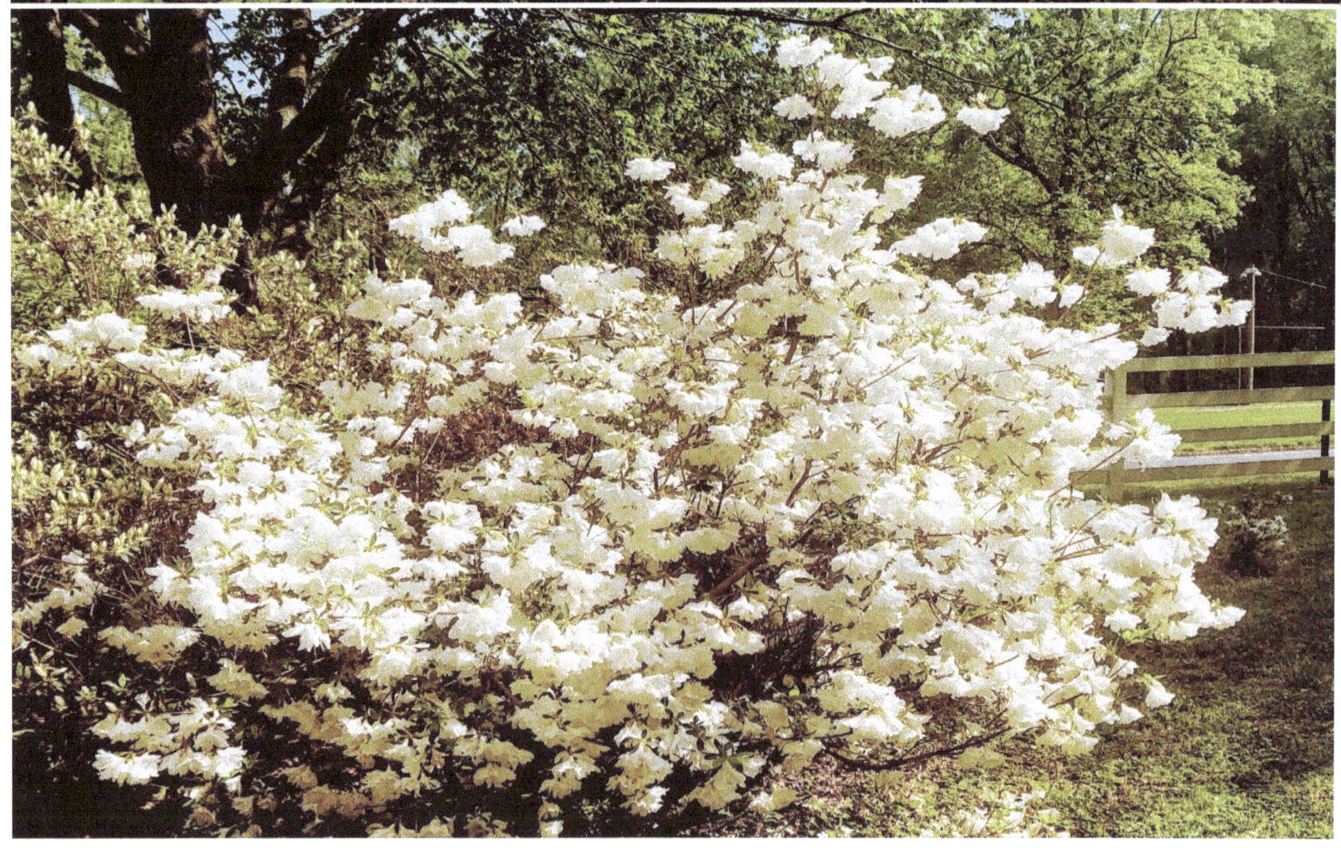

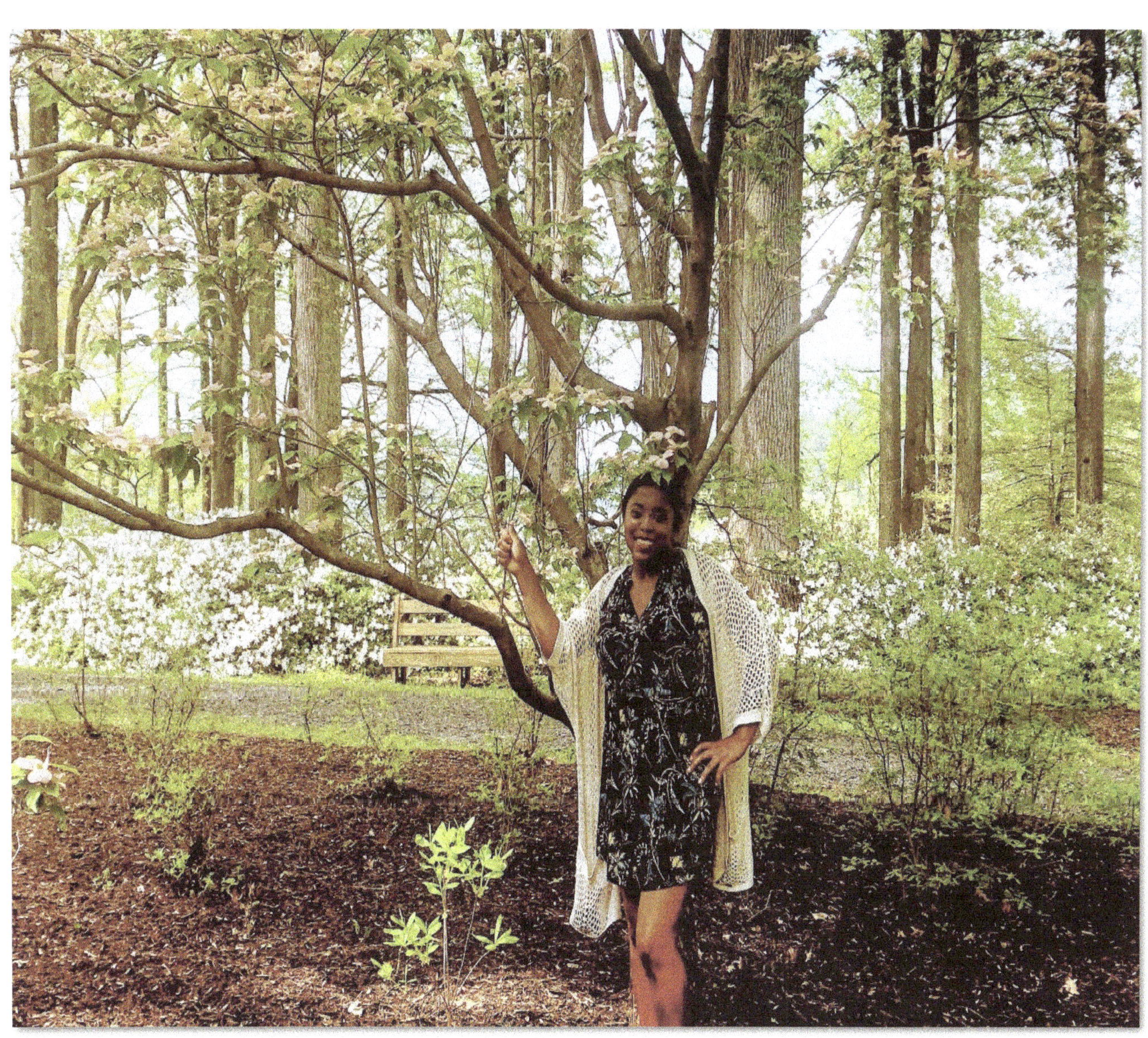

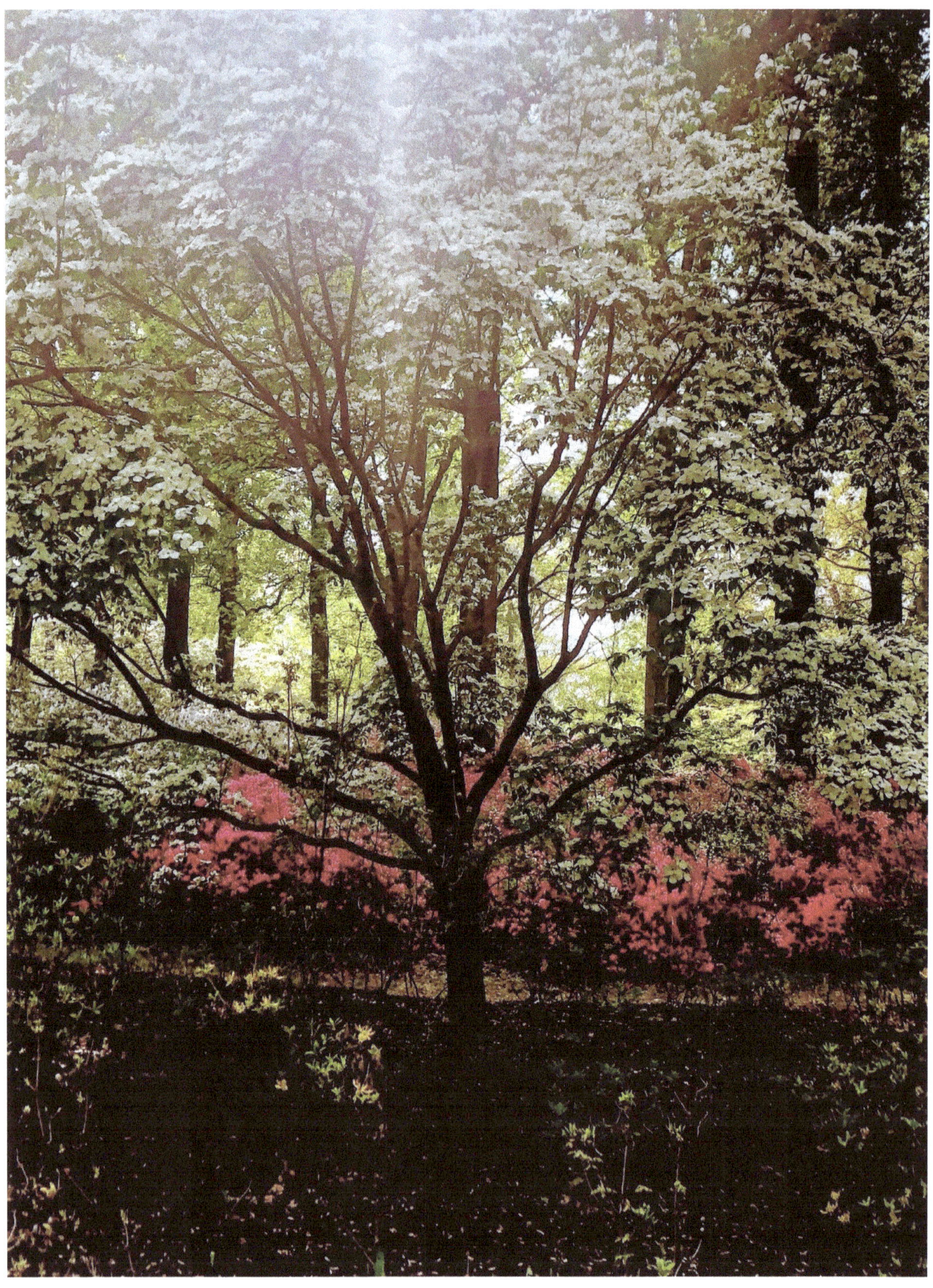

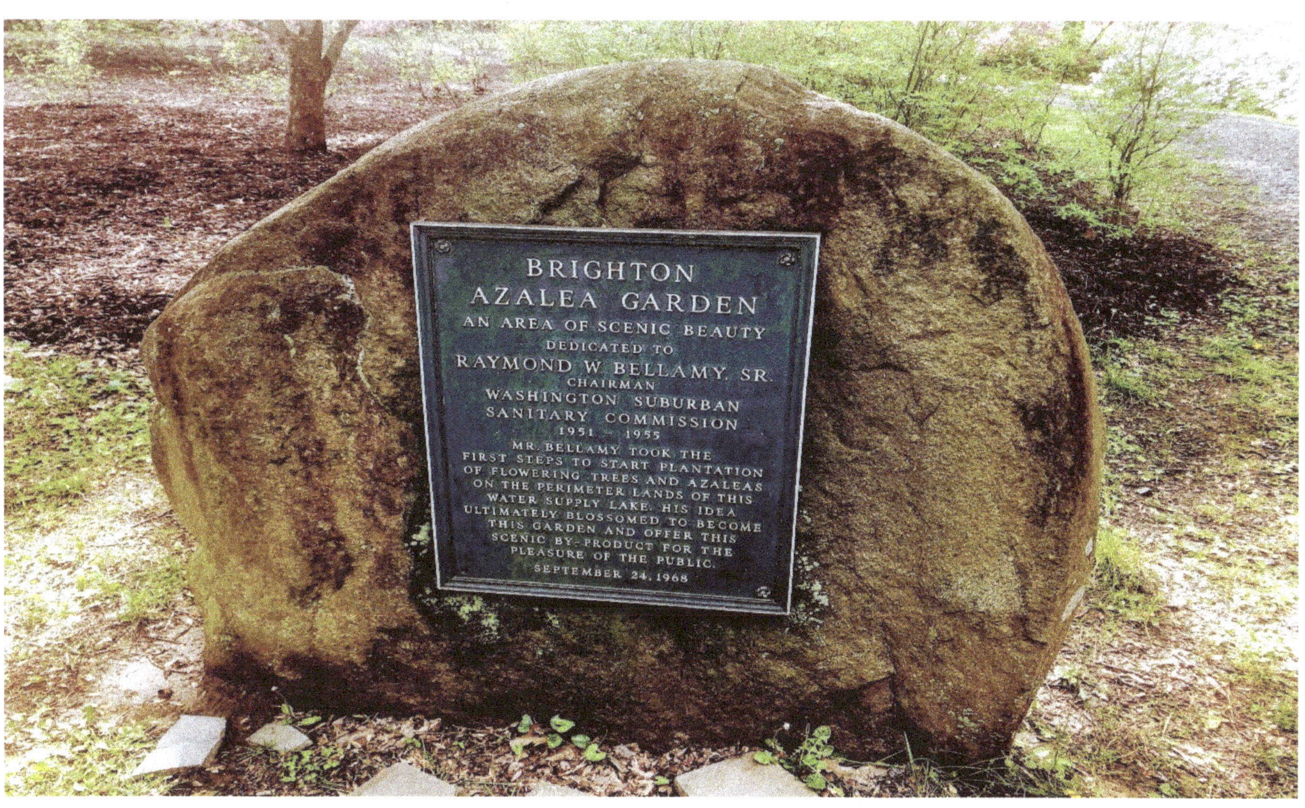

BRIGHTON
AZALEA GARDEN
AN AREA OF SCENIC BEAUTY
DEDICATED TO
RAYMOND W. BELLAMY, SR.
CHAIRMAN
WASHINGTON SUBURBAN
SANITARY COMMISSION
1951 — 1955
MR. BELLAMY TOOK THE
FIRST STEPS TO START PLANTATION
OF FLOWERING TREES AND AZALEAS
ON THE PERIMETER LANDS OF THIS
WATER SUPPLY LAKE. HIS IDEA
ULTIMATELY BLOSSOMED TO BECOME
THIS GARDEN AND OFFER THIS
SCENIC BY-PRODUCT FOR THE
PLEASURE OF THE PUBLIC.
SEPTEMBER 24, 1968

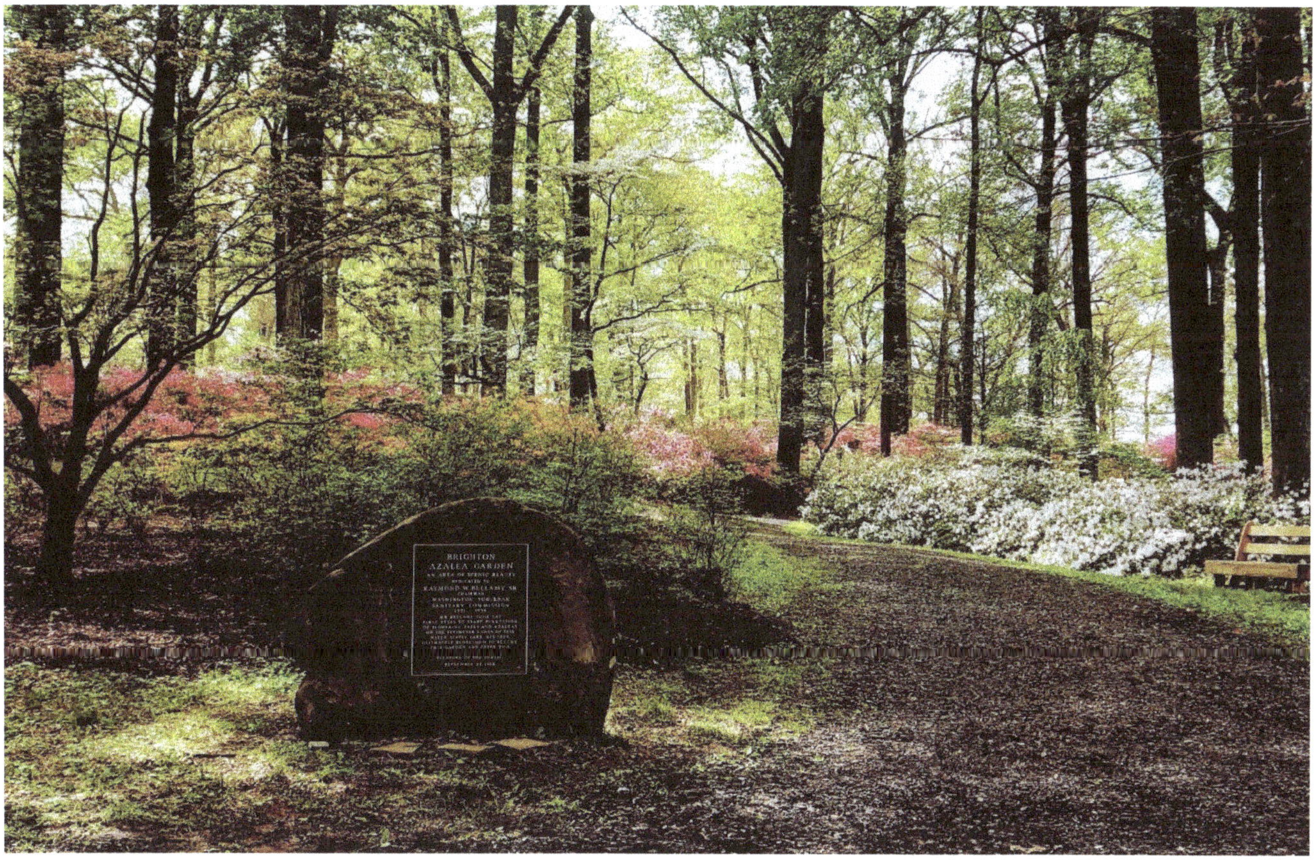

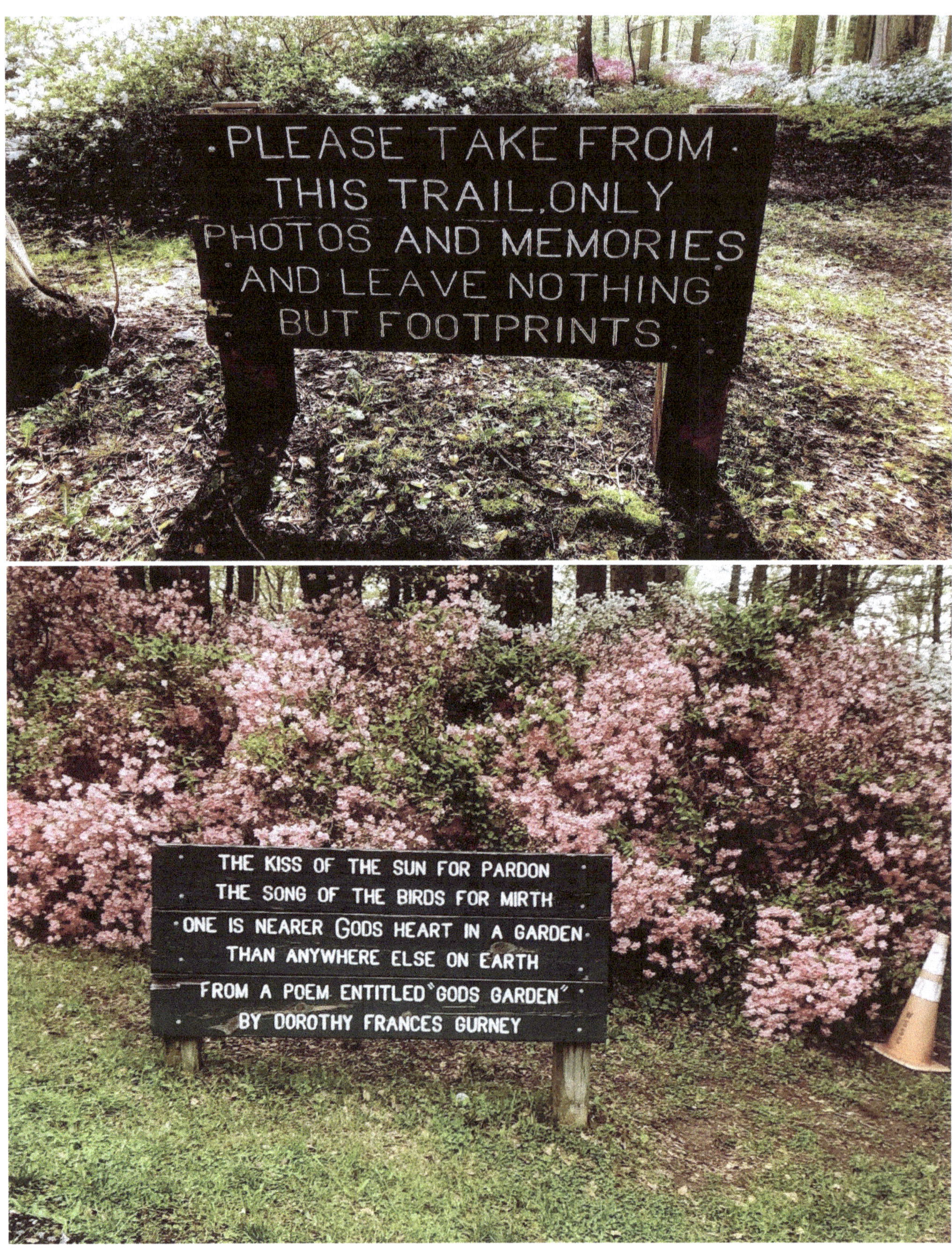

· PLEASE TAKE FROM ·
THIS TRAIL, ONLY
PHOTOS AND MEMORIES
AND LEAVE NOTHING
BUT FOOTPRINTS

THE KISS OF THE SUN FOR PARDON
THE SONG OF THE BIRDS FOR MIRTH
· ONE IS NEARER GODS HEART IN A GARDEN ·
THAN ANYWHERE ELSE ON EARTH
FROM A POEM ENTITLED "GODS GARDEN"
· BY DOROTHY FRANCES GURNEY

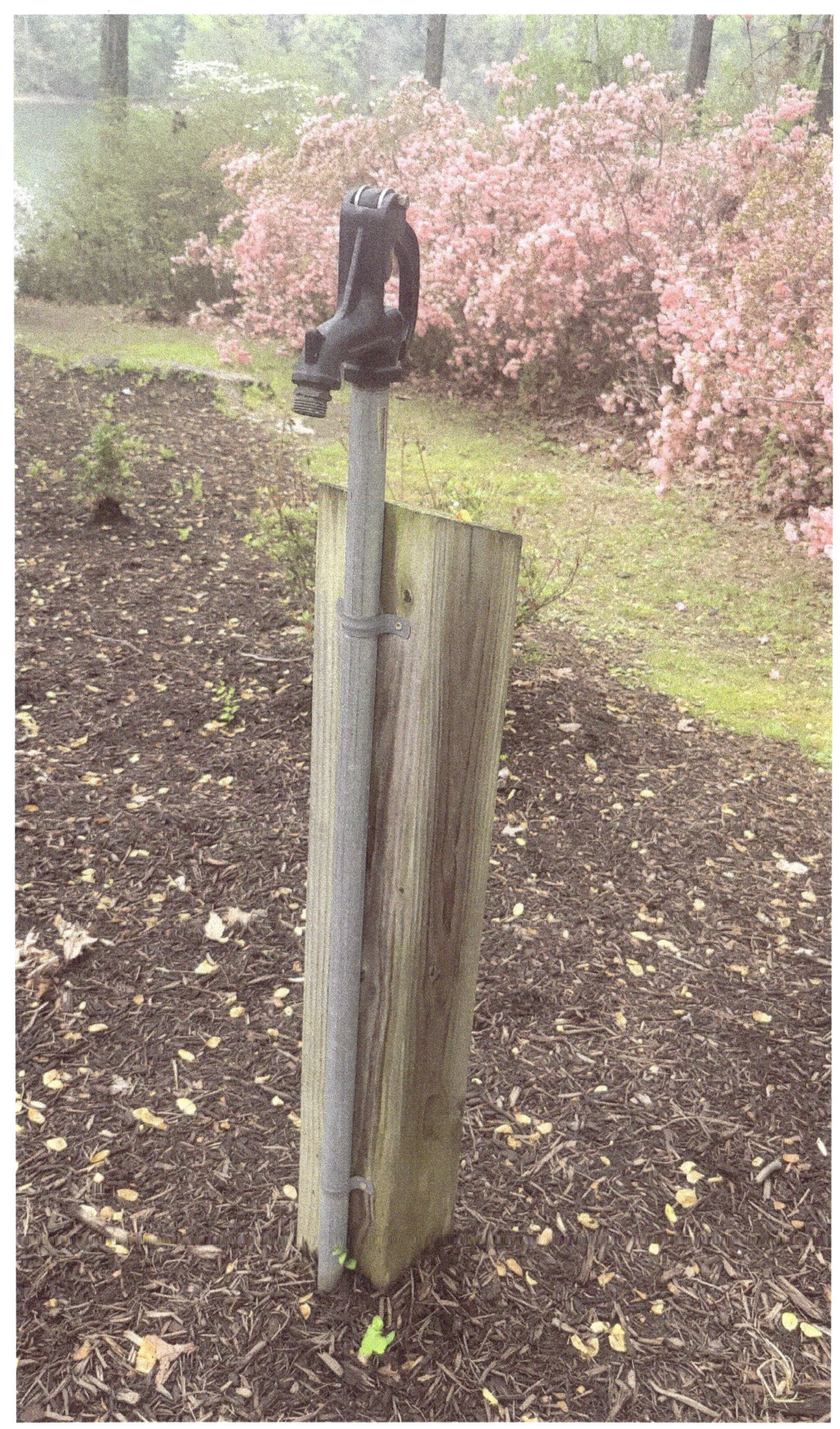

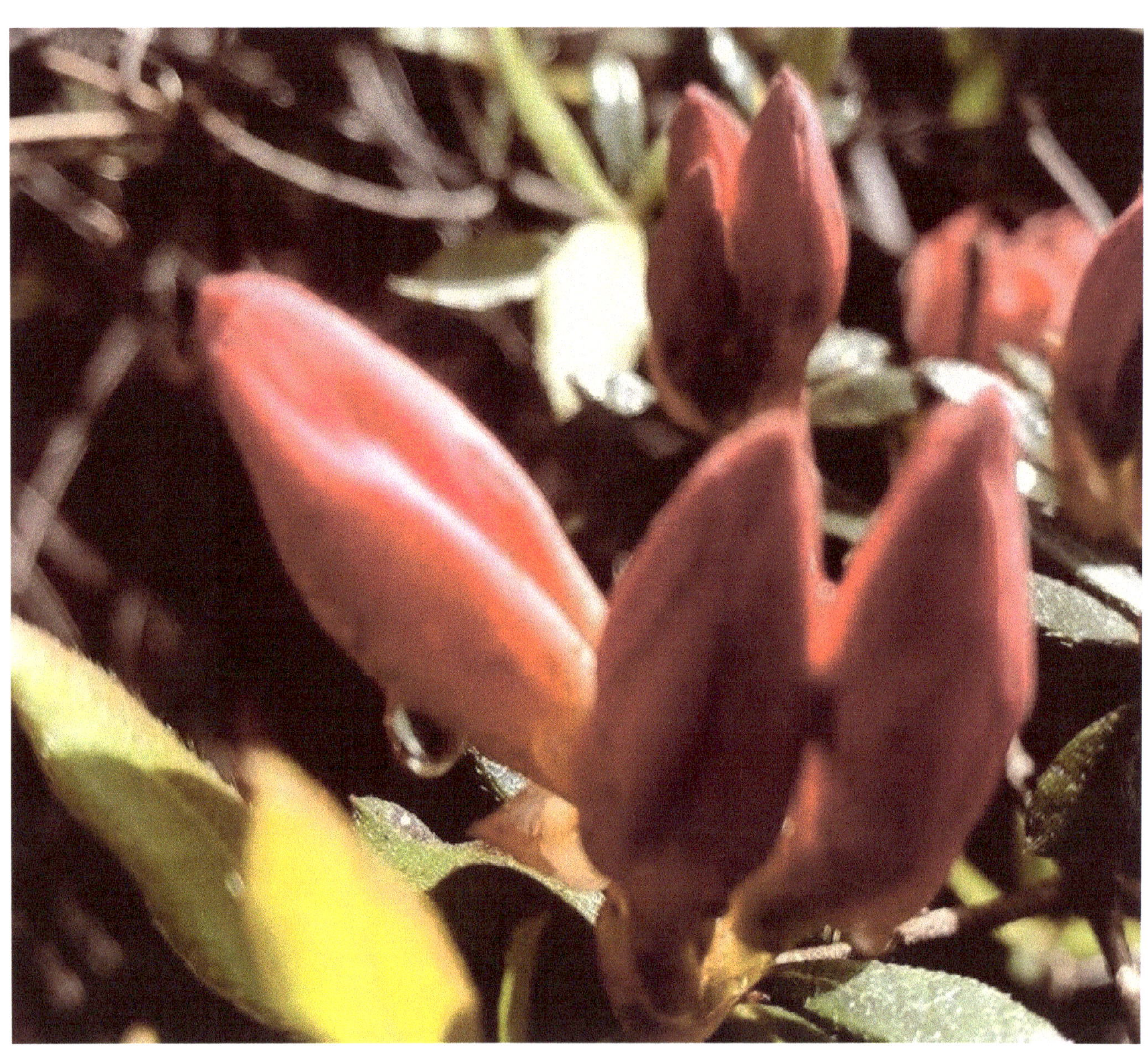

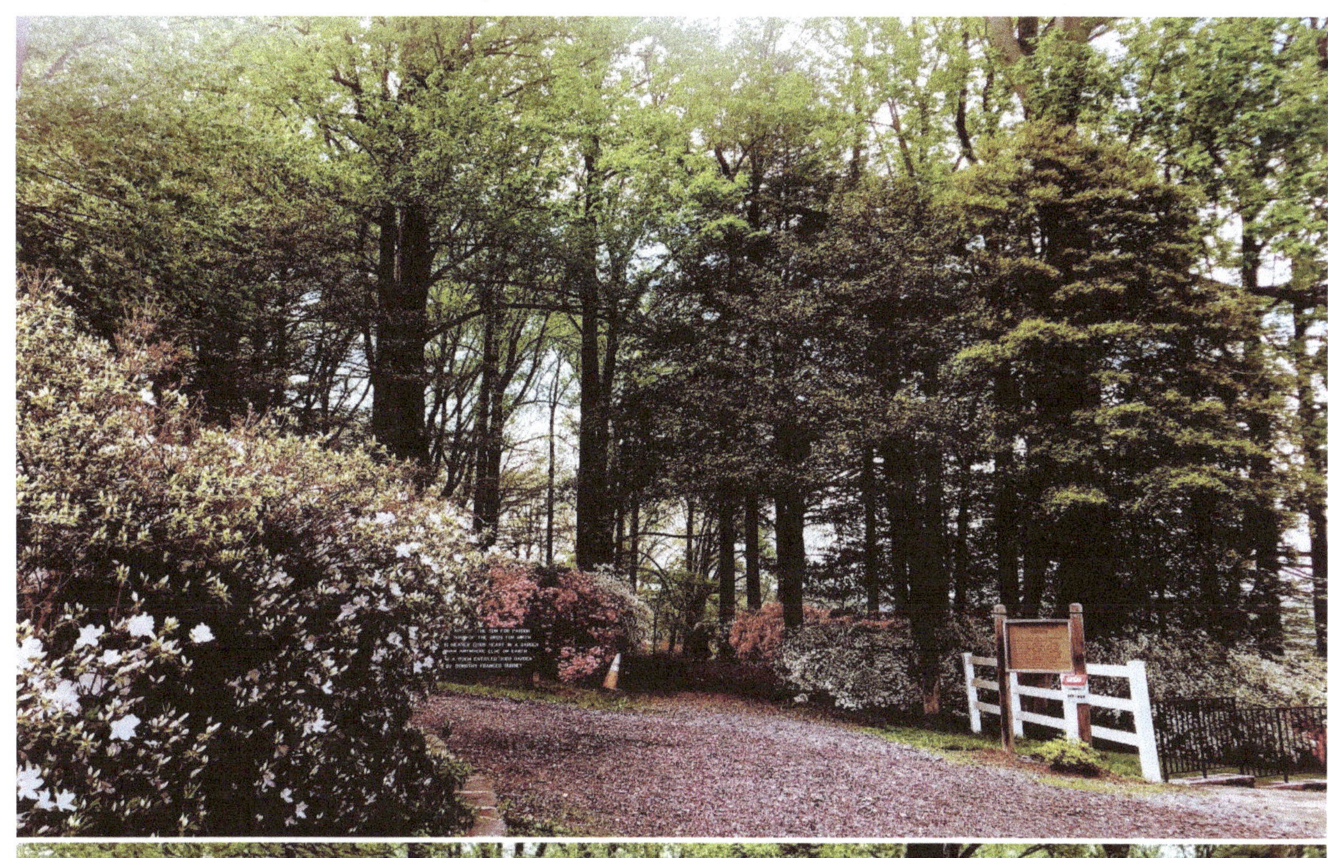

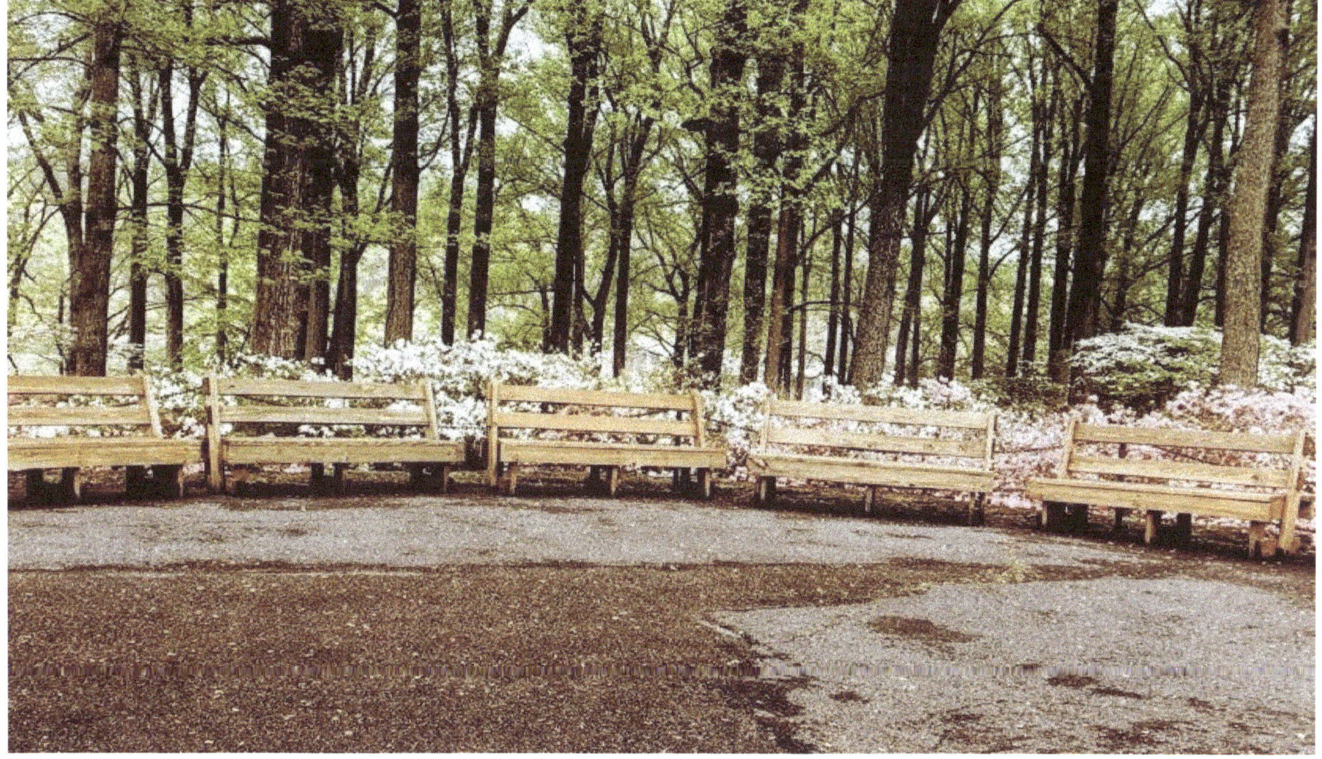

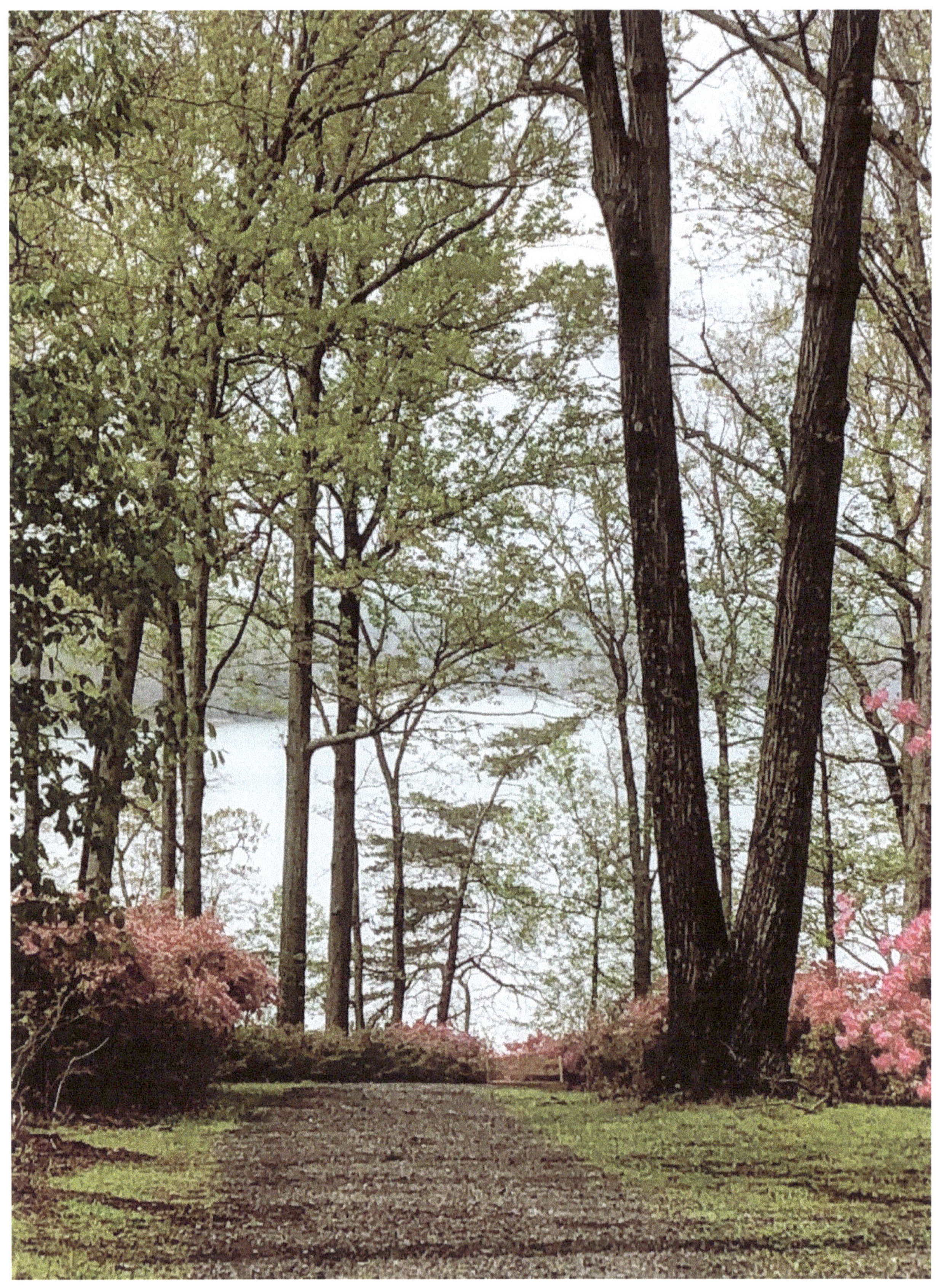

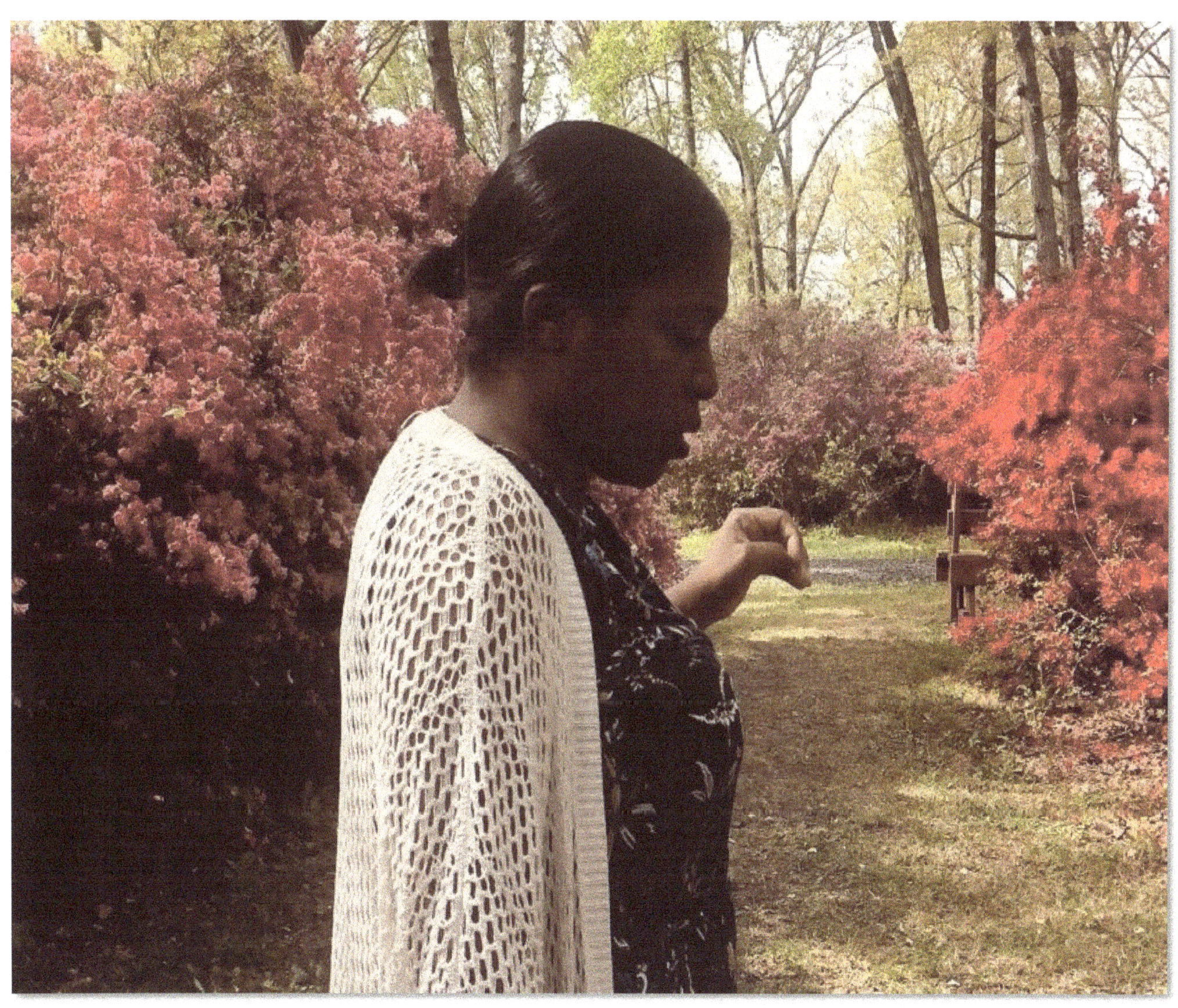

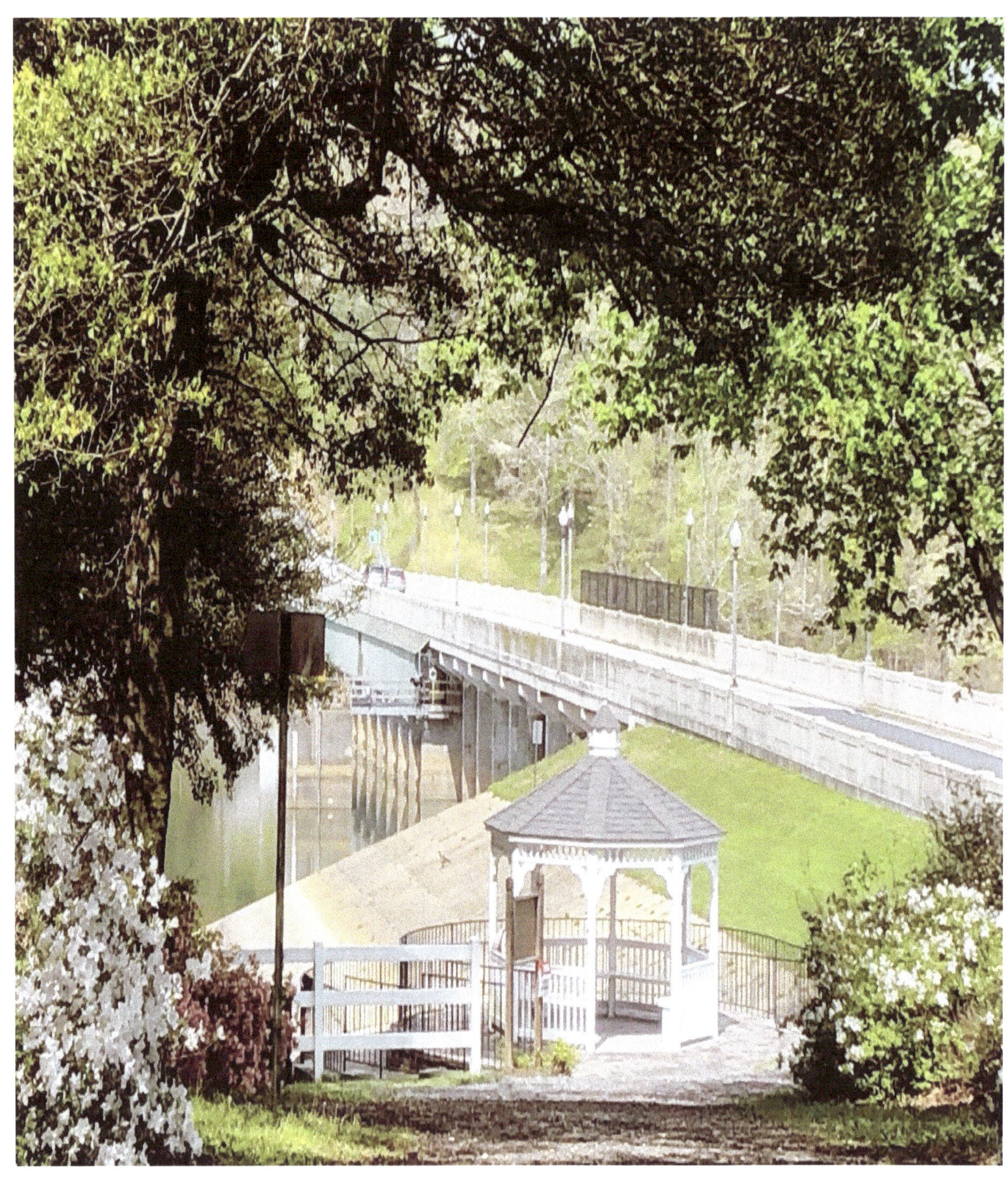

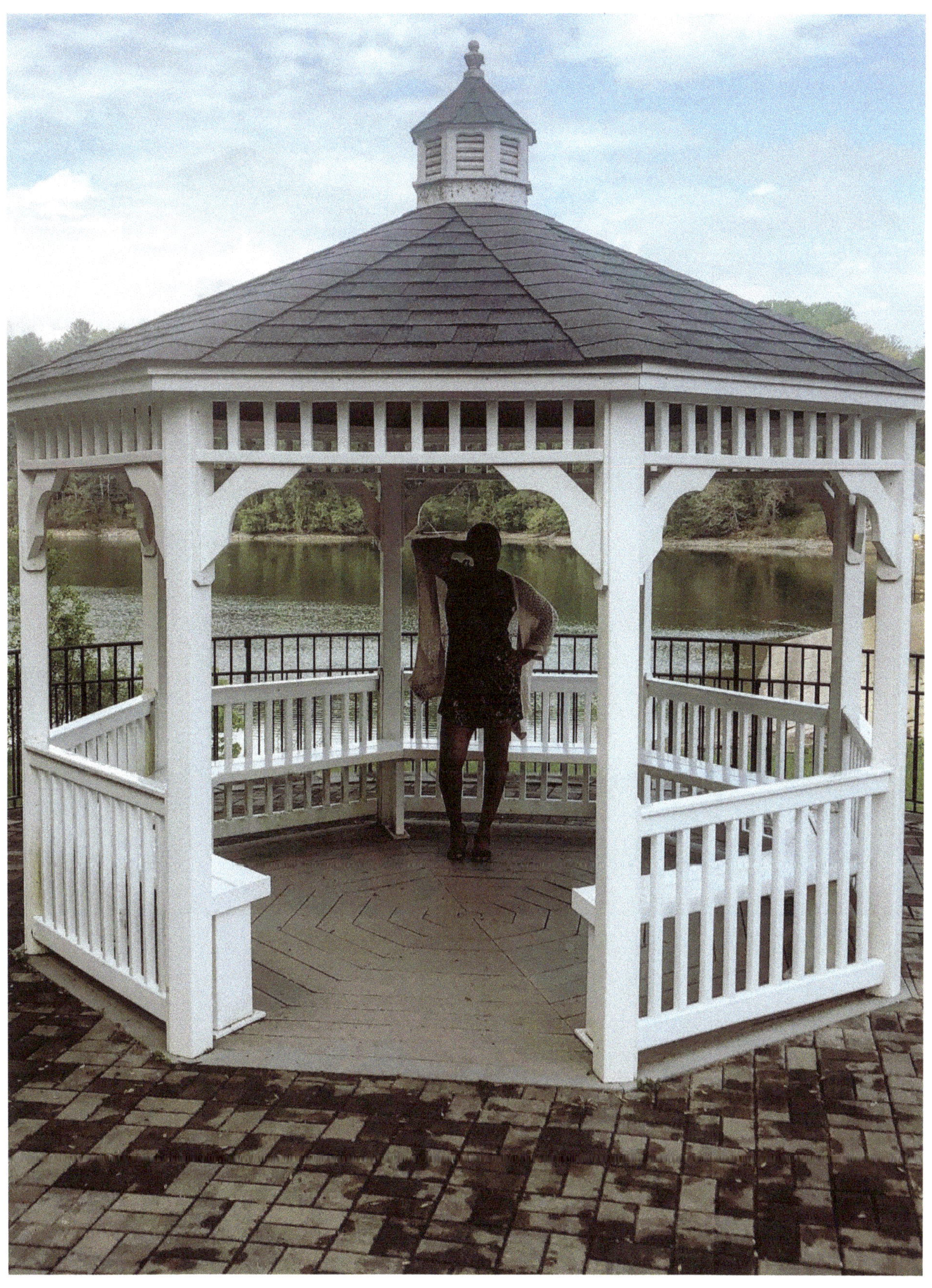

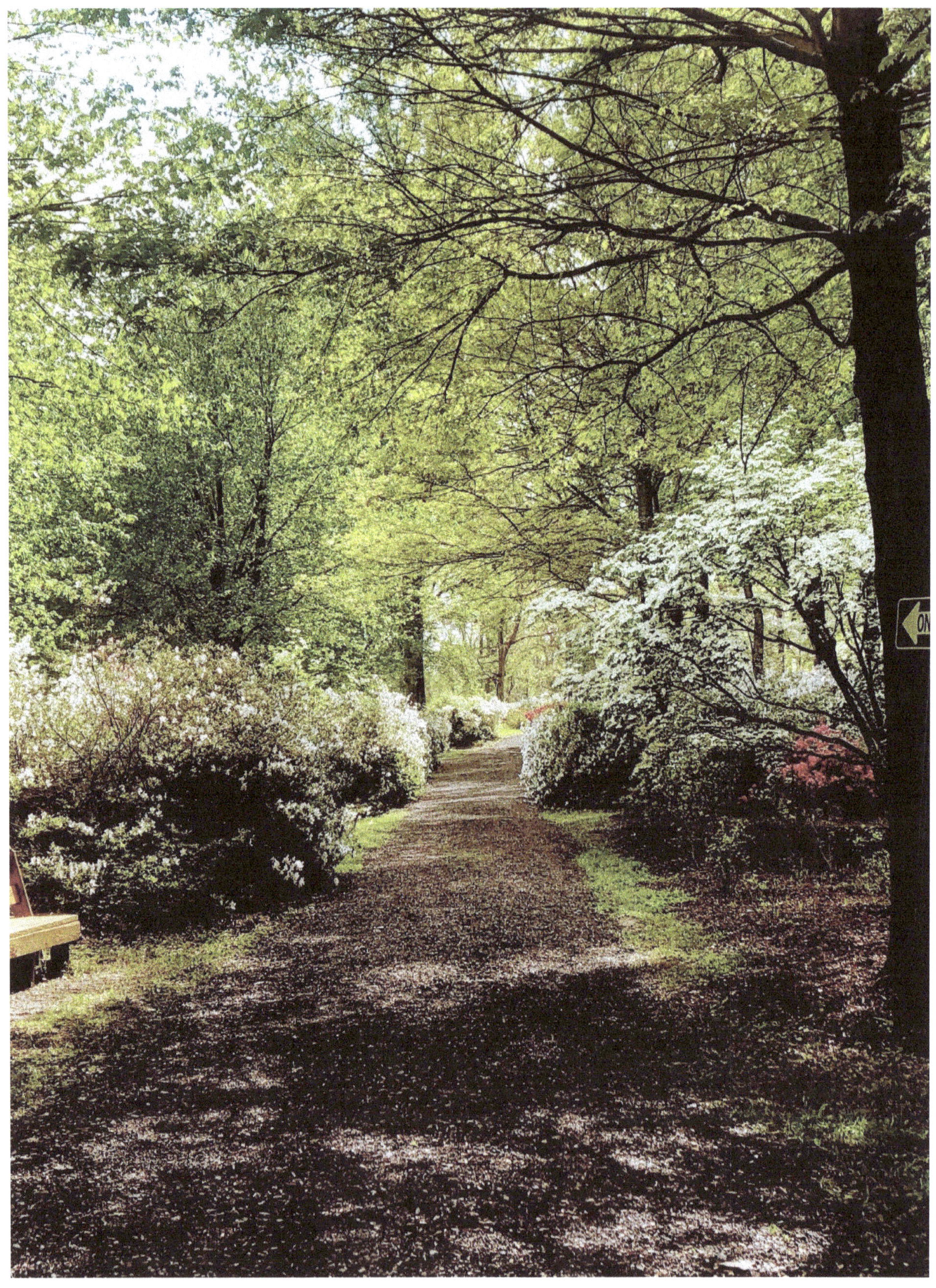
ON

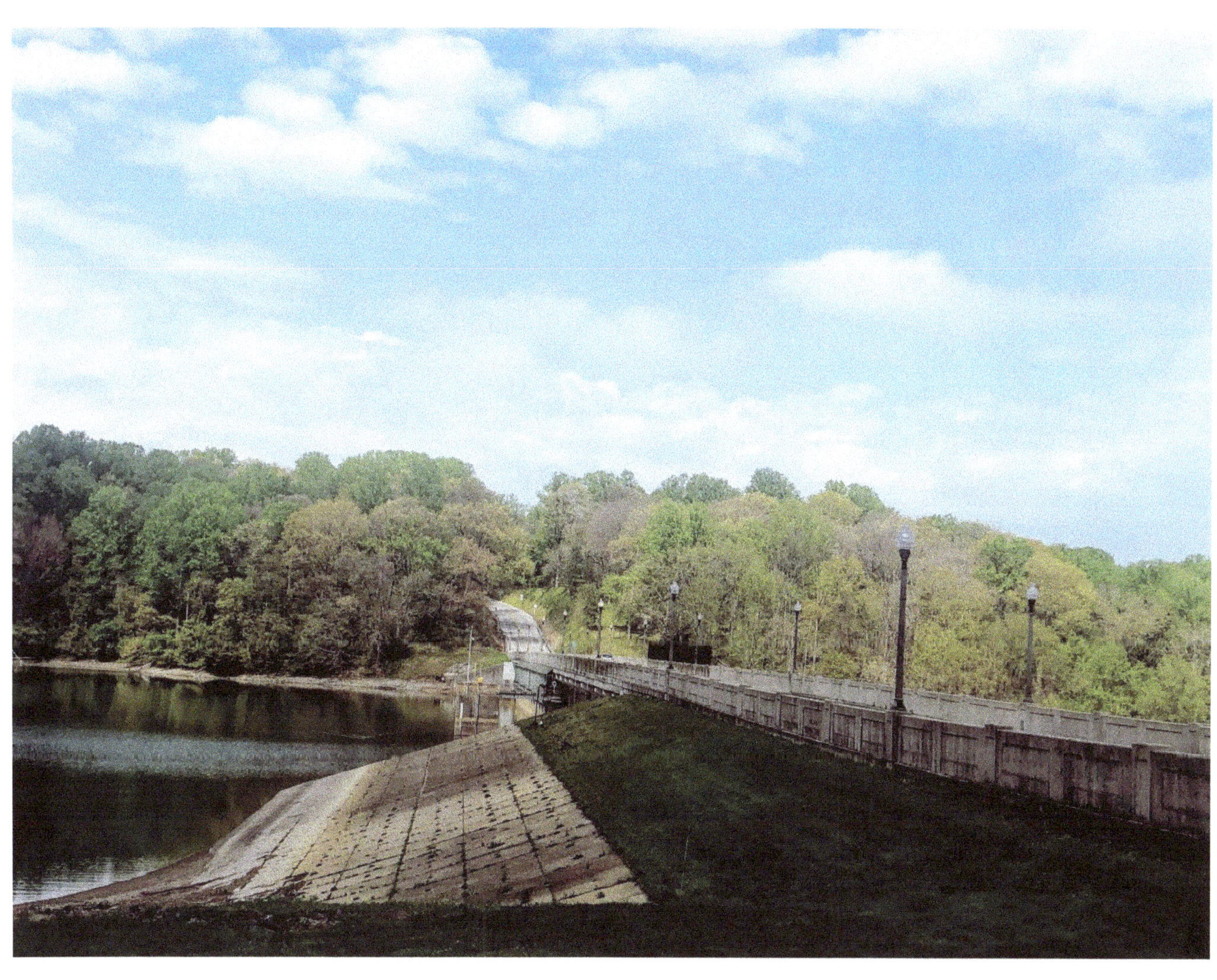

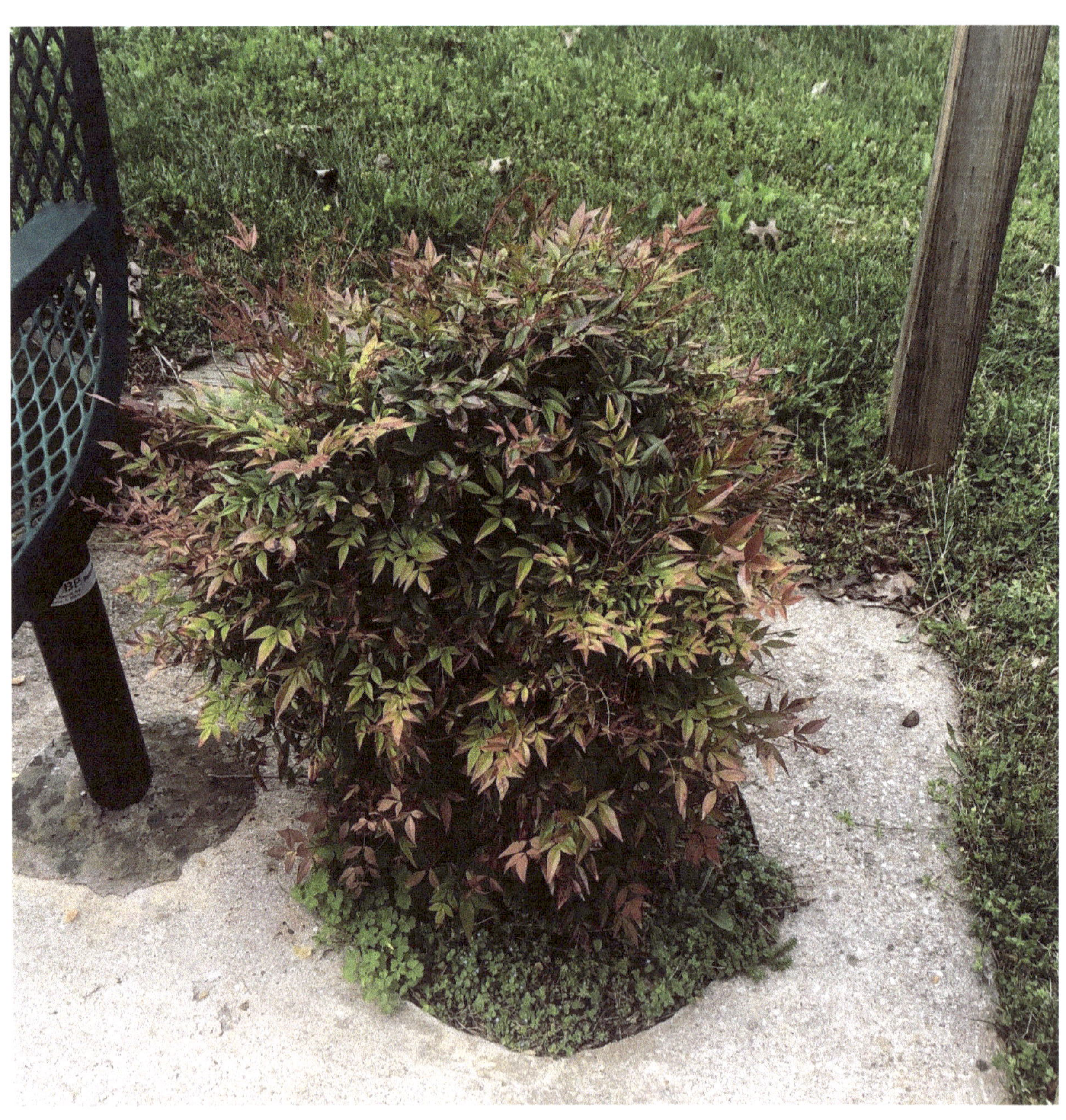

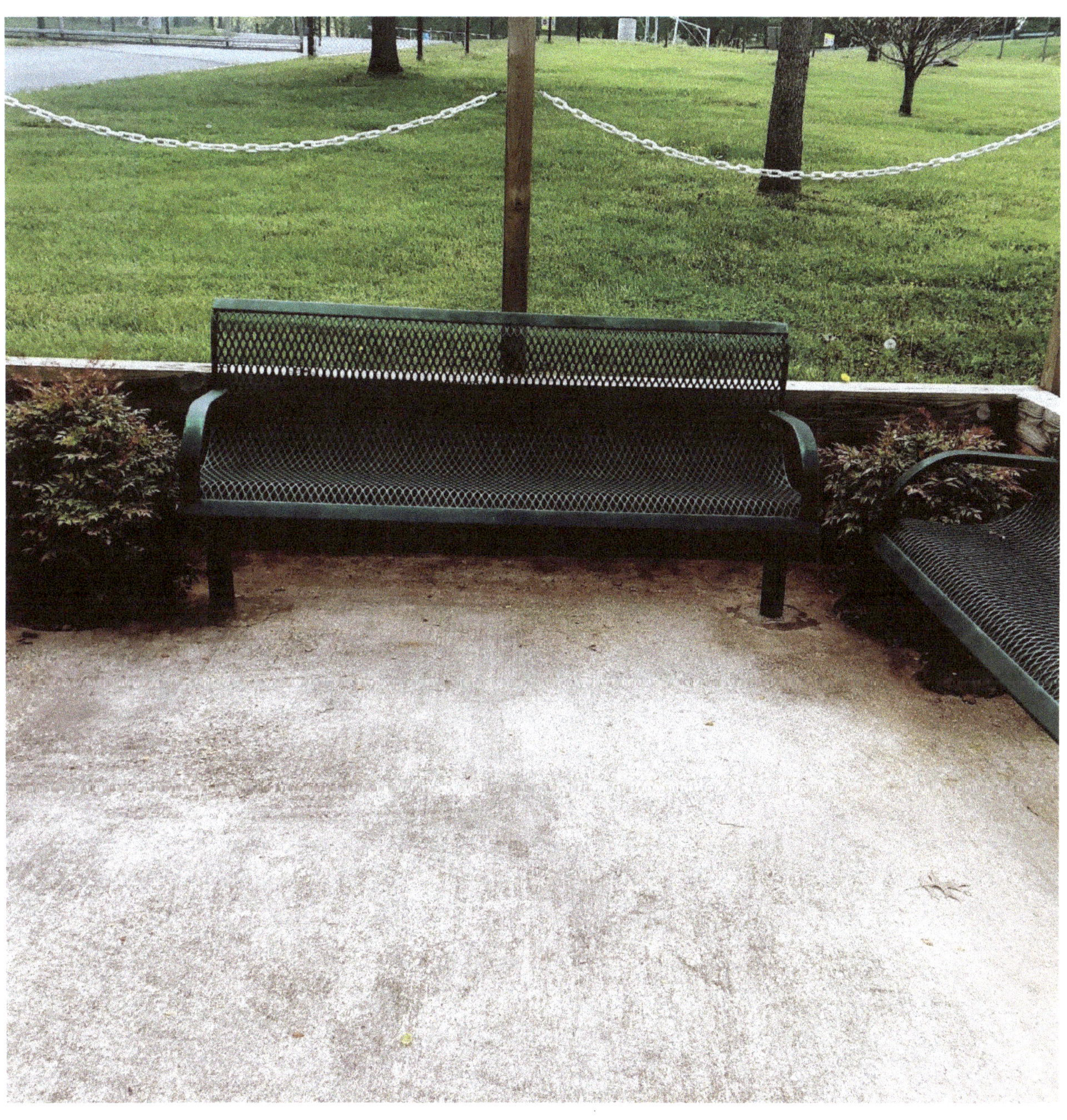

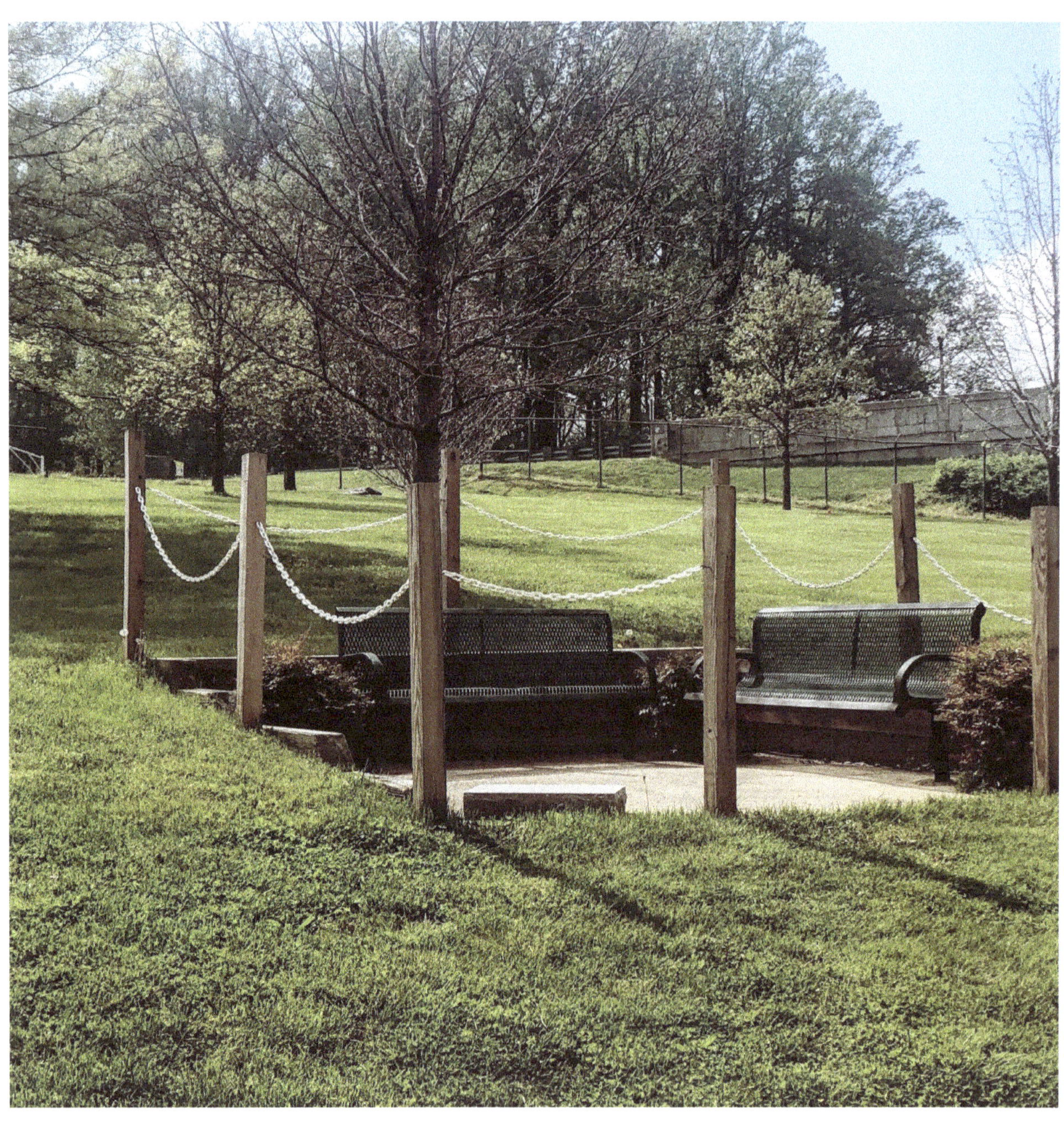

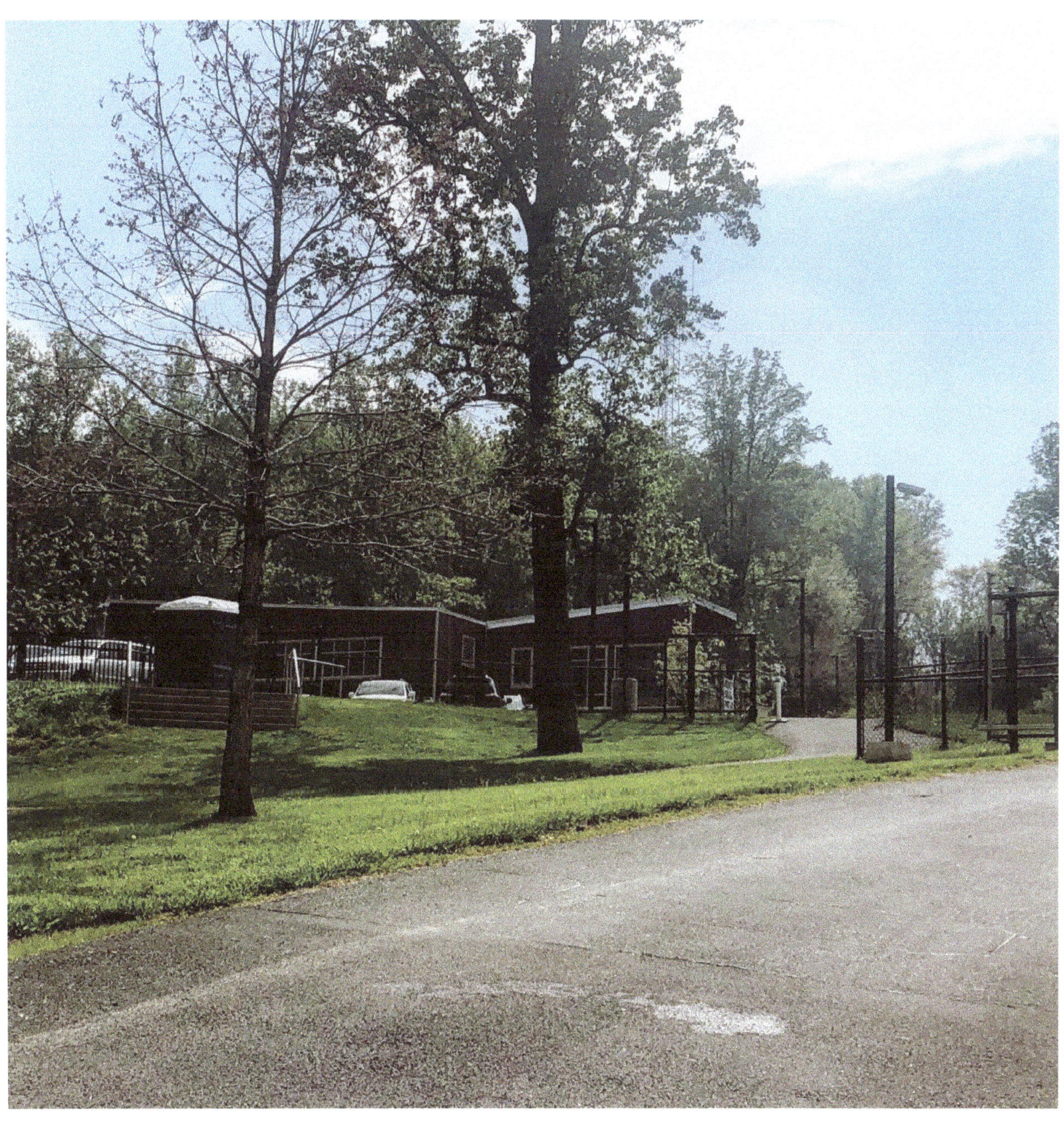

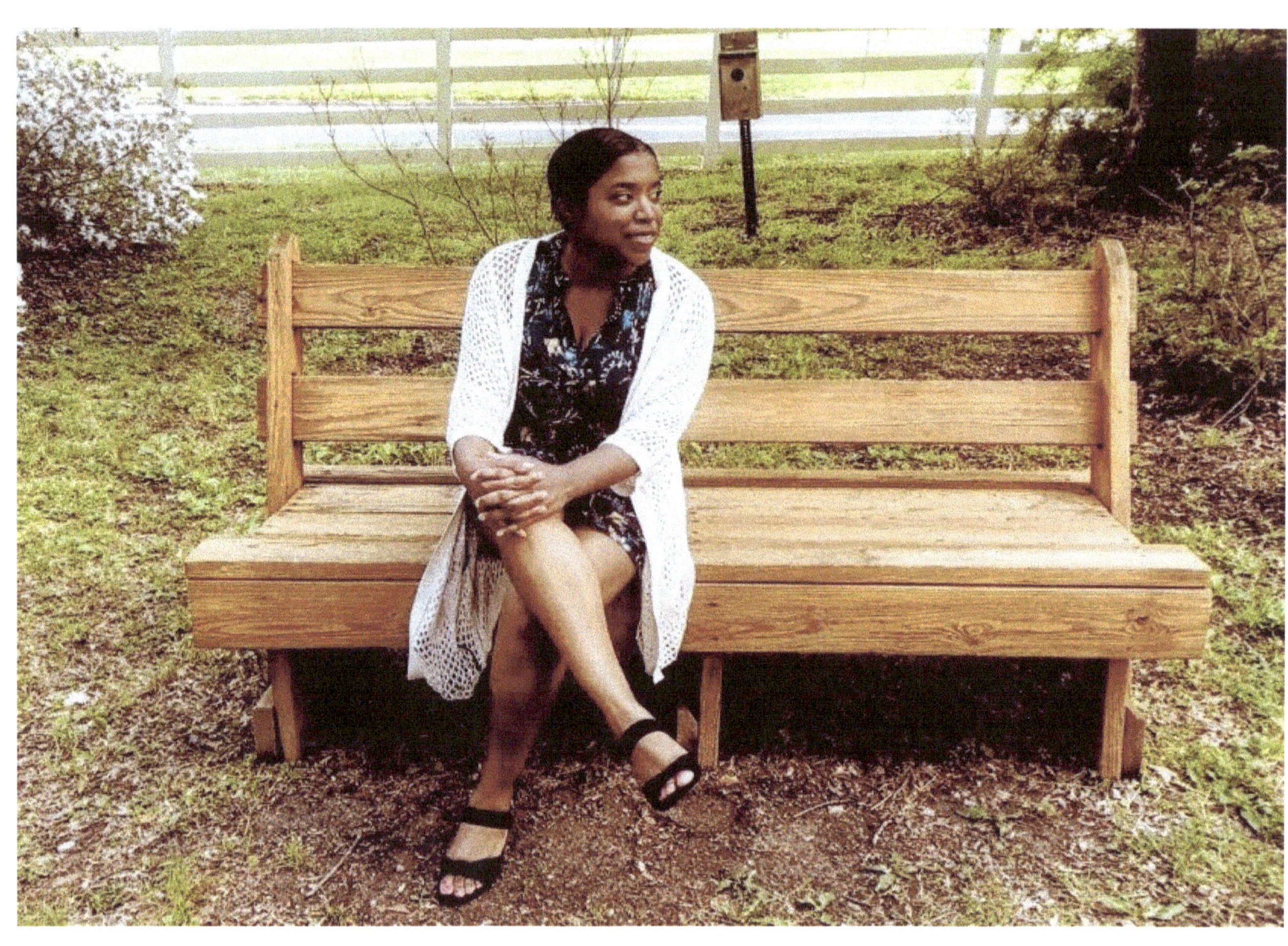

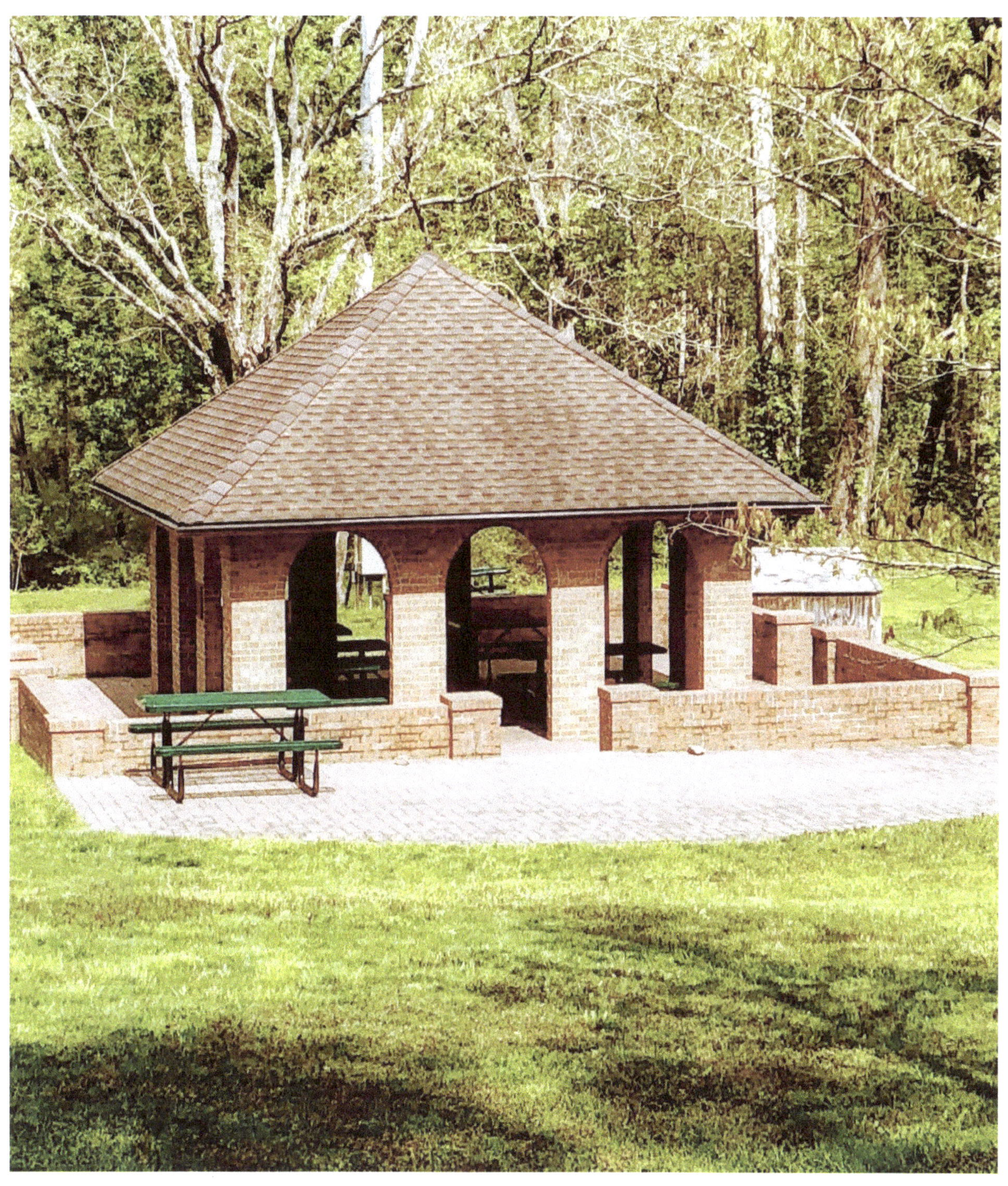

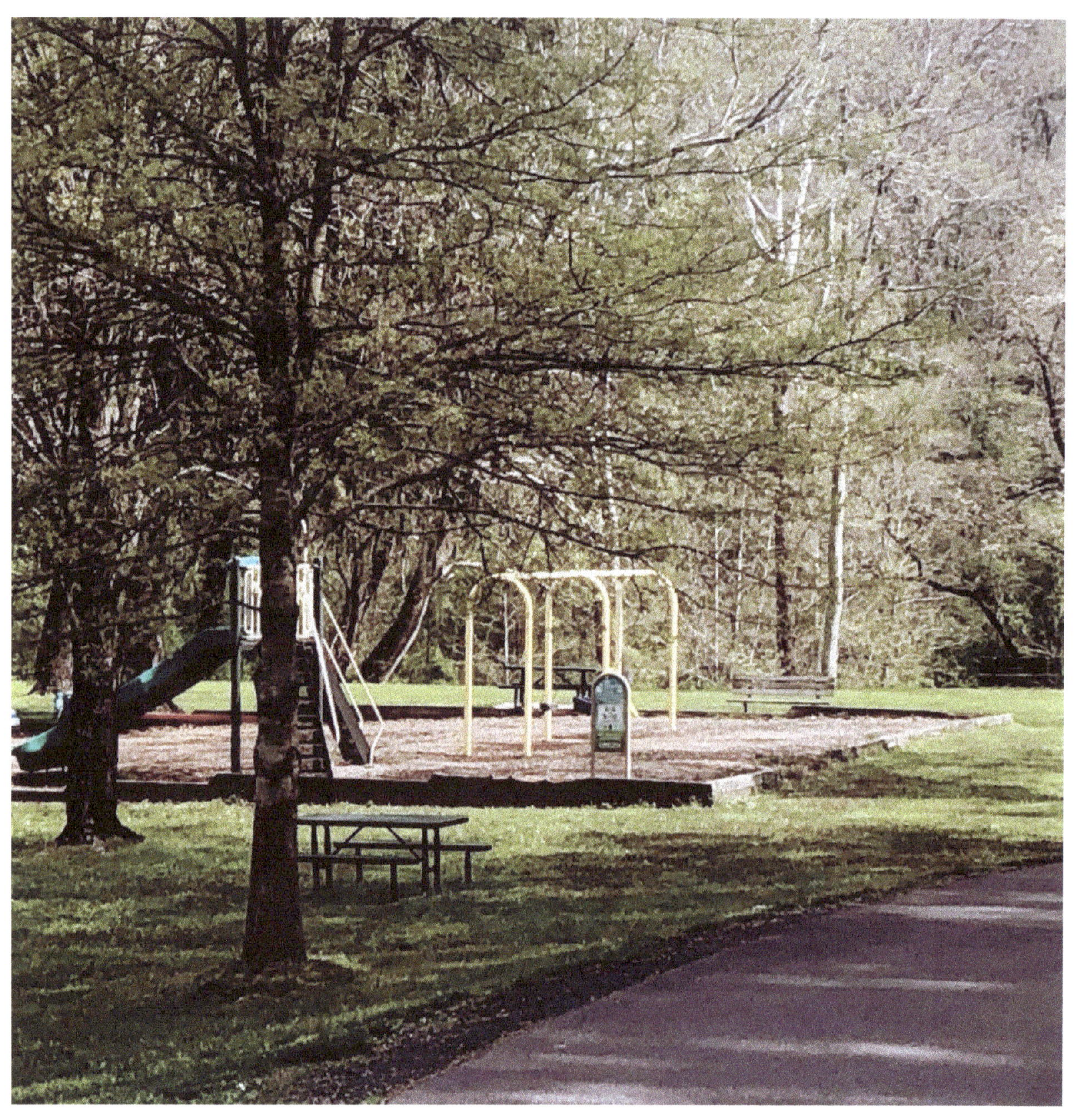

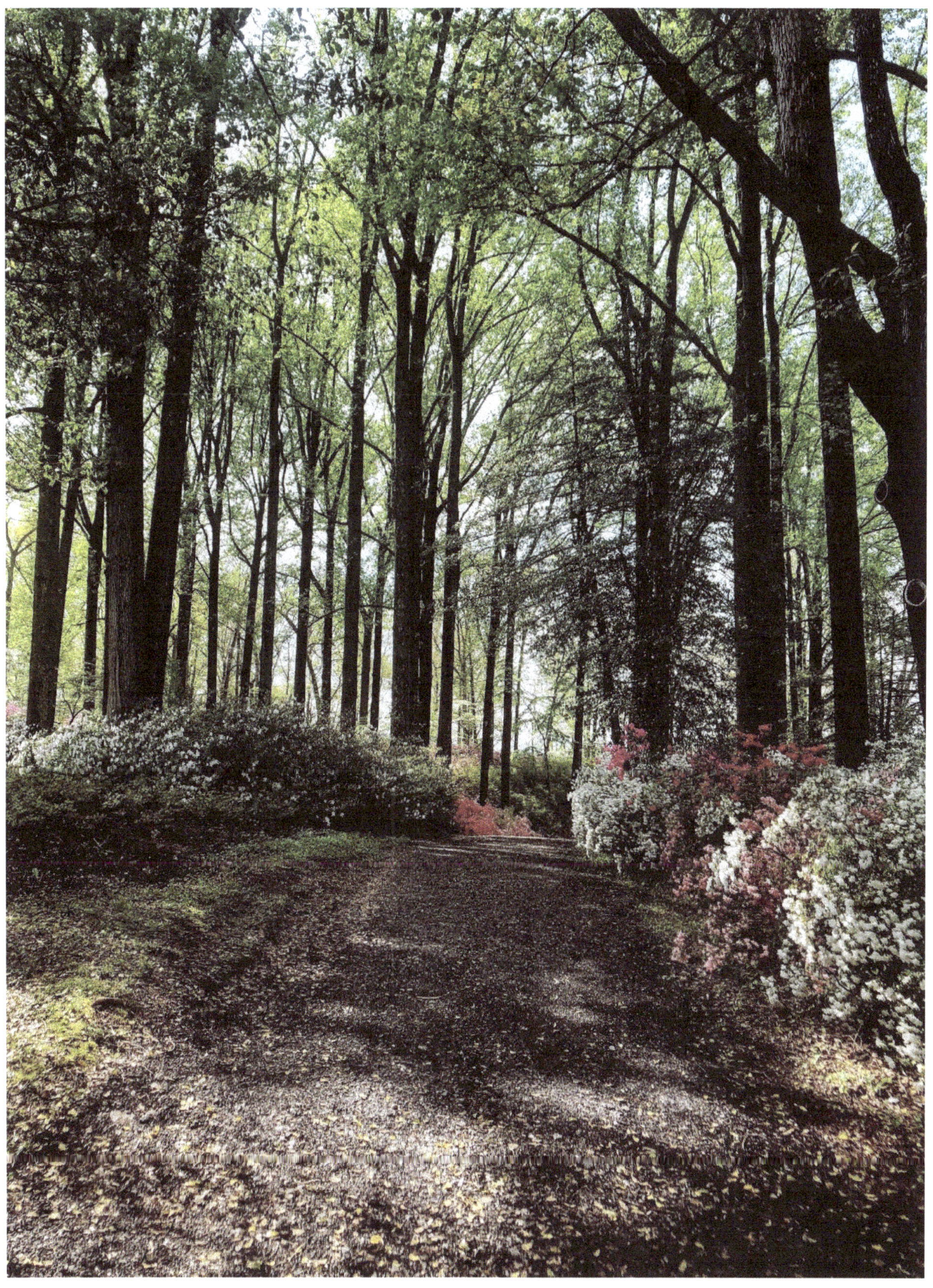

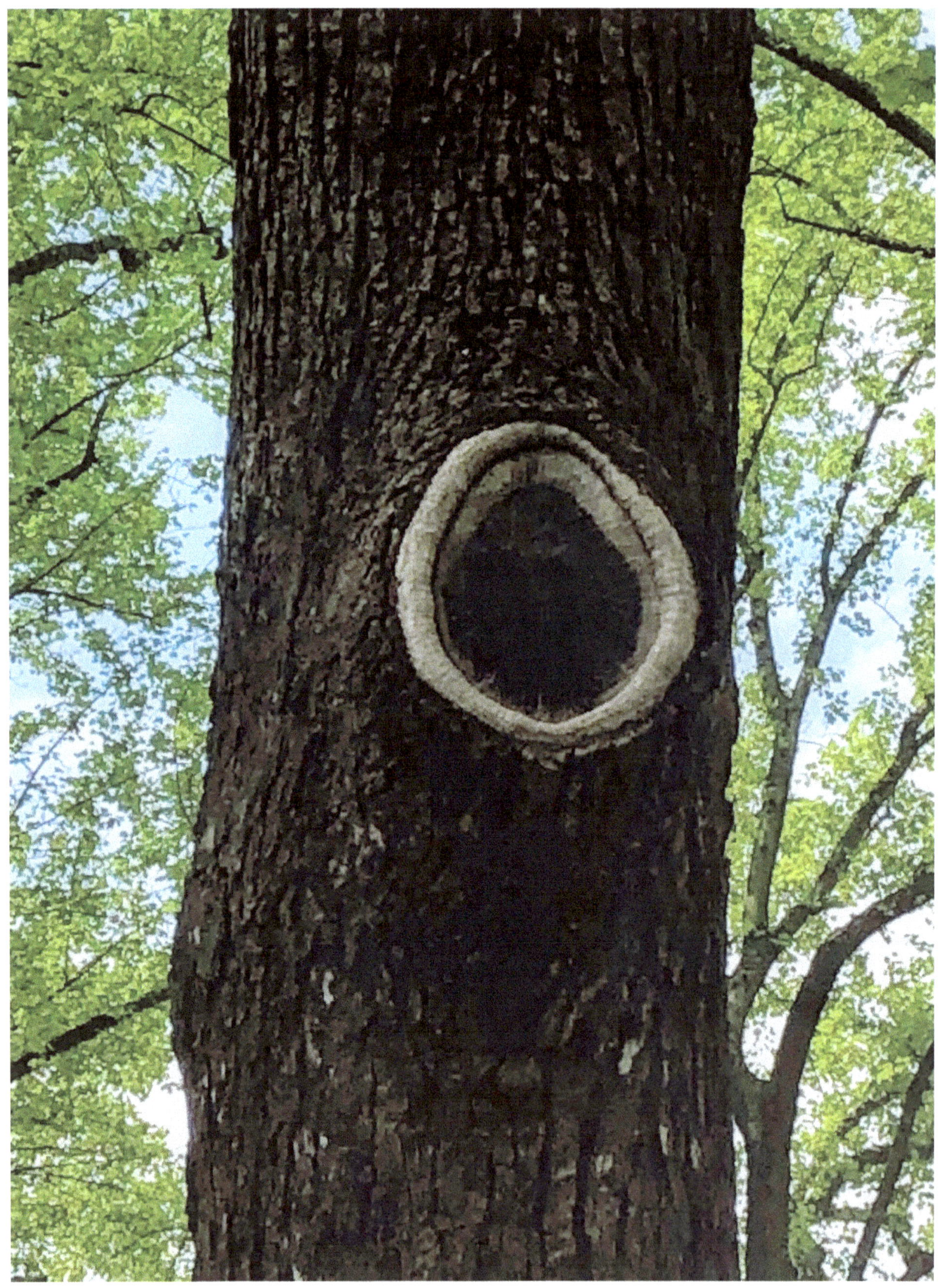

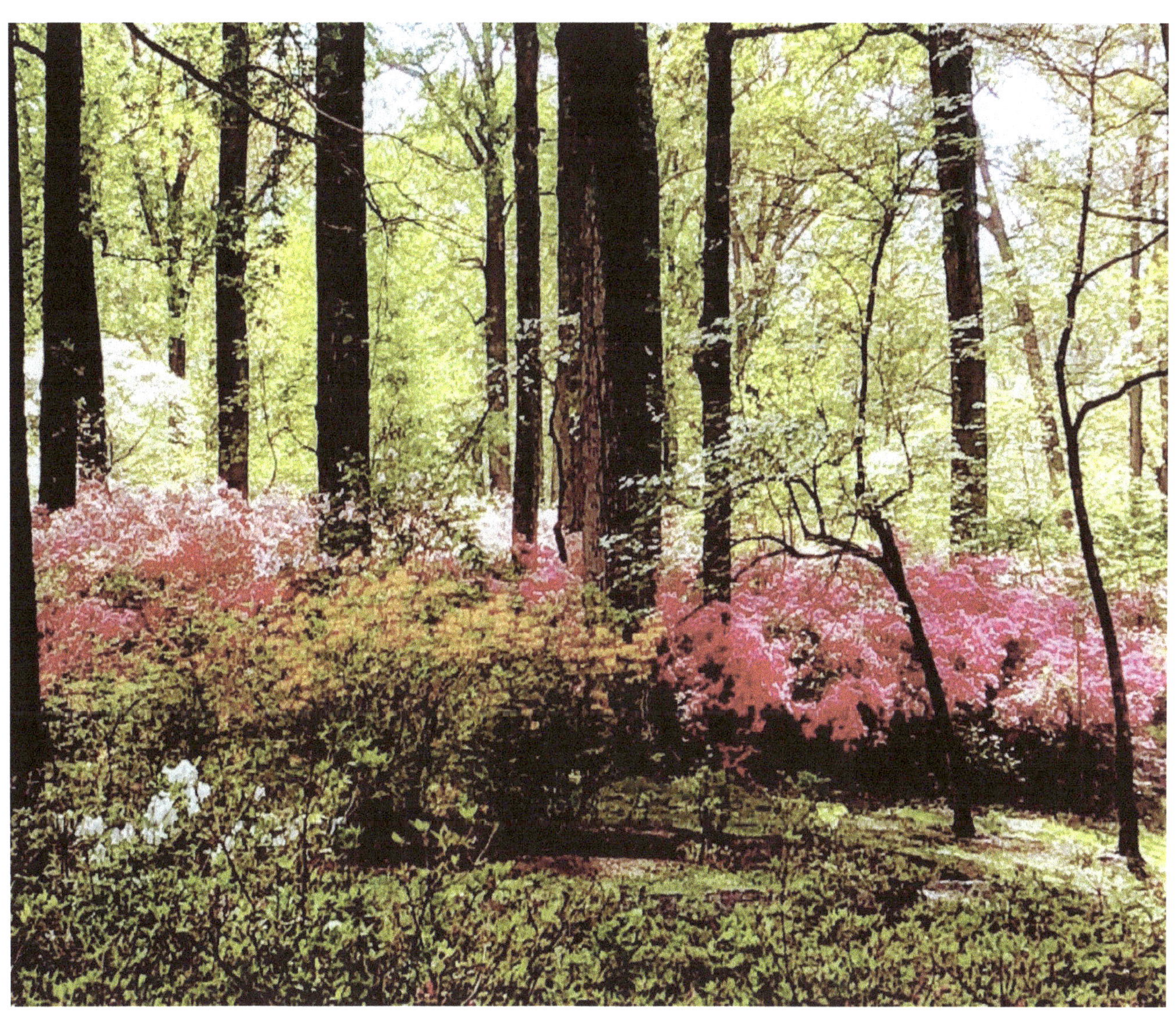

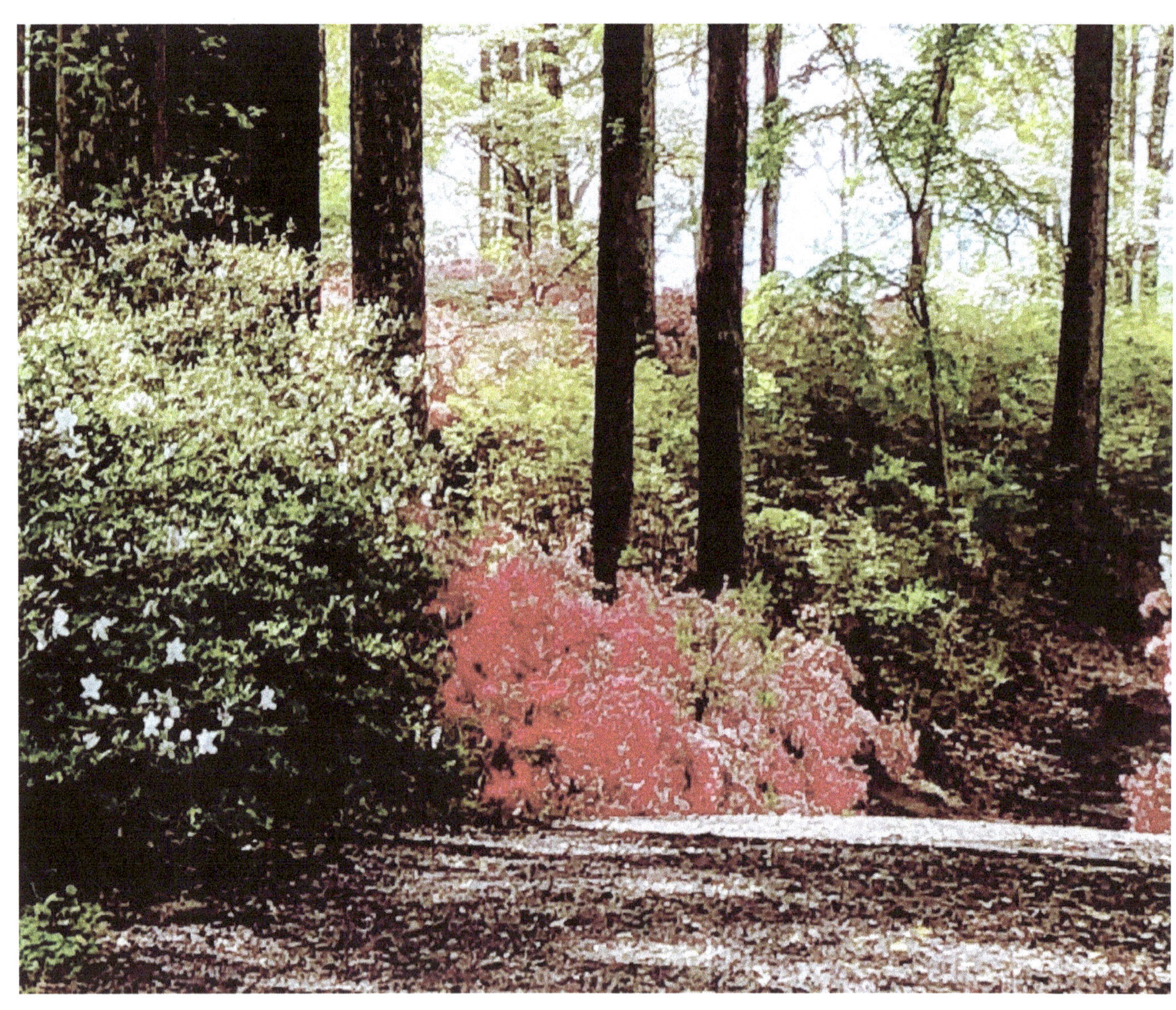

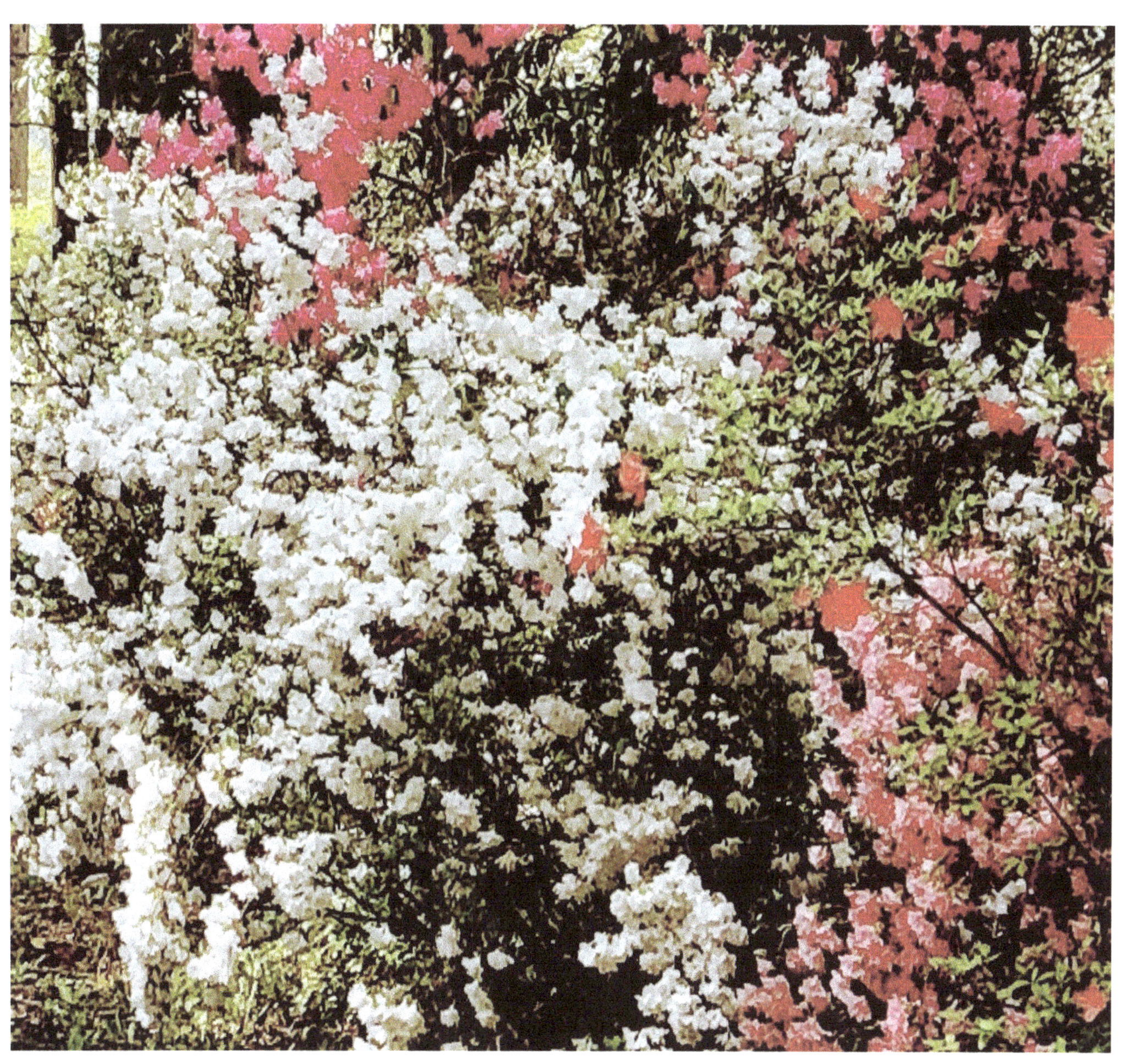

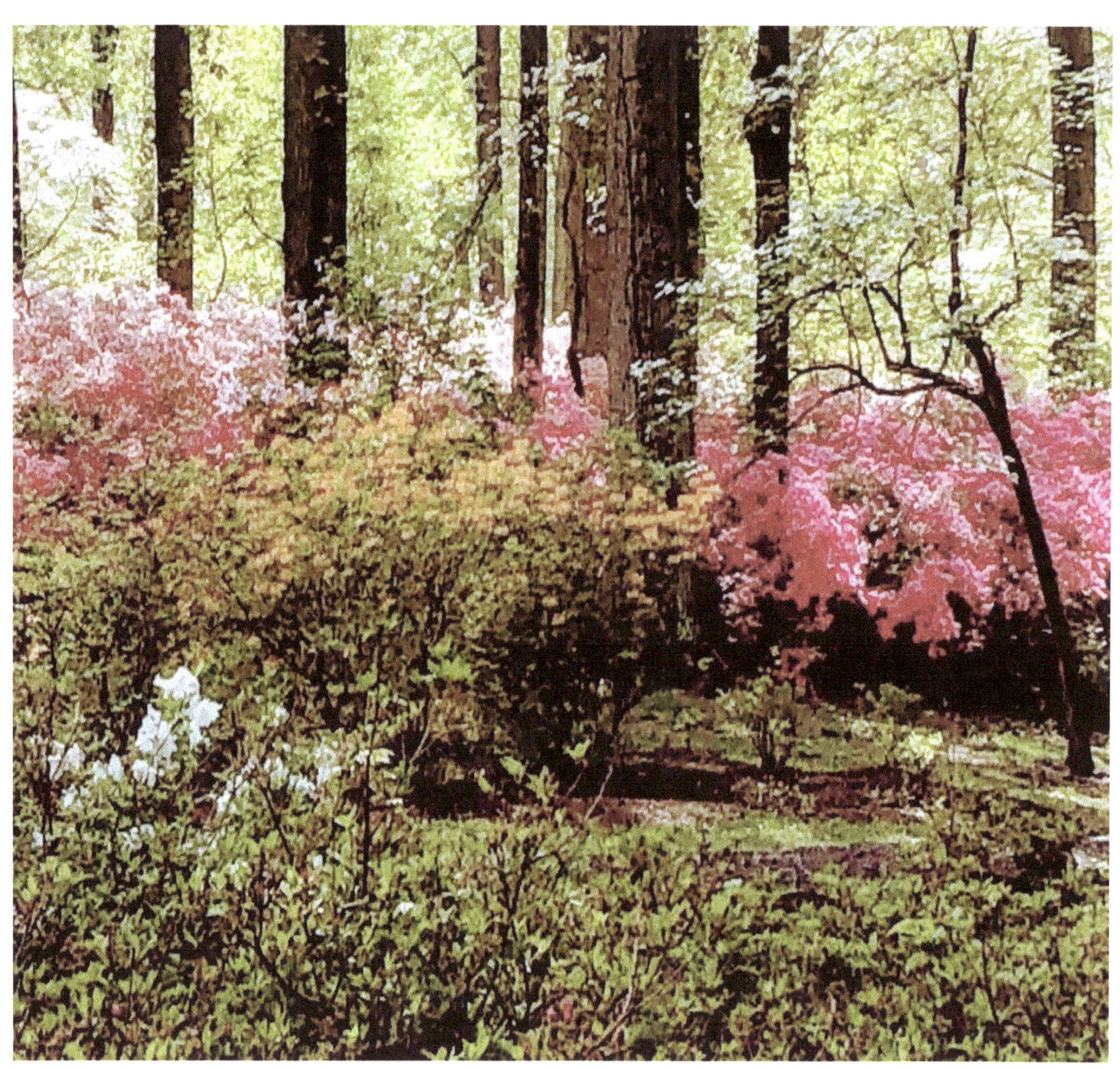

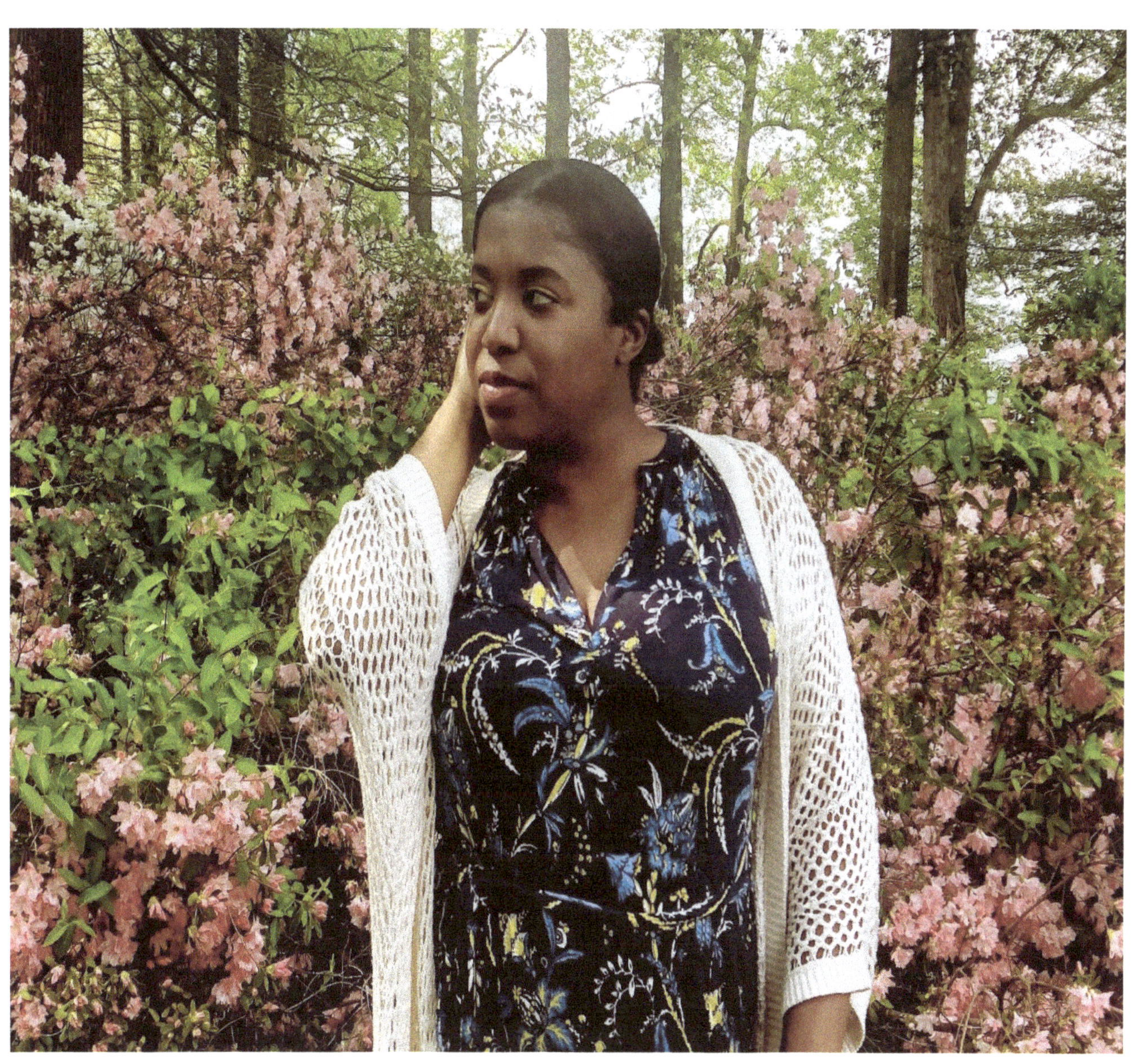

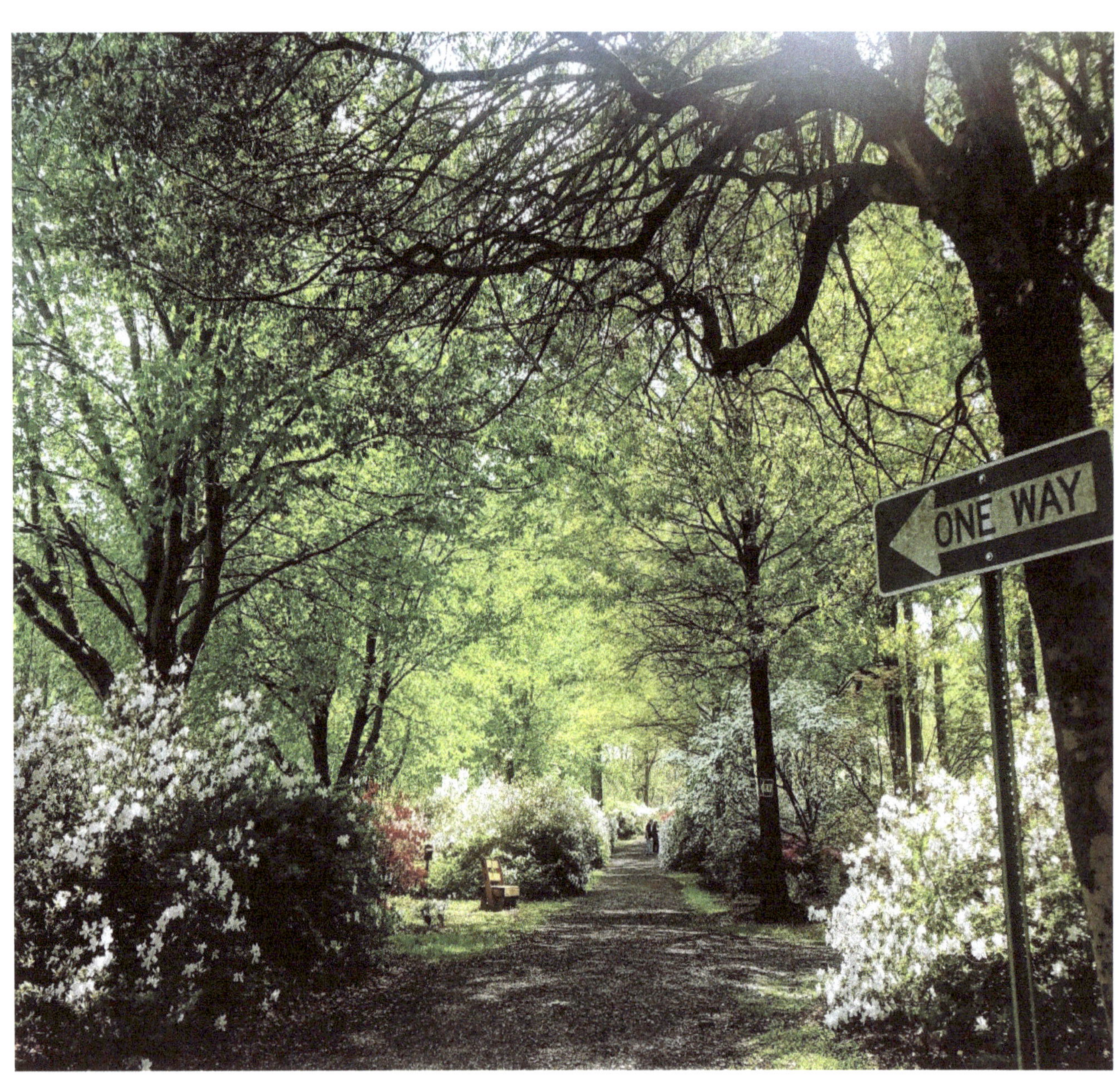

ONE WAY

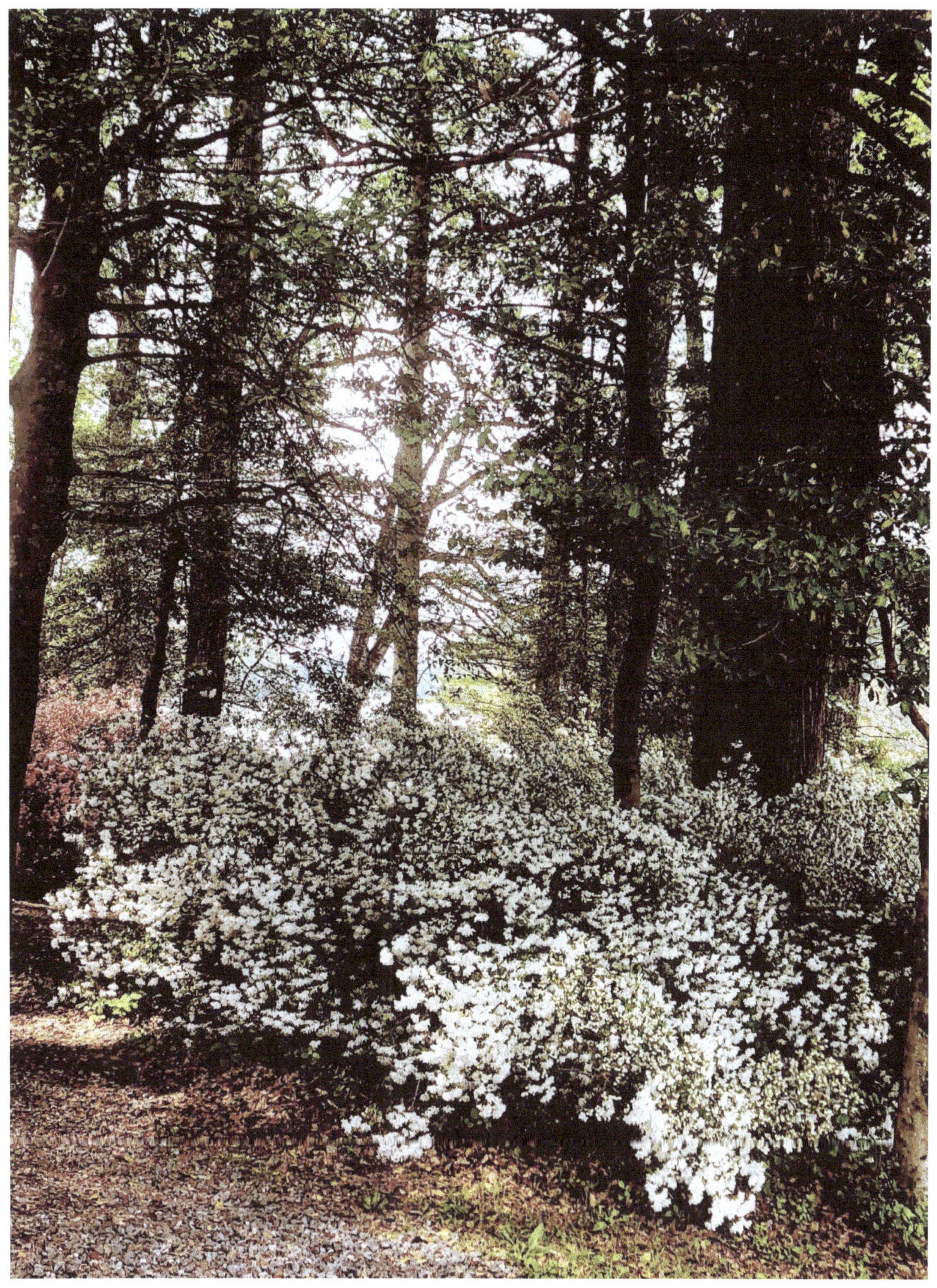

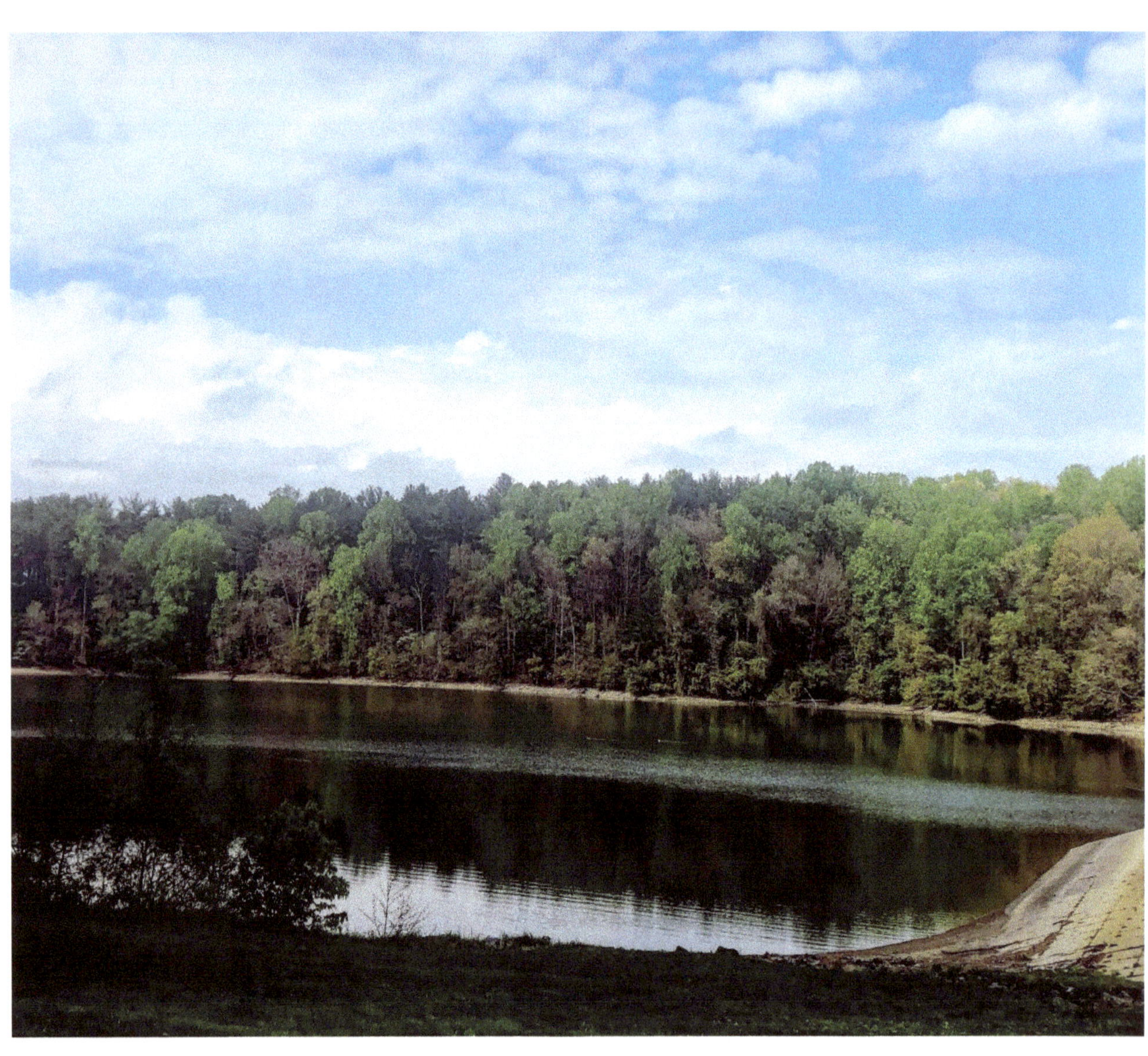

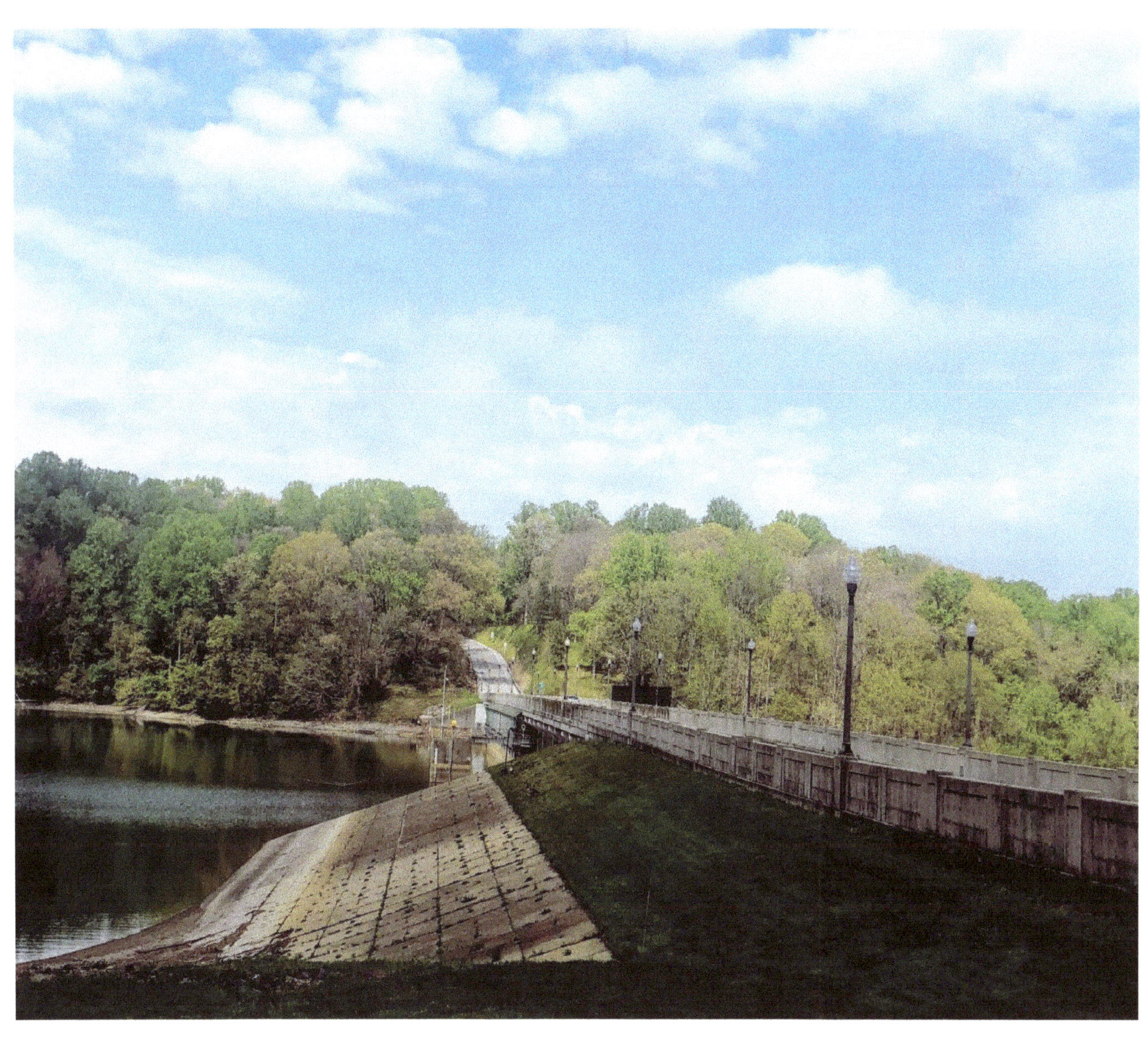

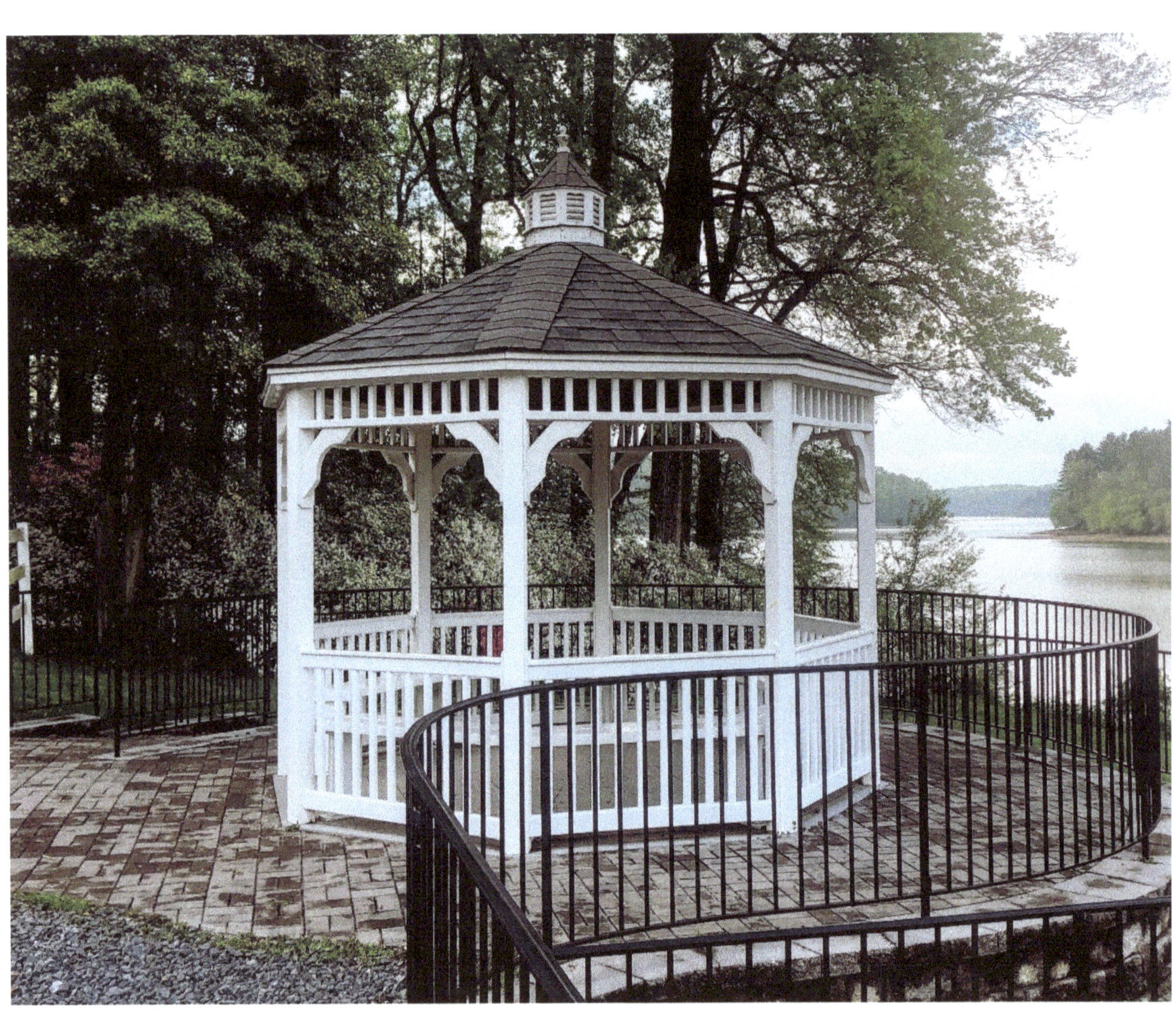

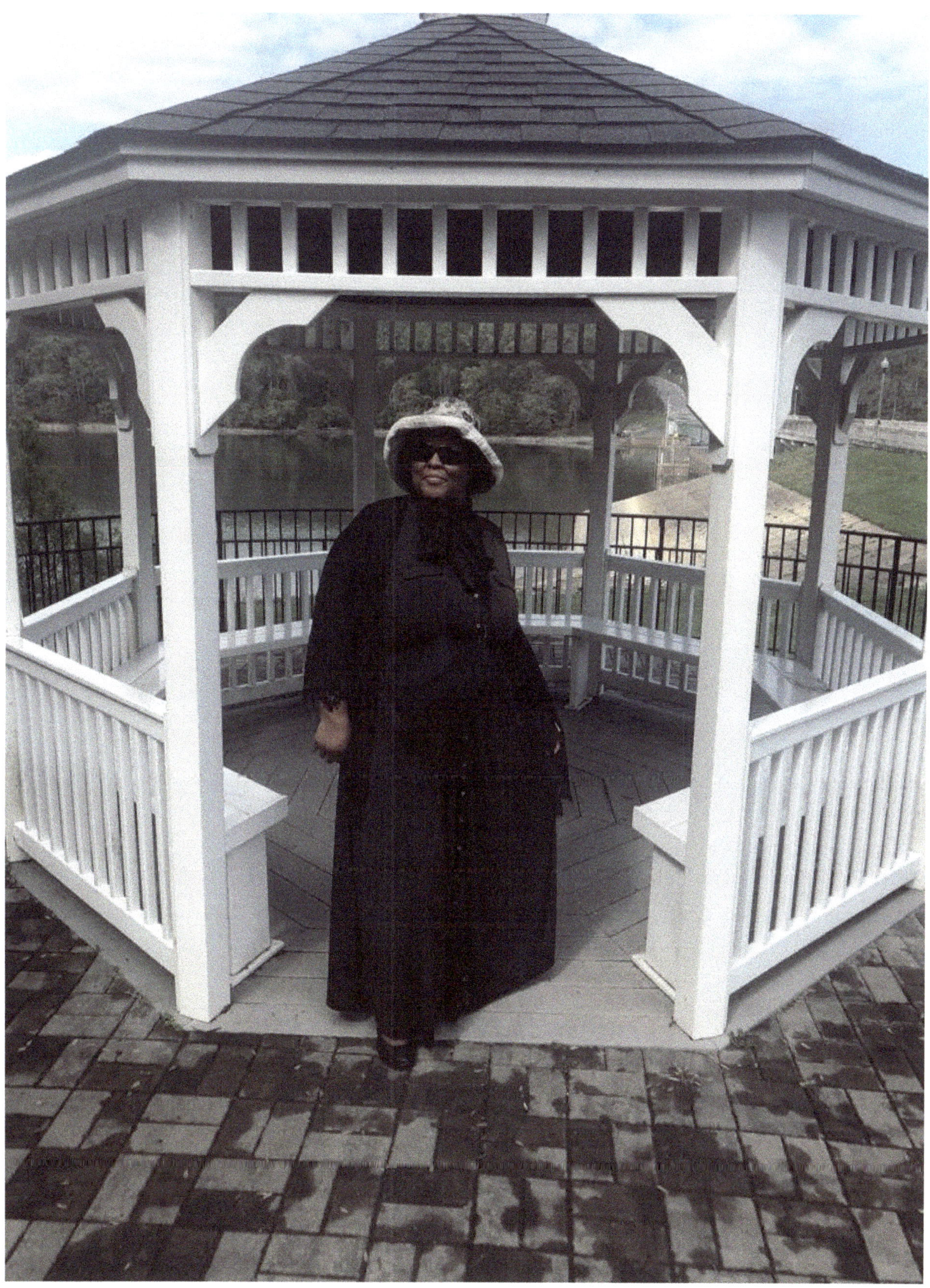

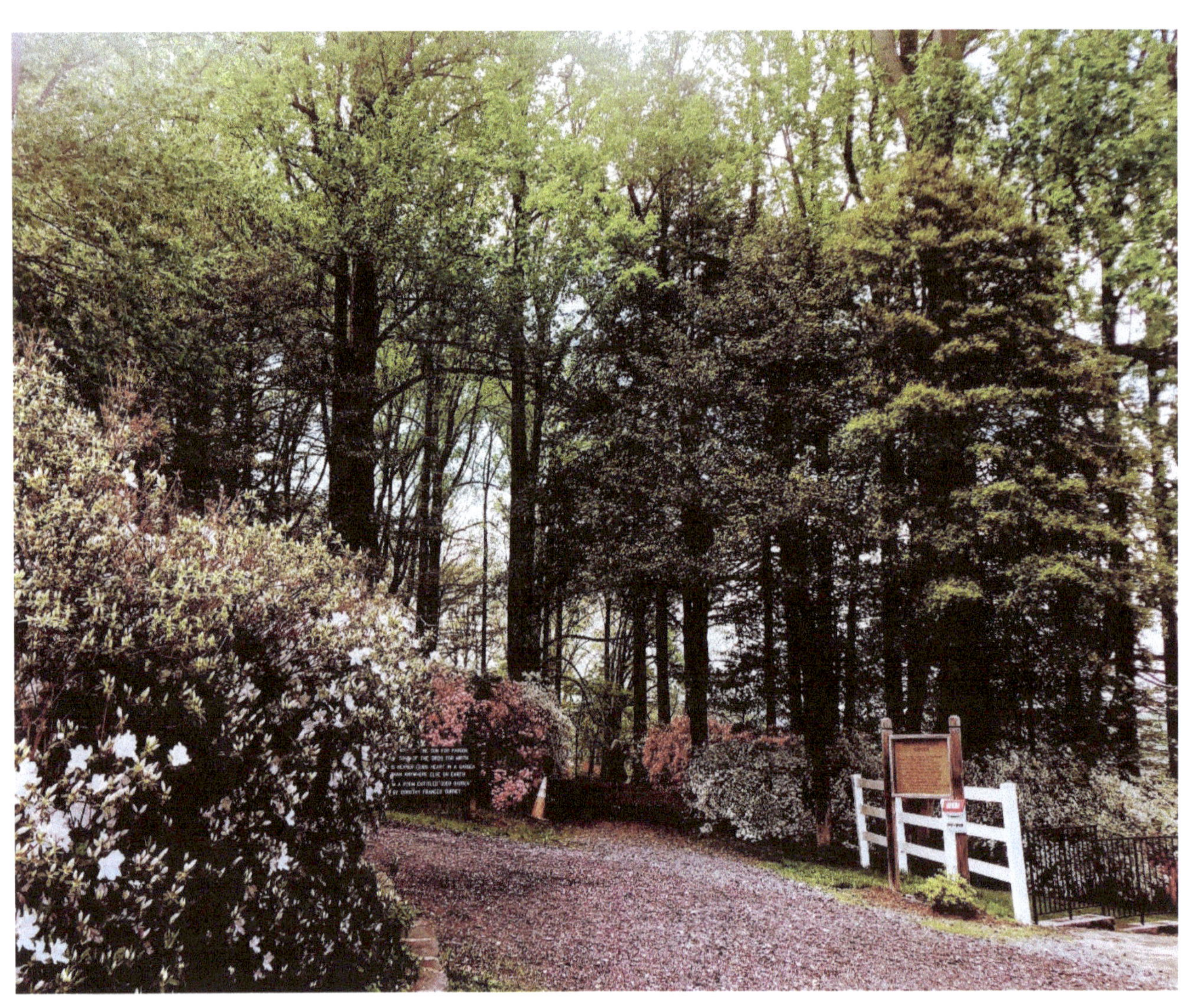

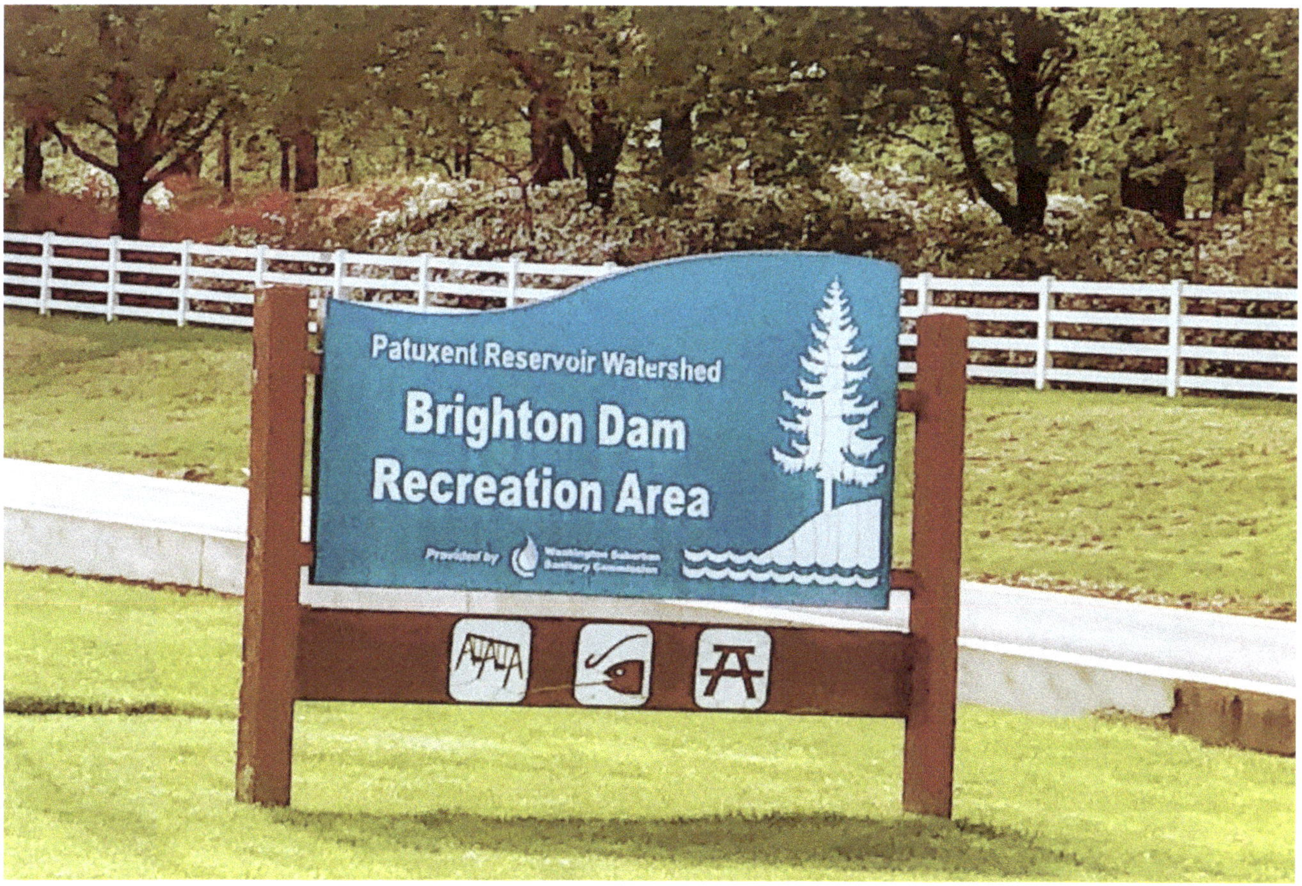

Patuxent Reservoir Watershed
Brighton Dam
Recreation Area
Provided by Washington Suburban Sanitary Commission

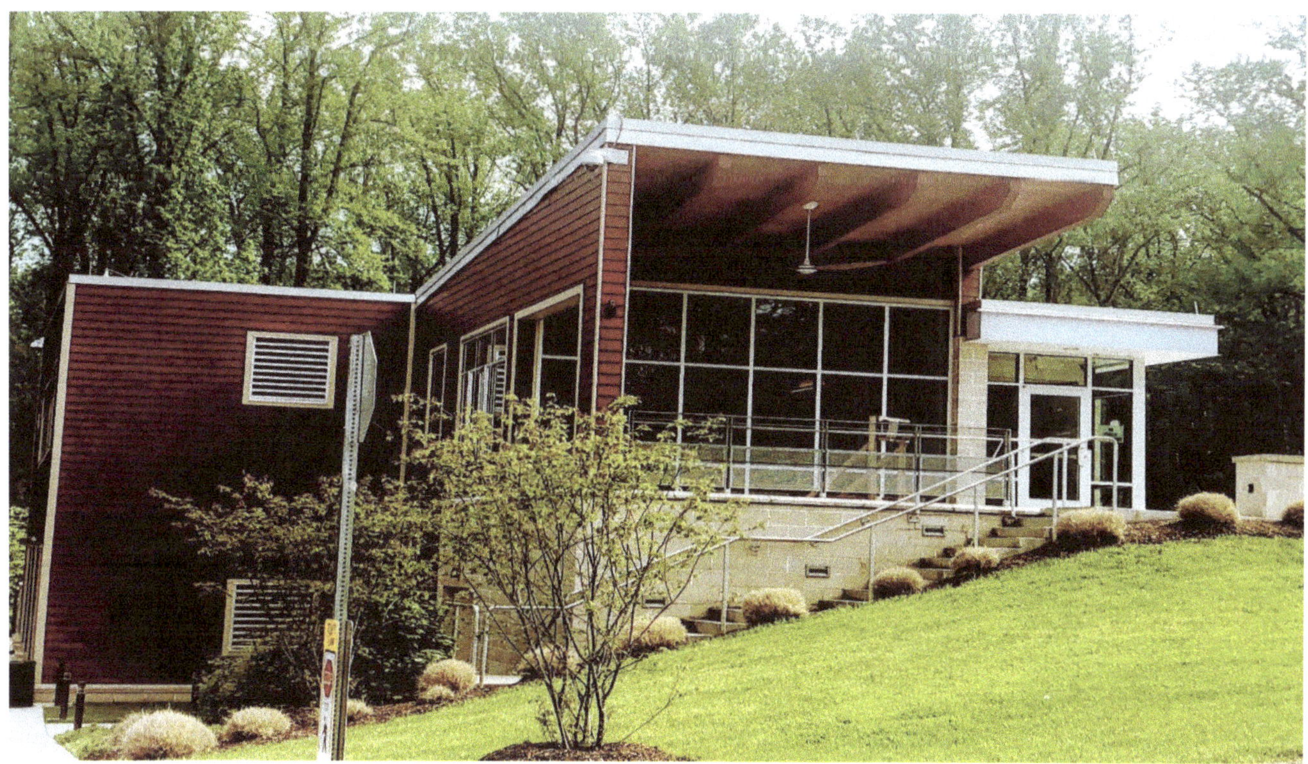

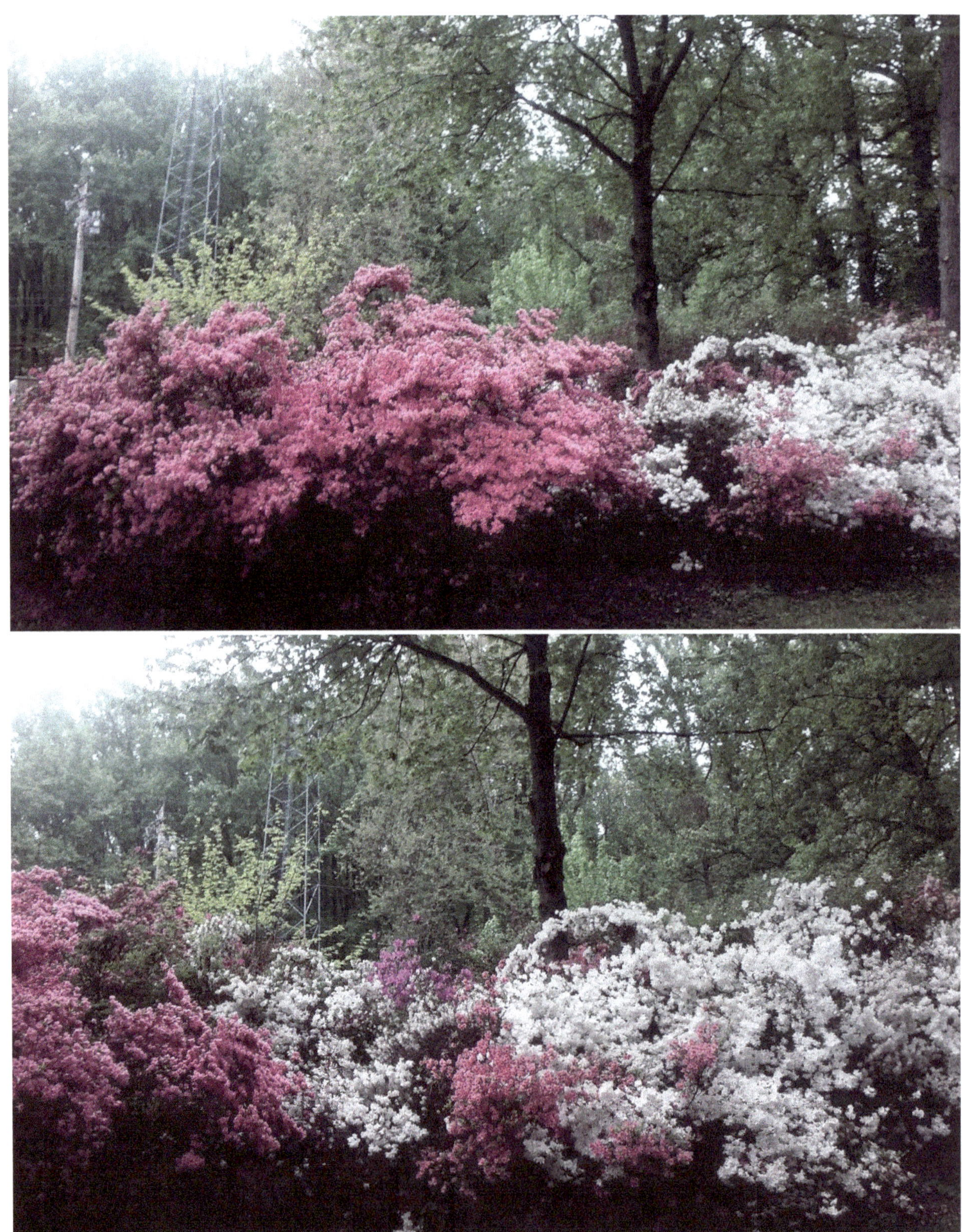

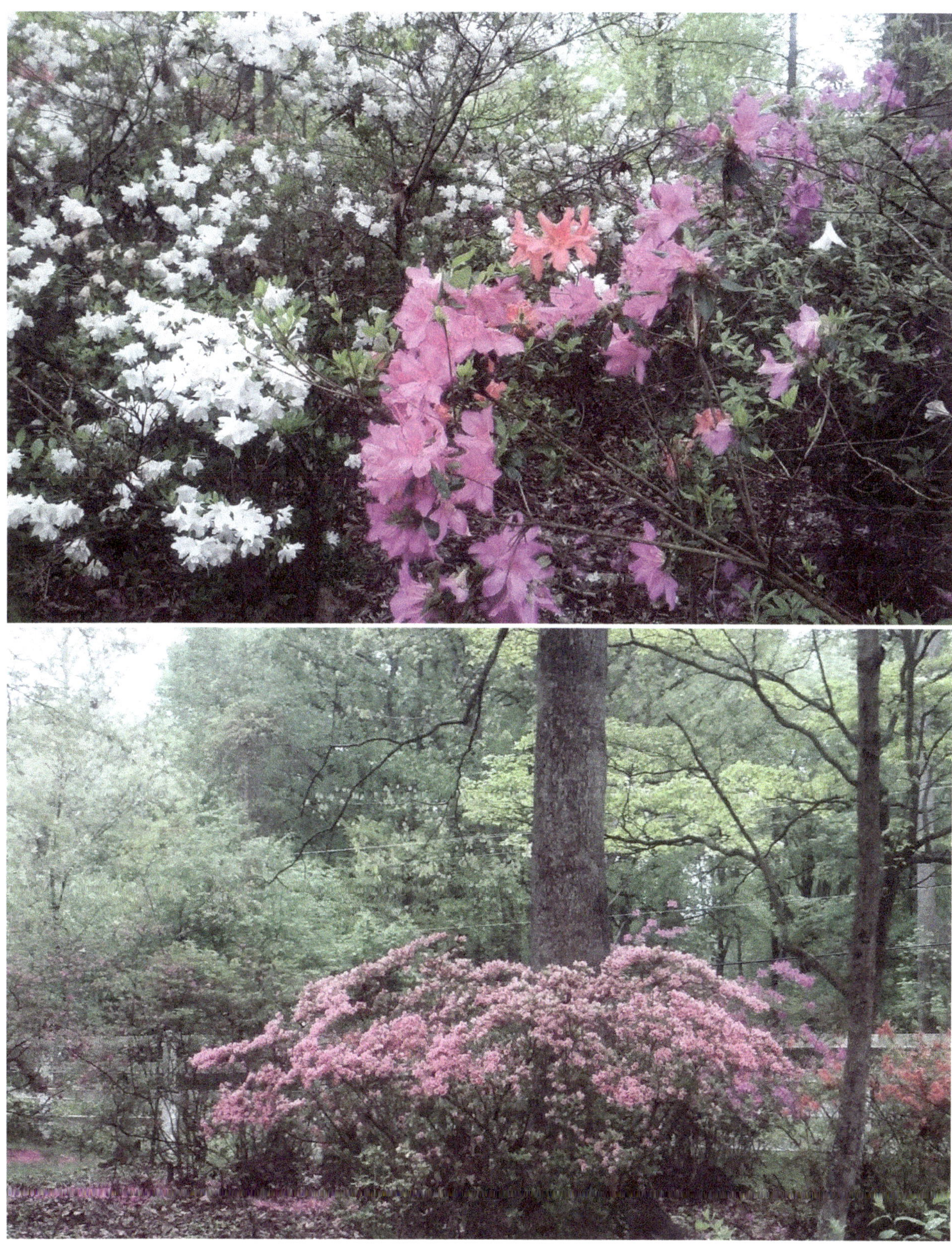

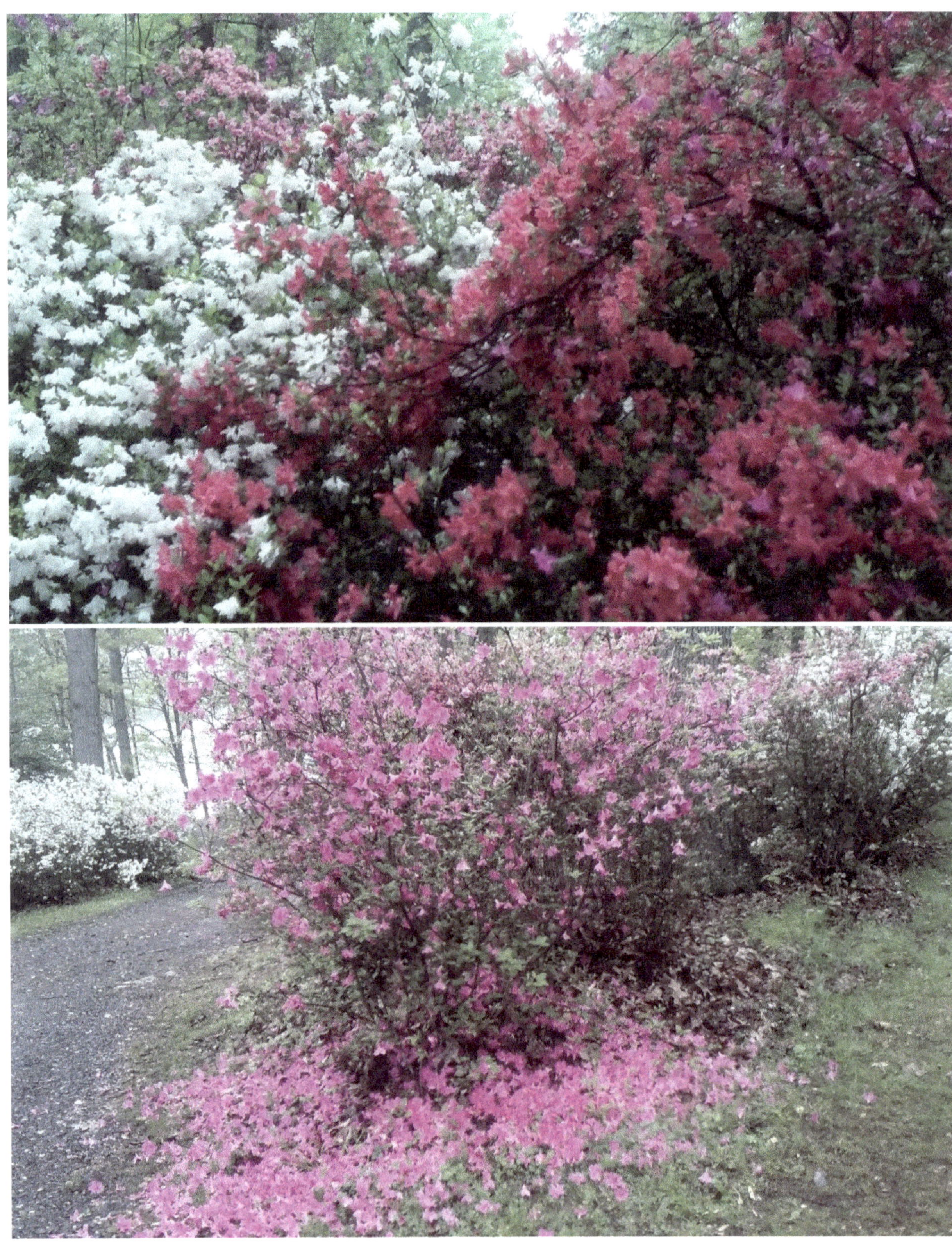

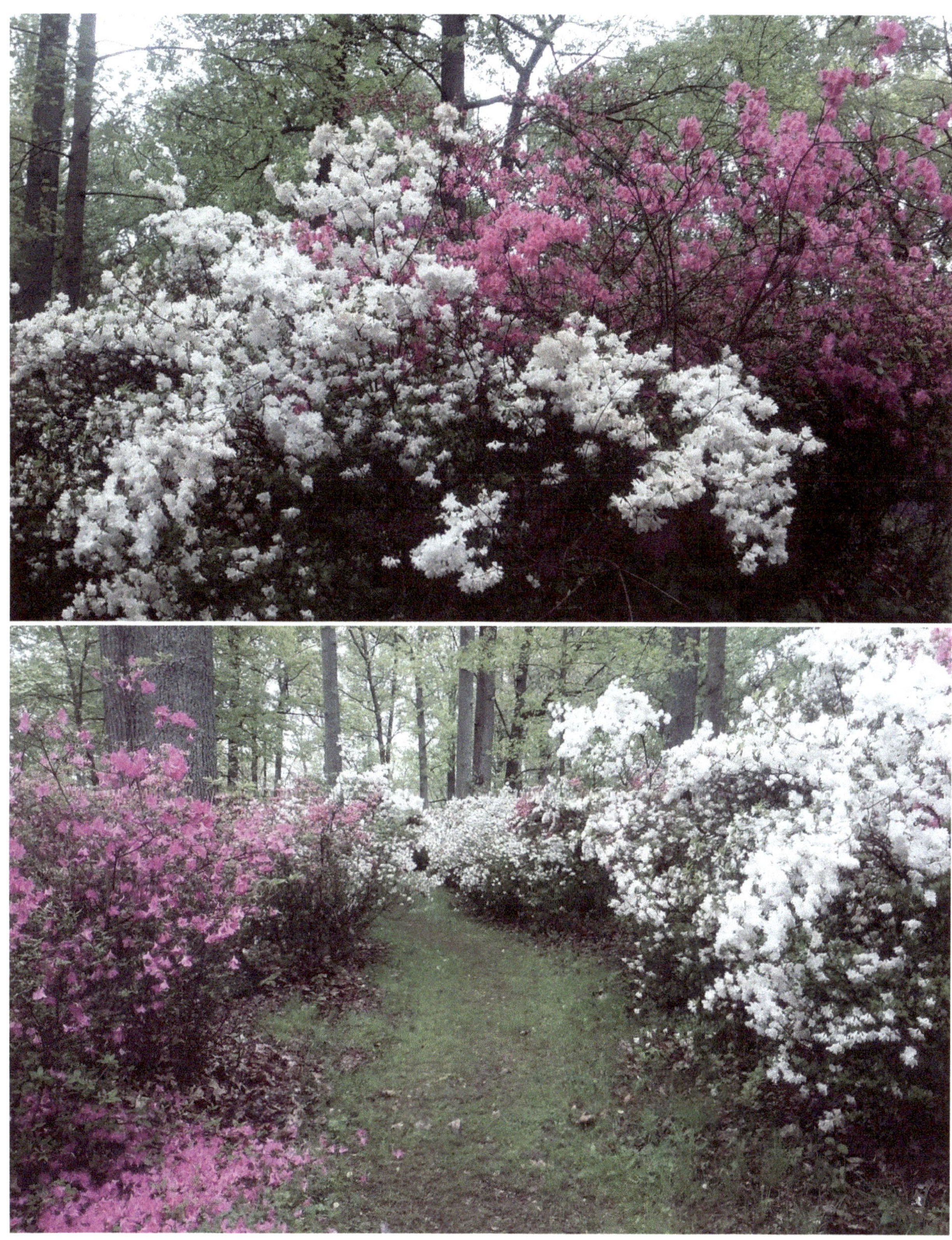

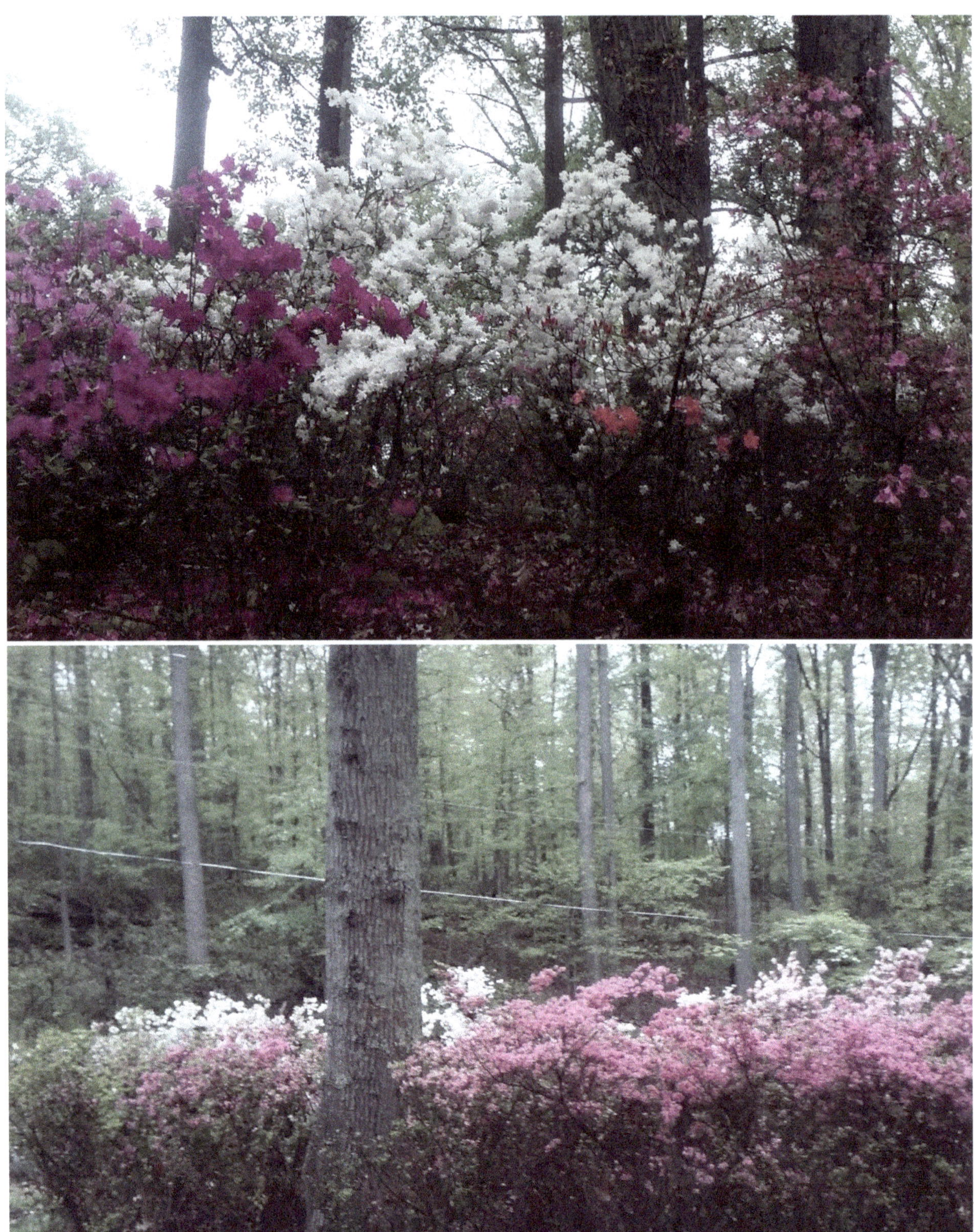

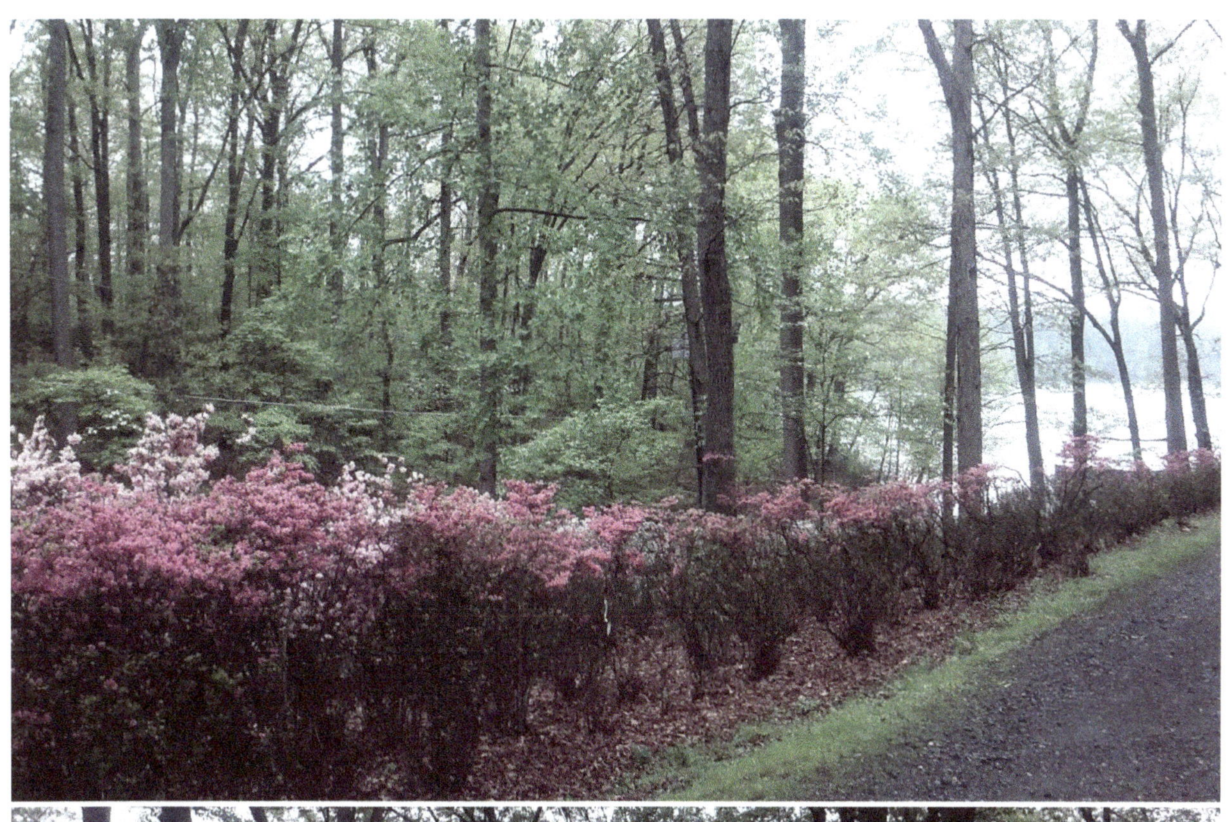

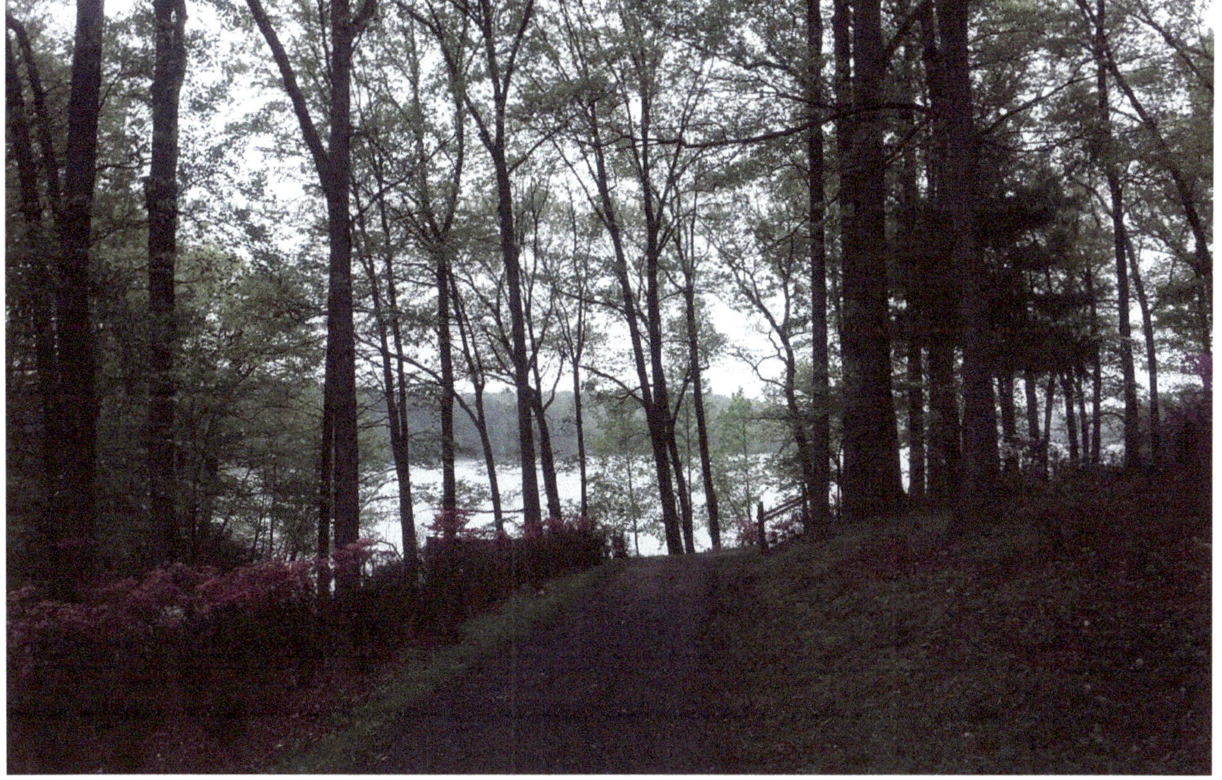

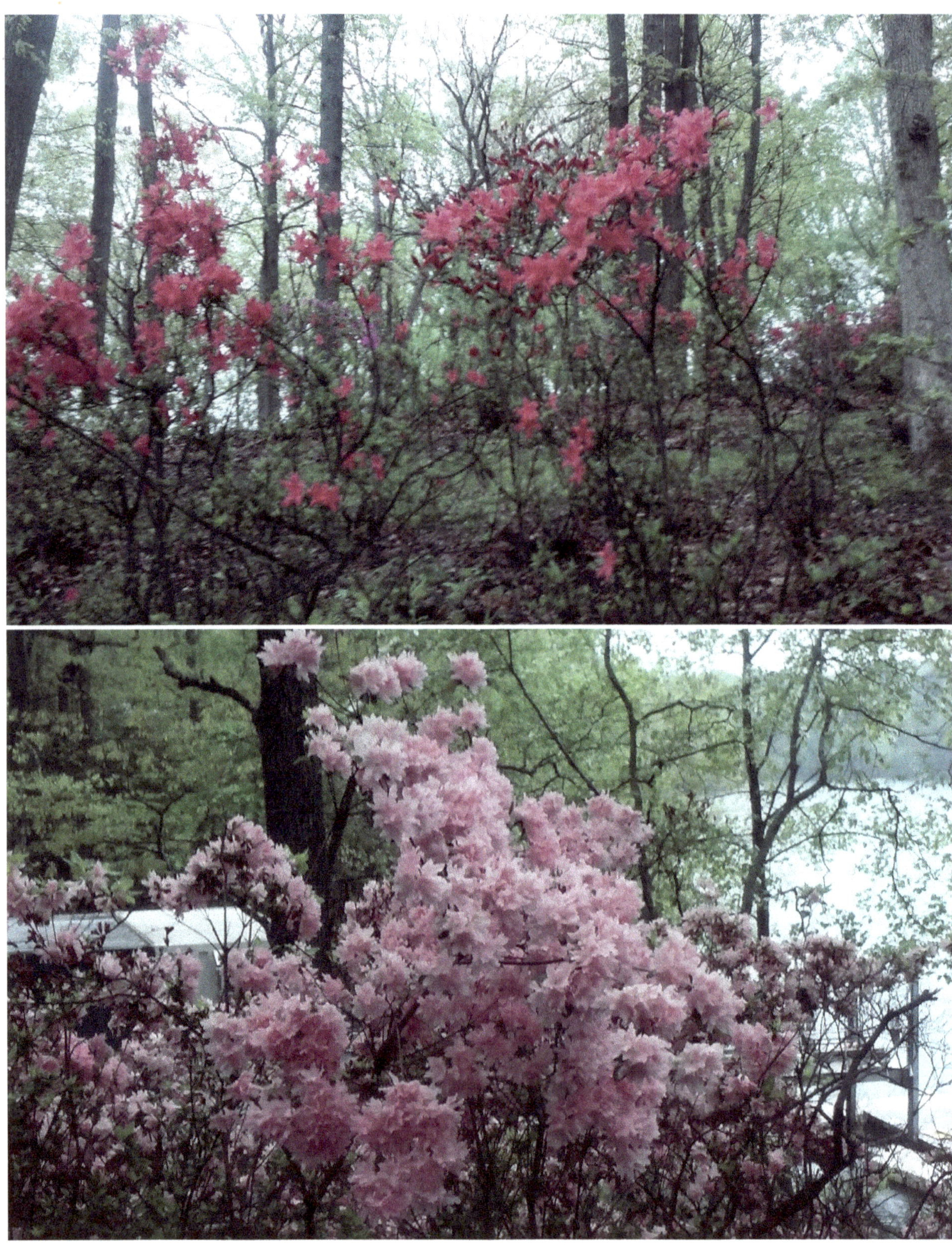

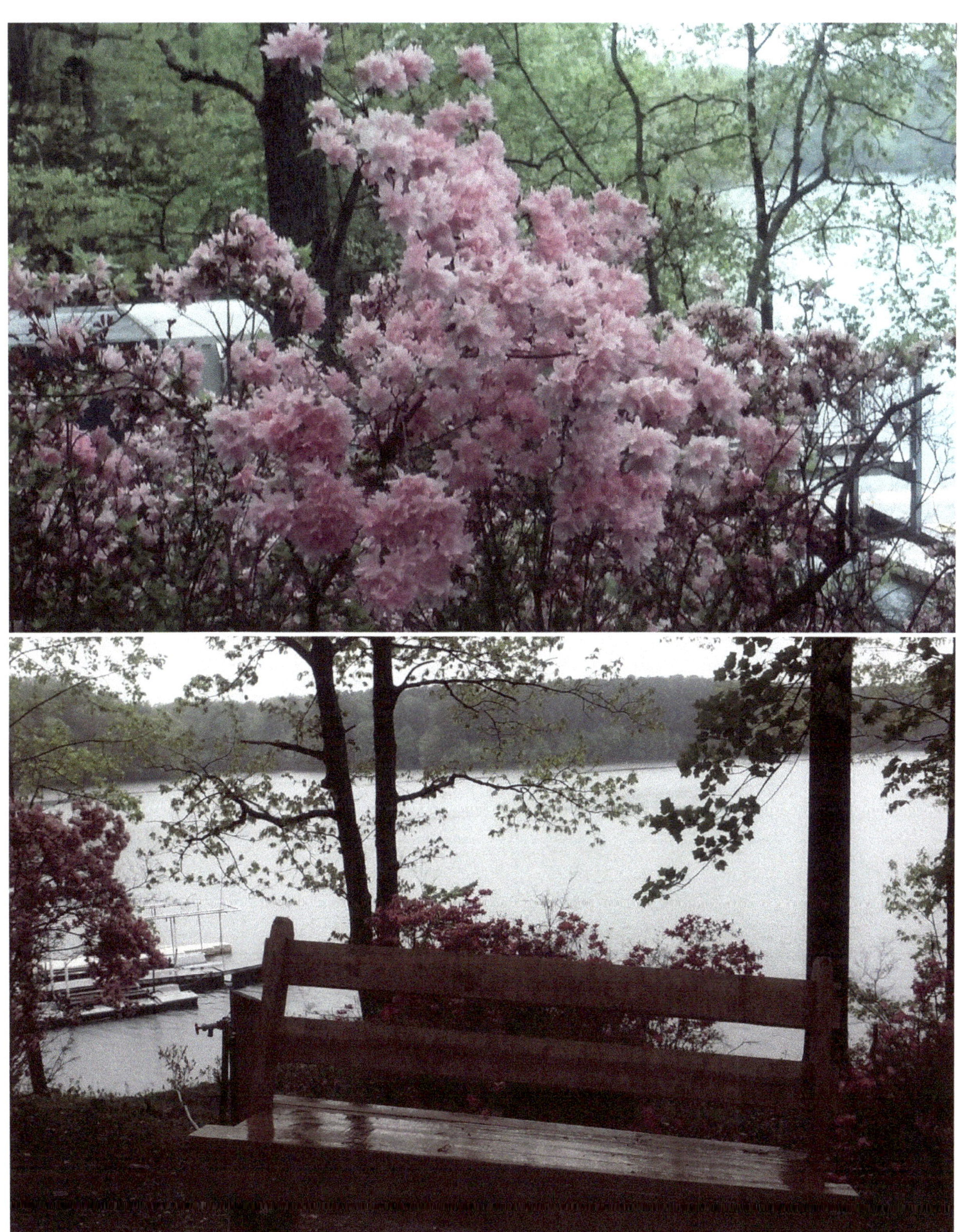

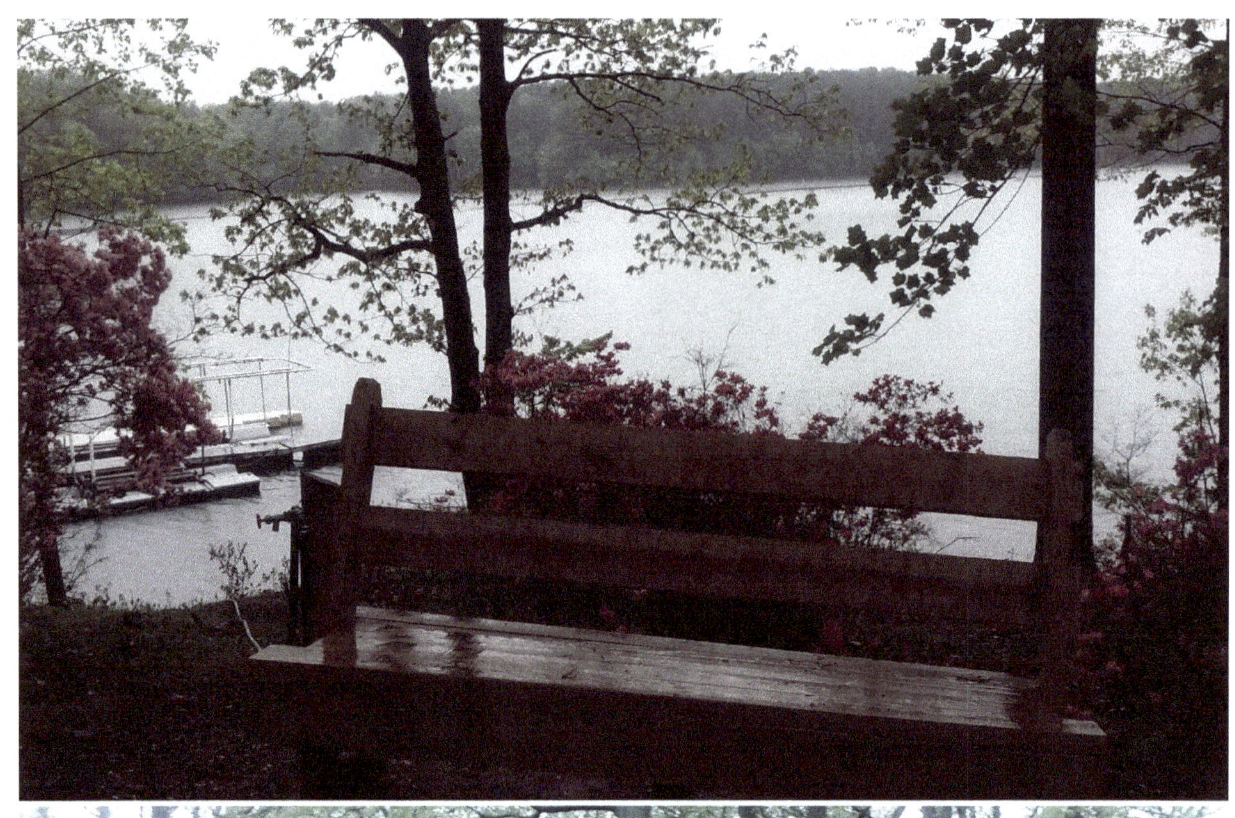

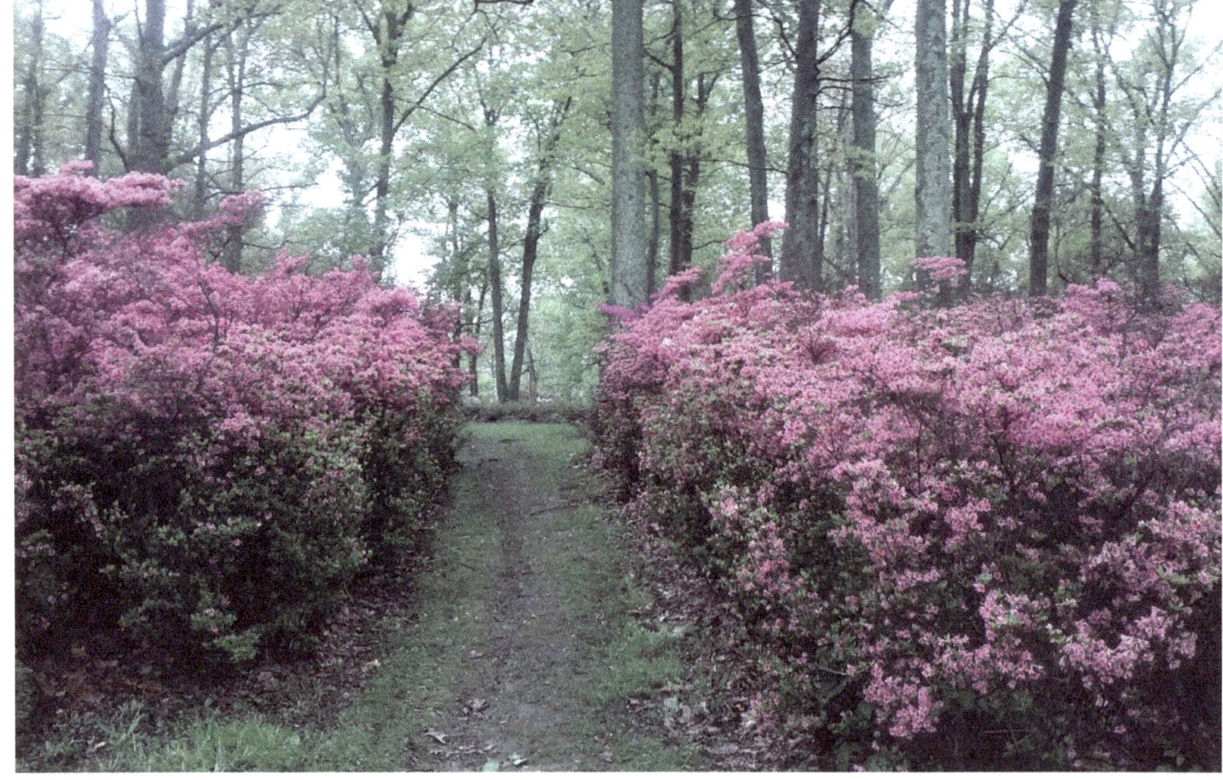

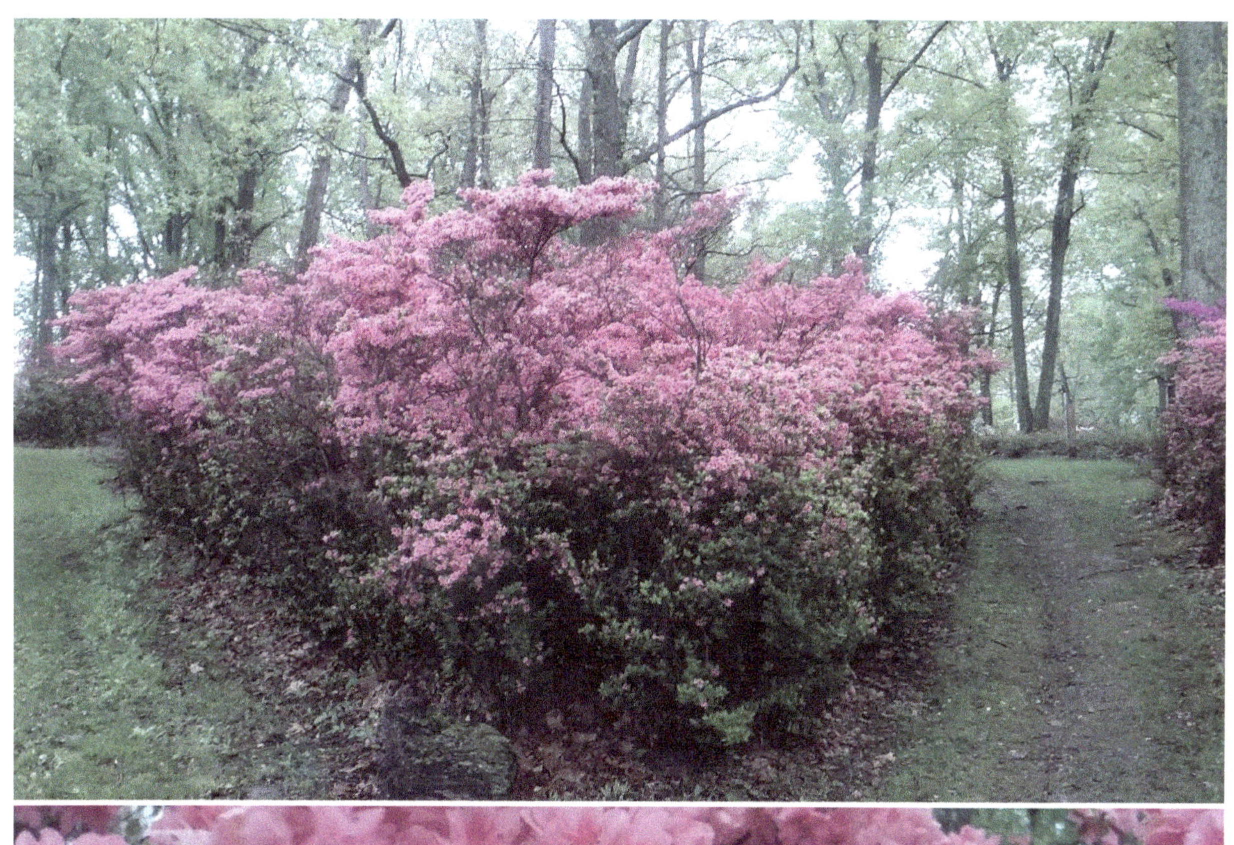

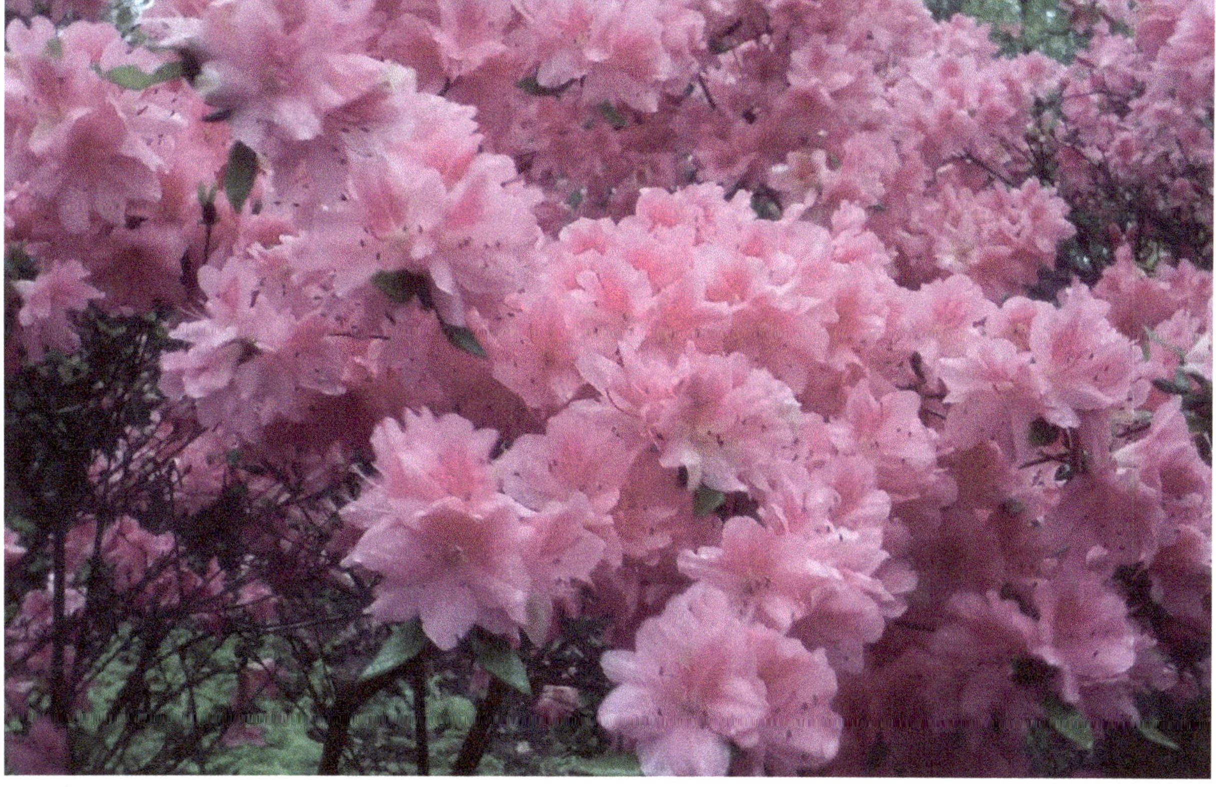

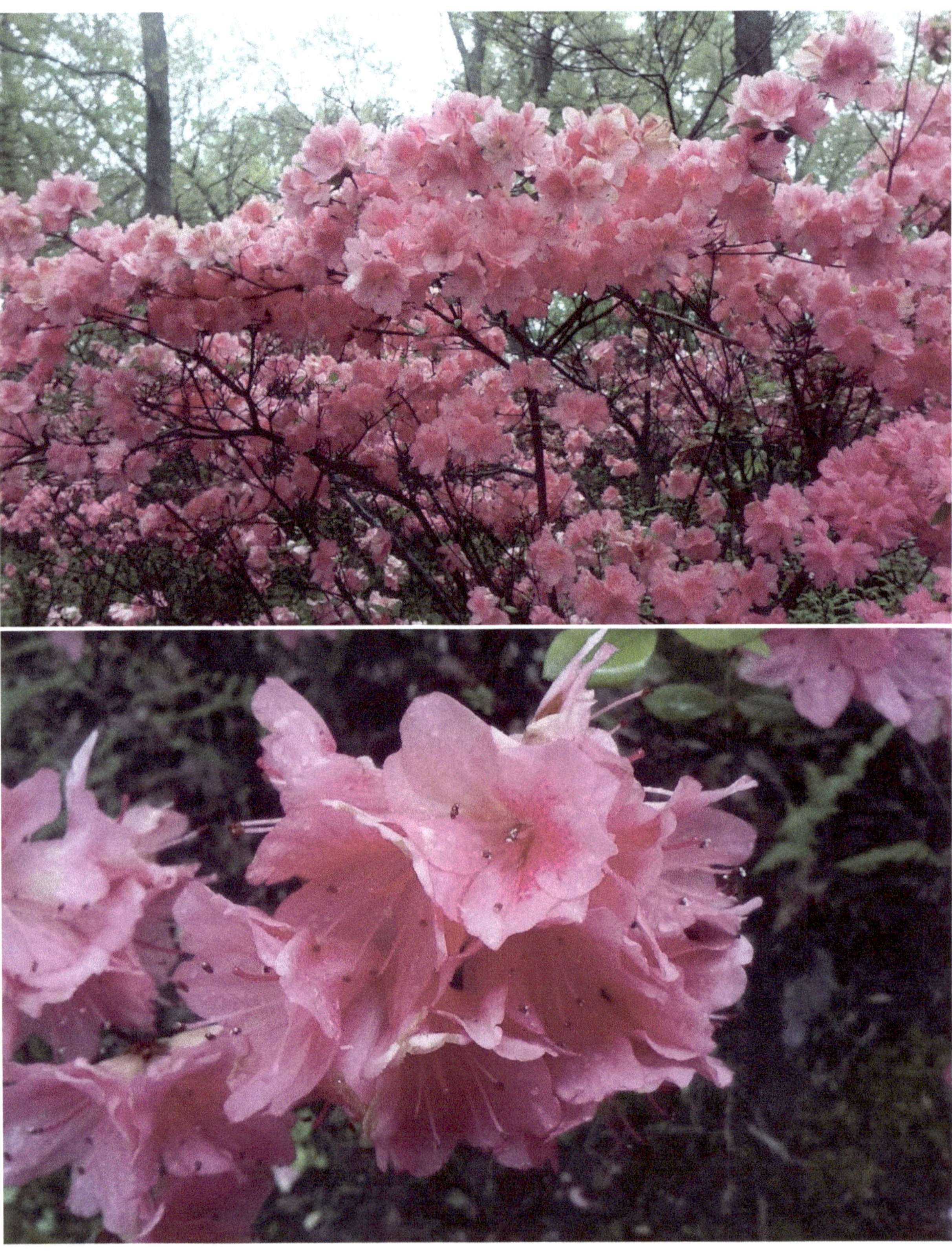

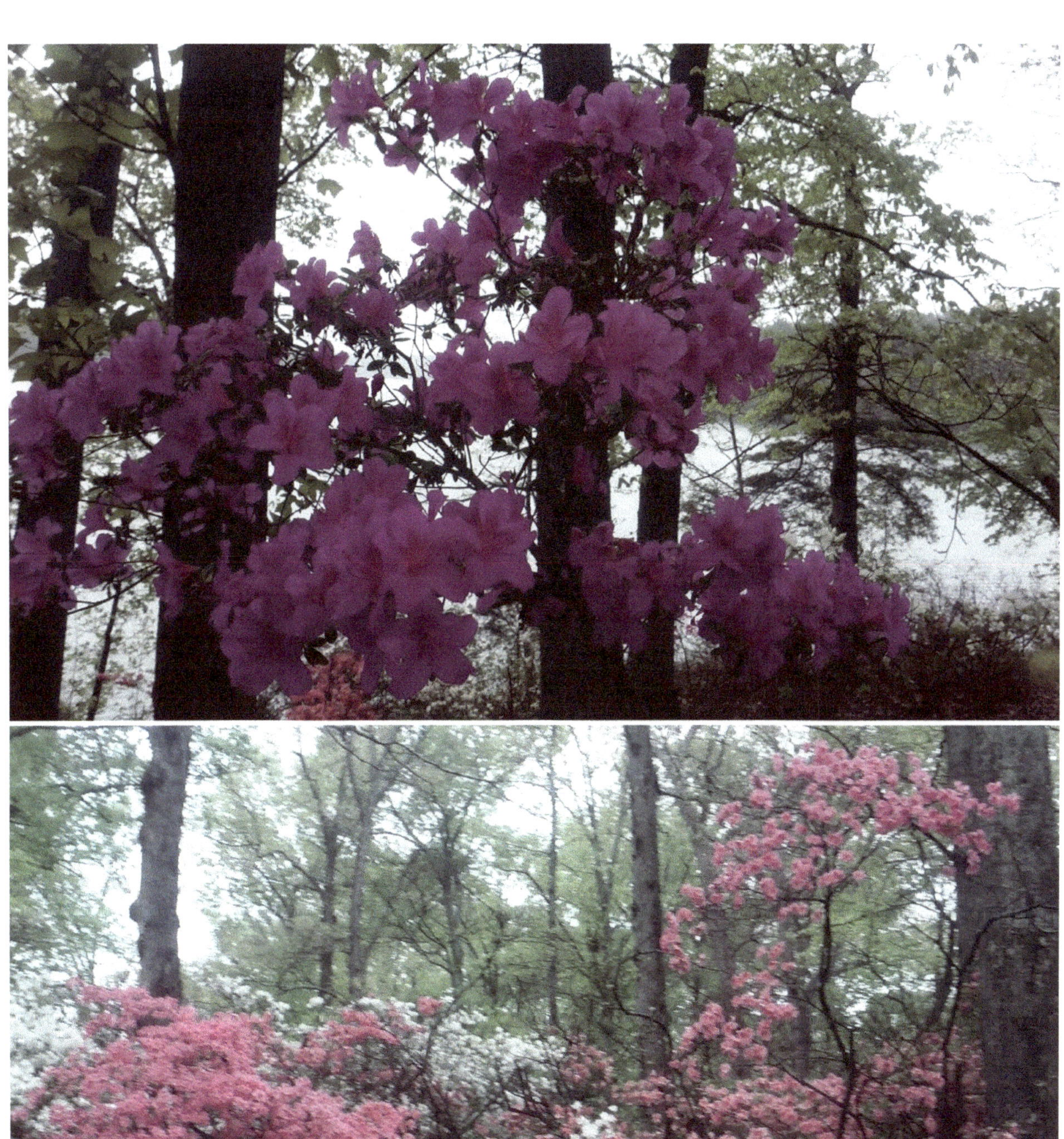

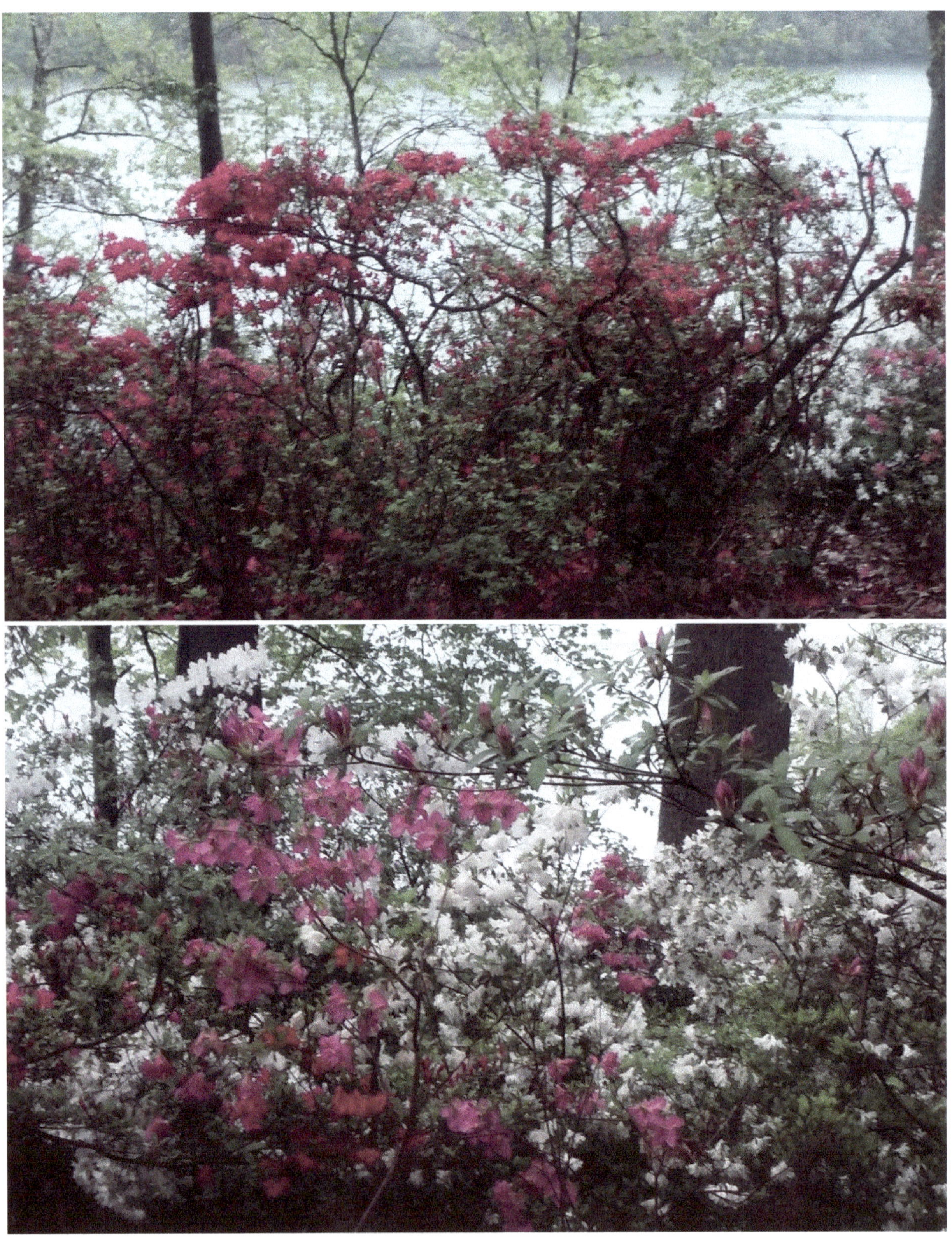

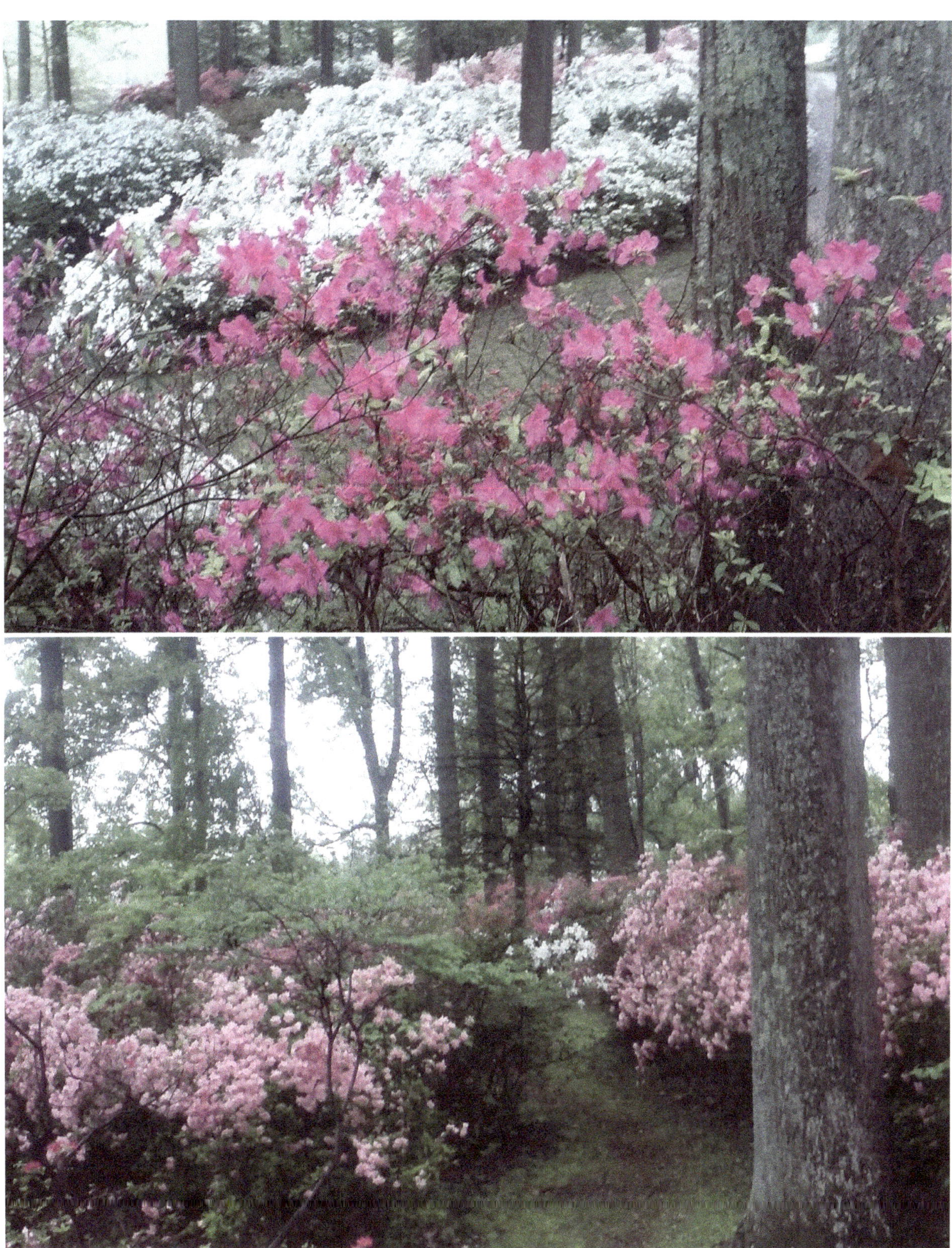

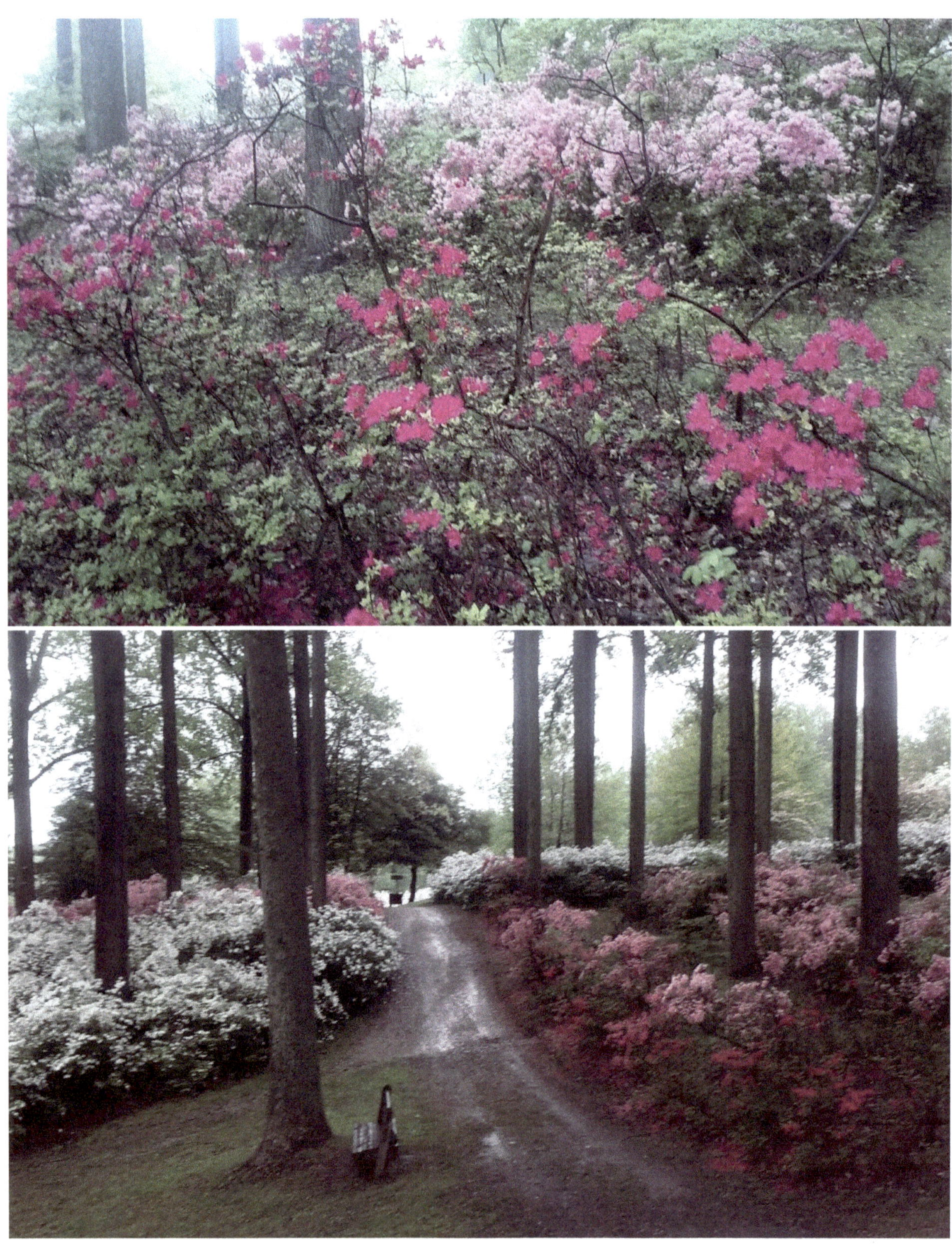

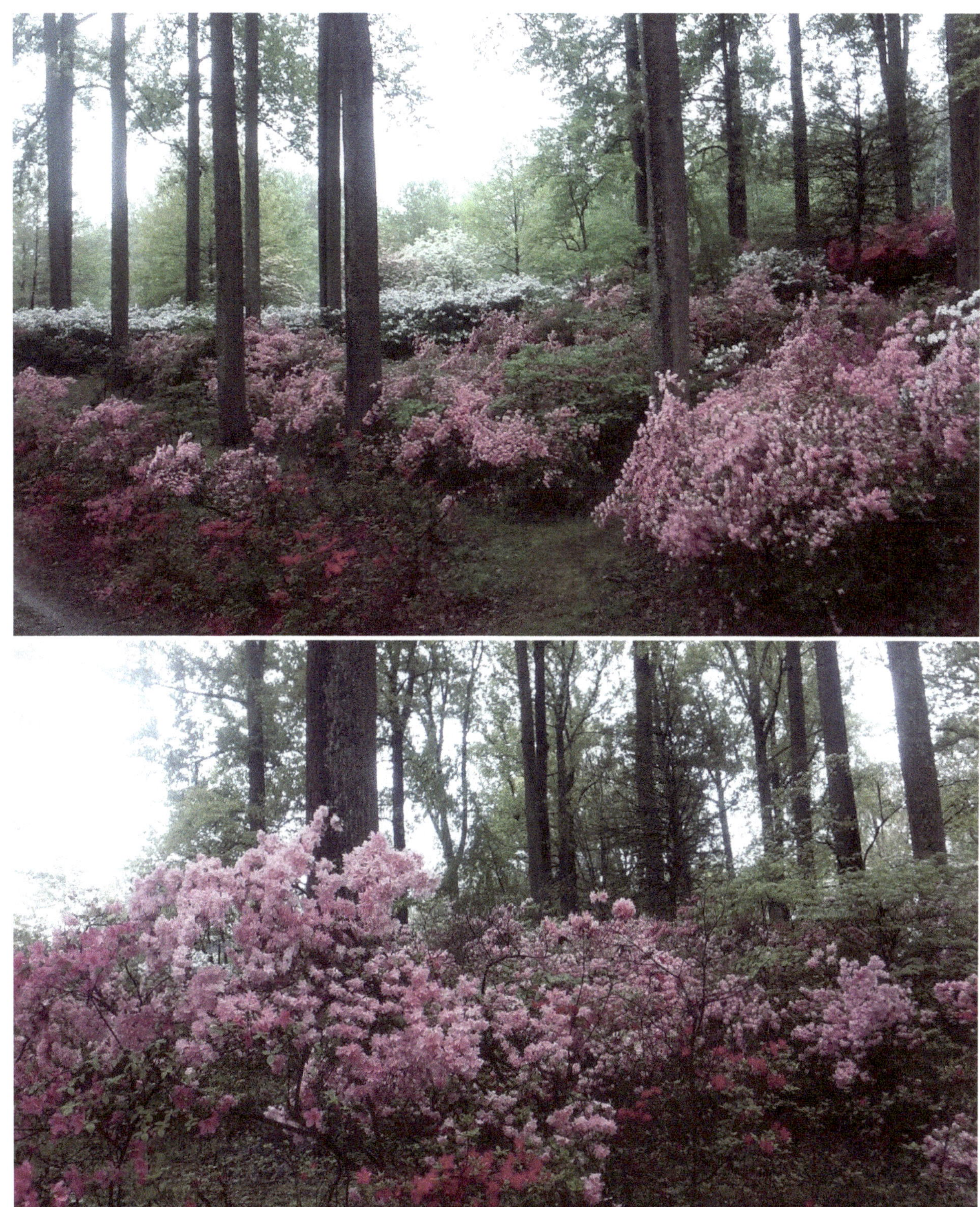

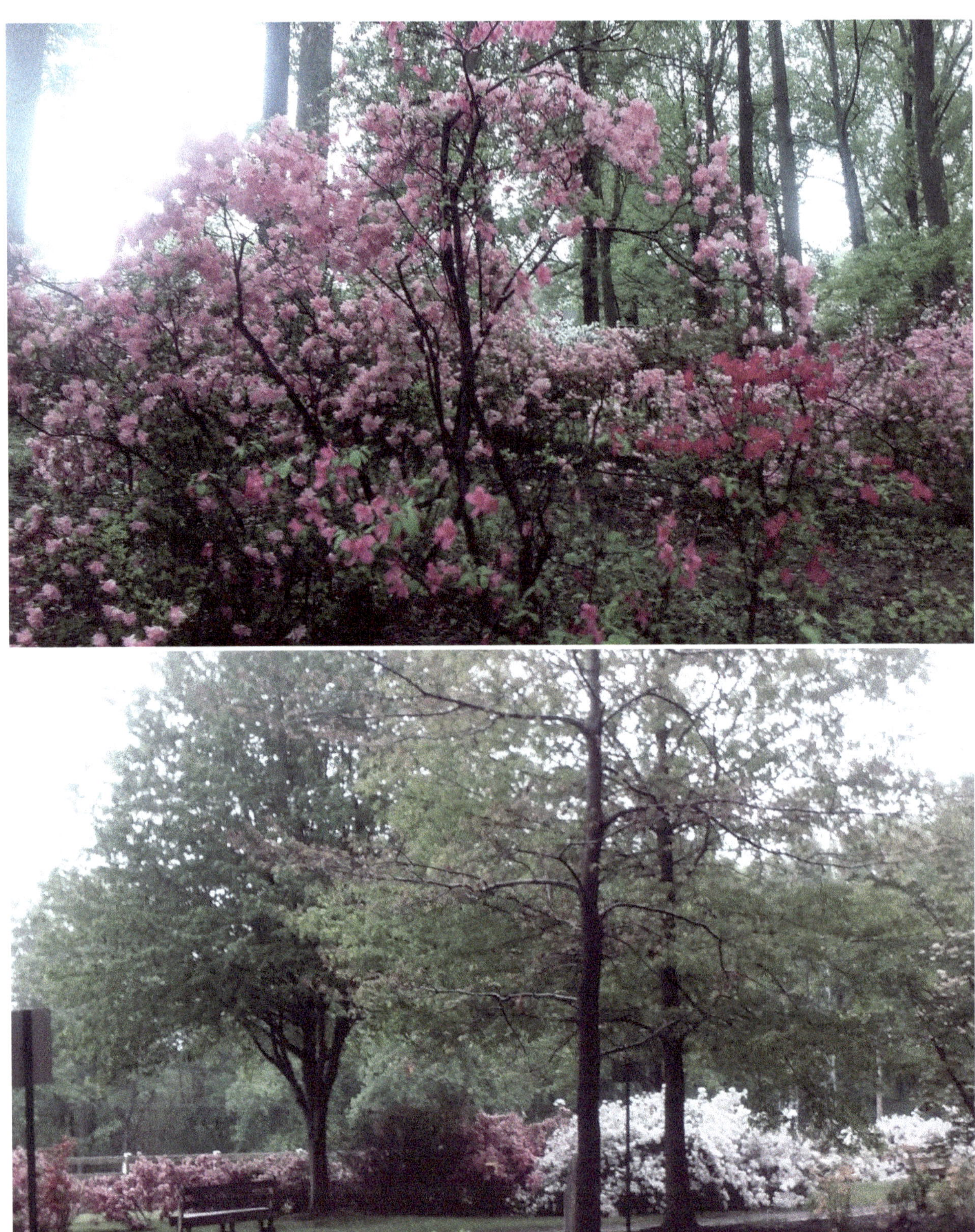

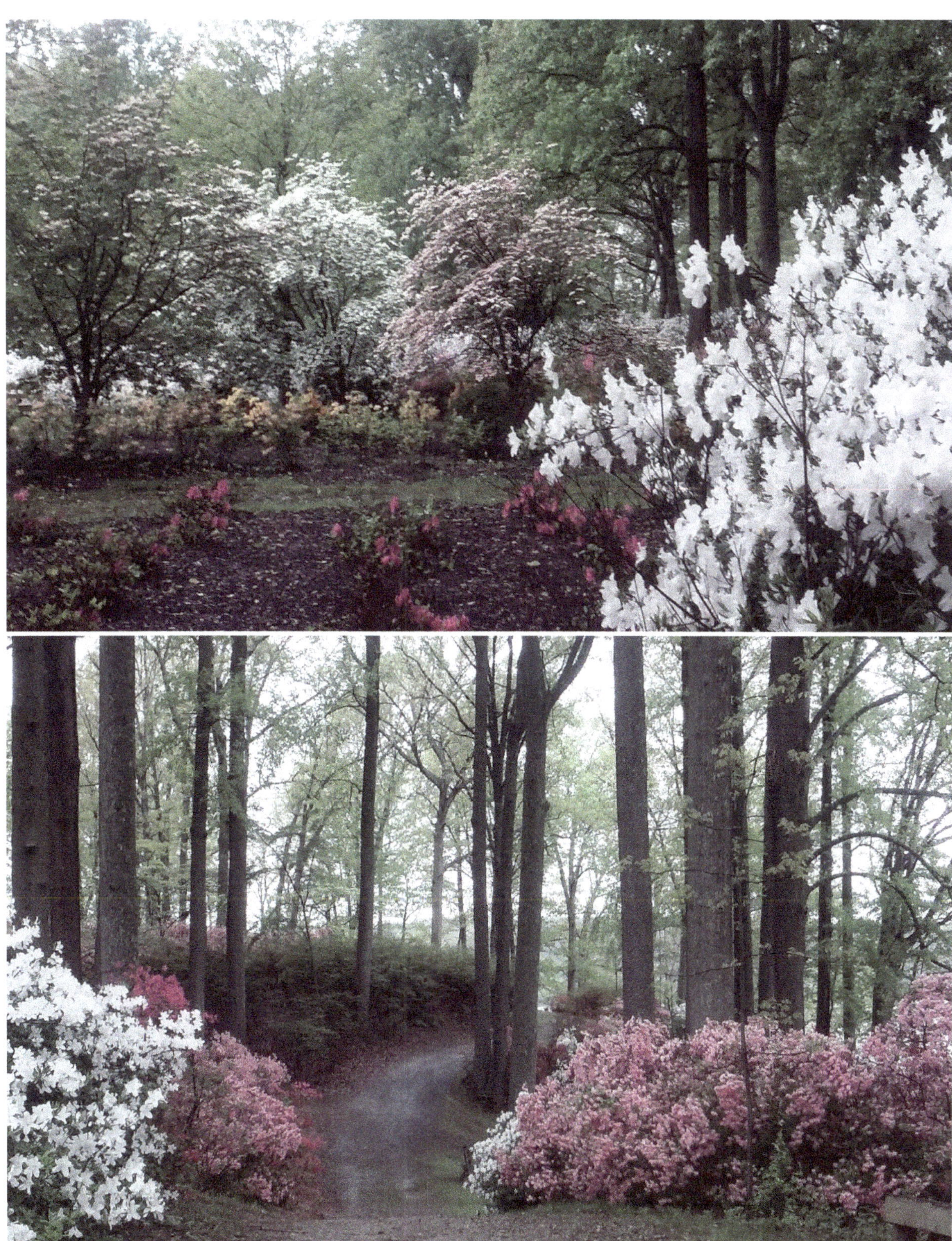

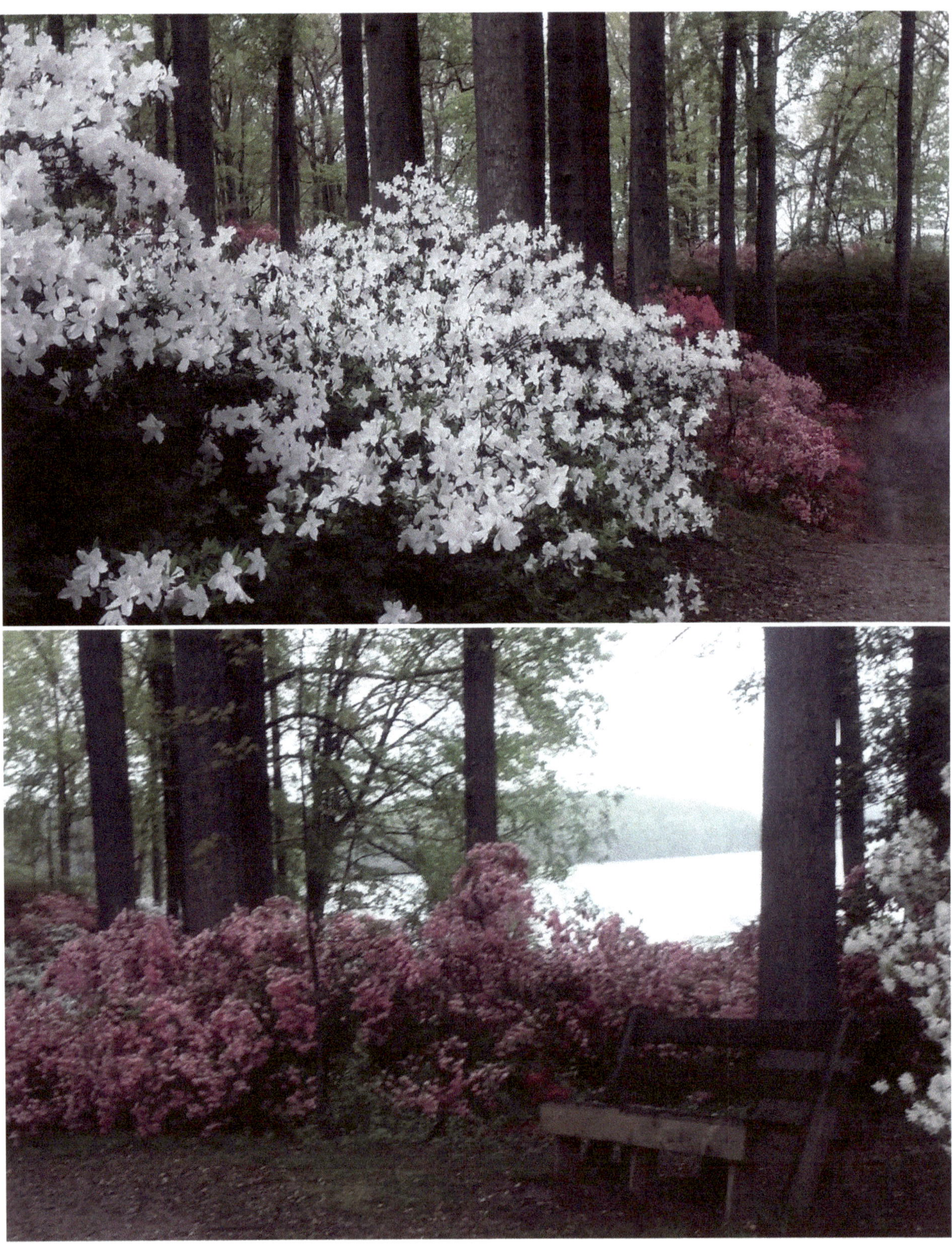

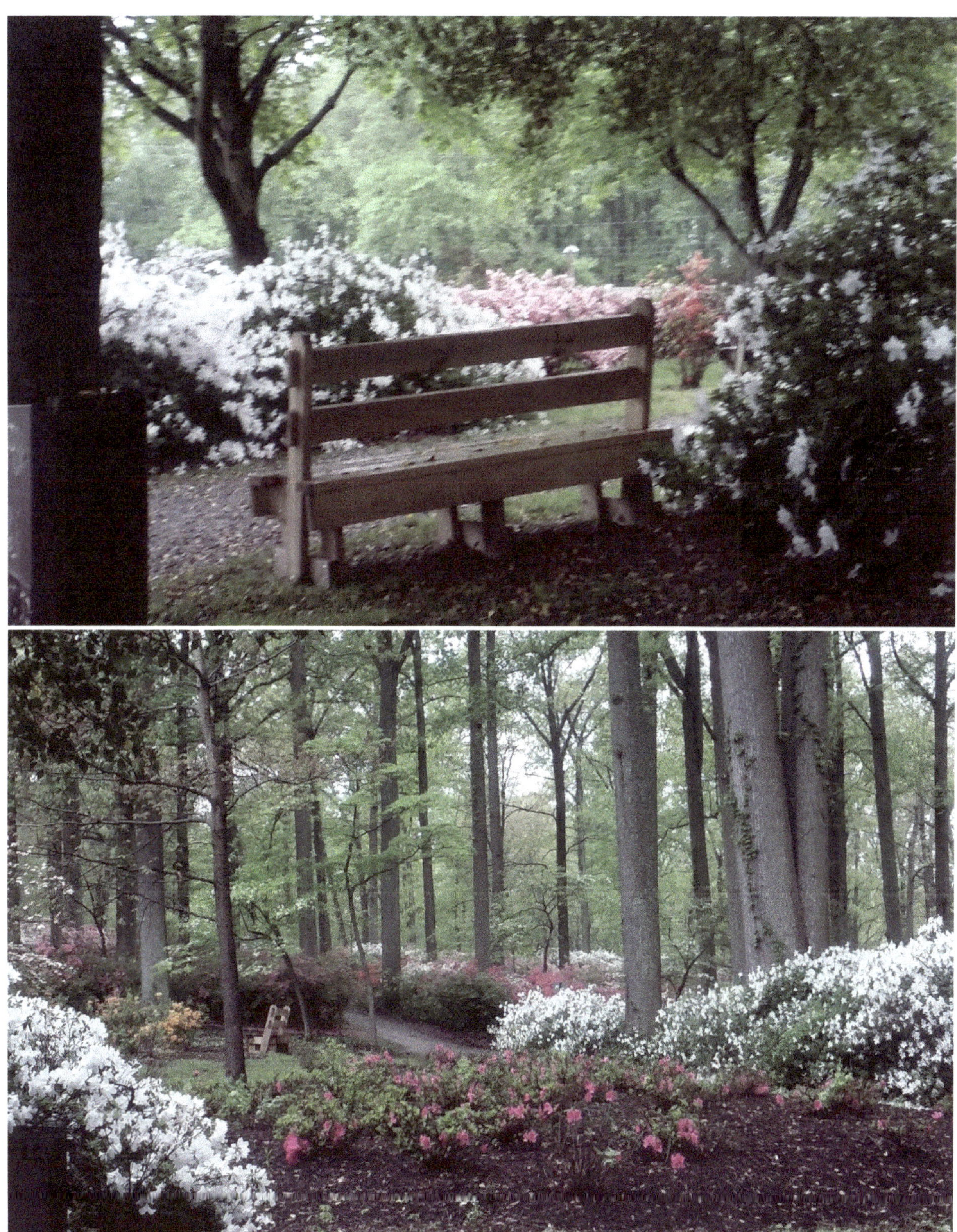

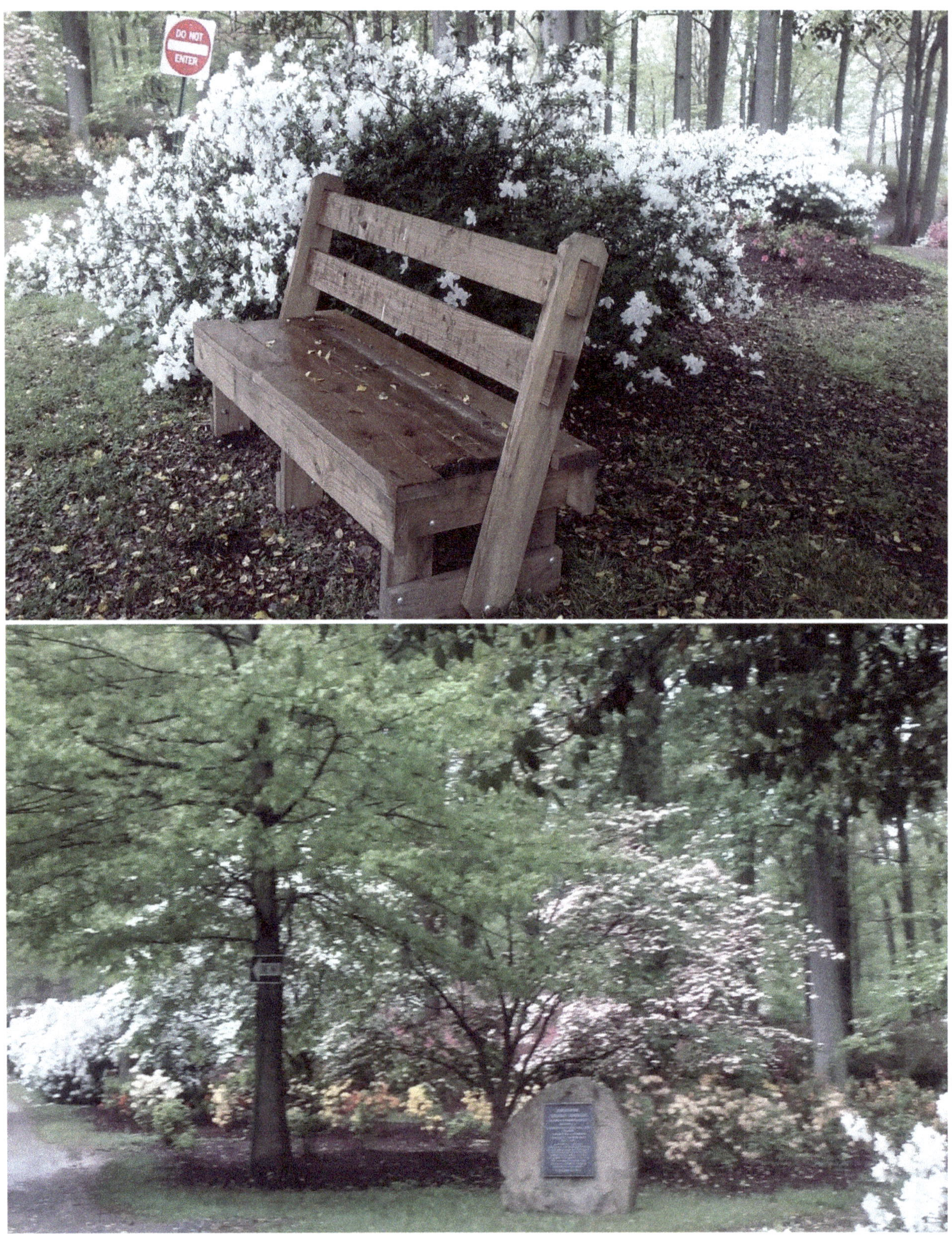
DO NOT
ENTER

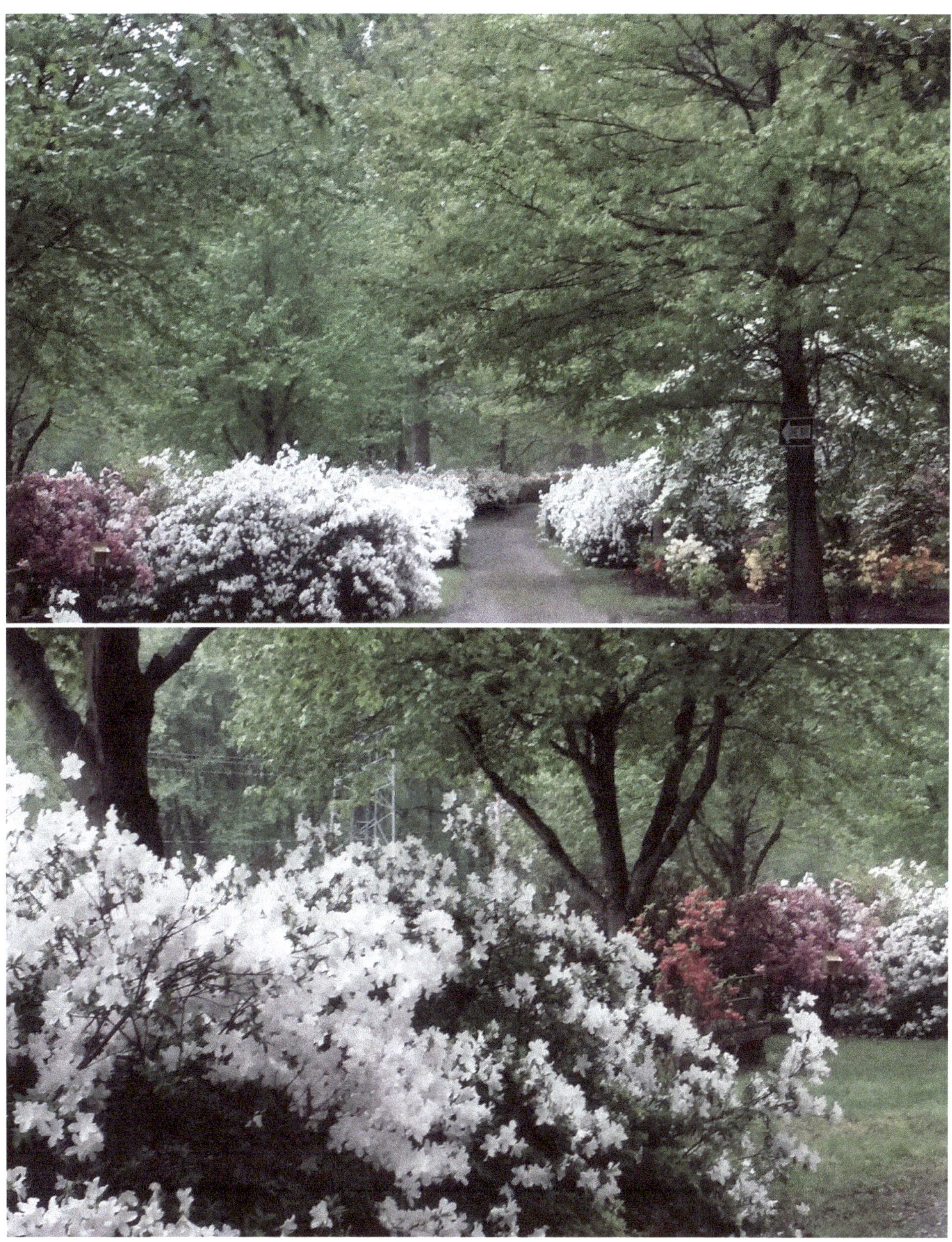

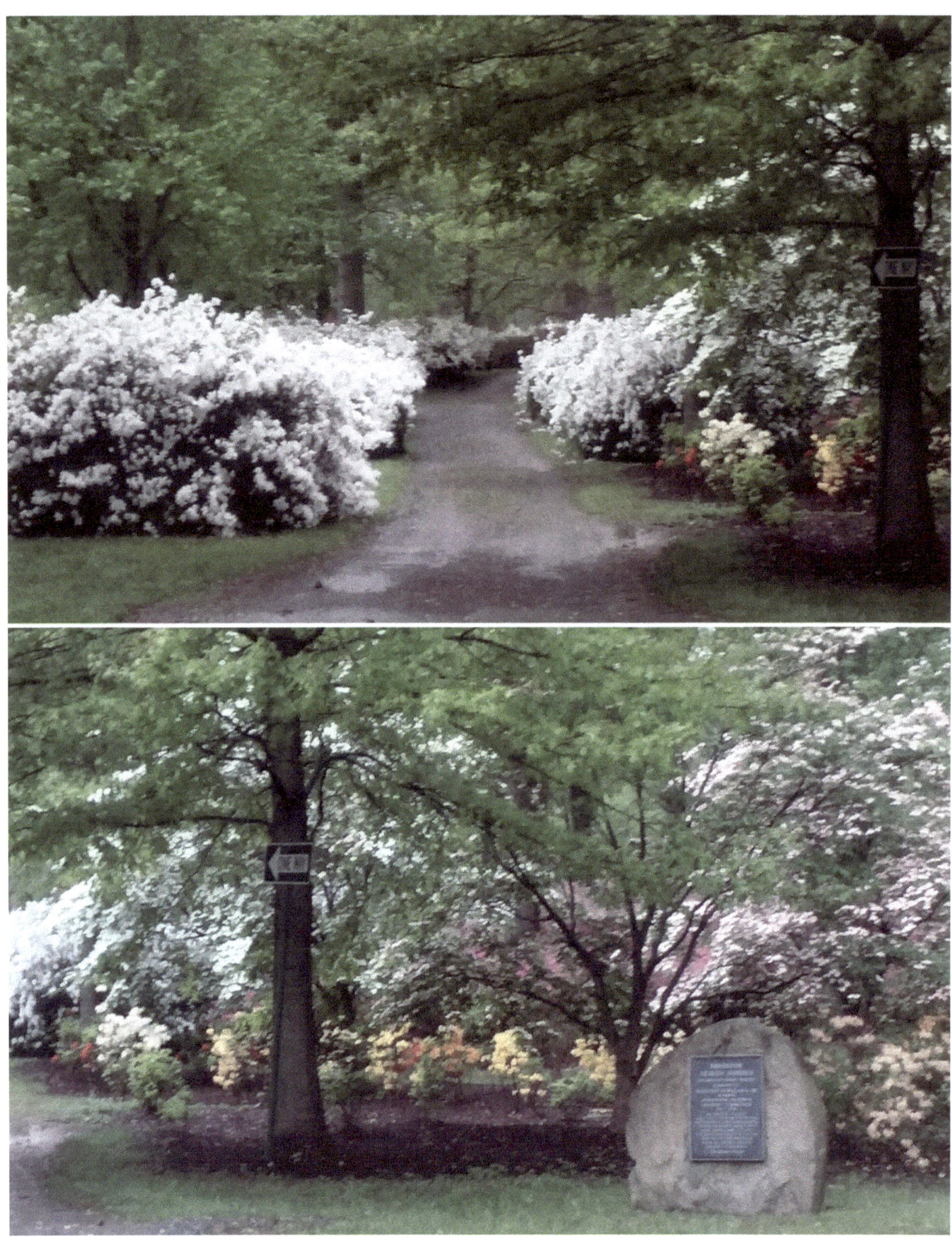

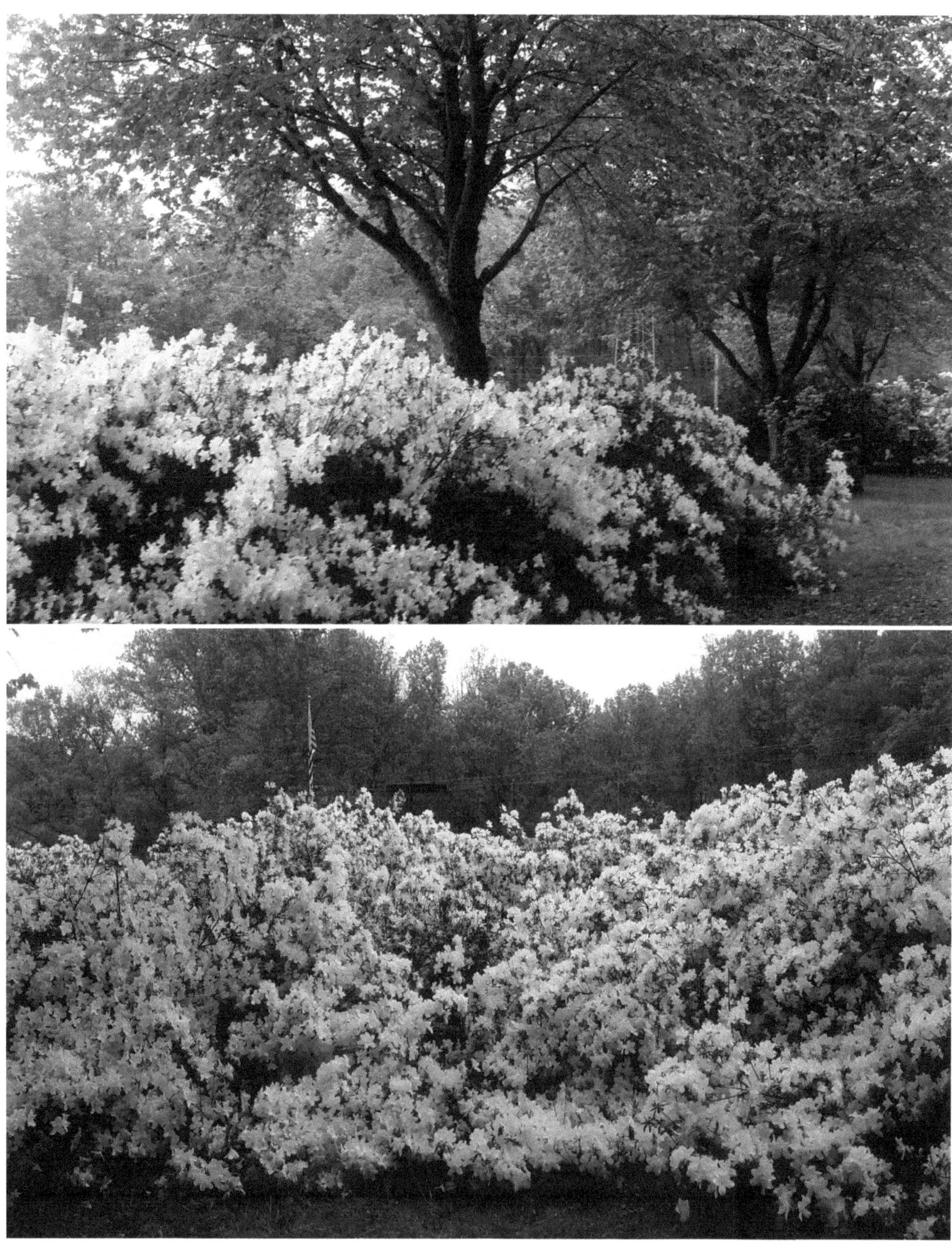

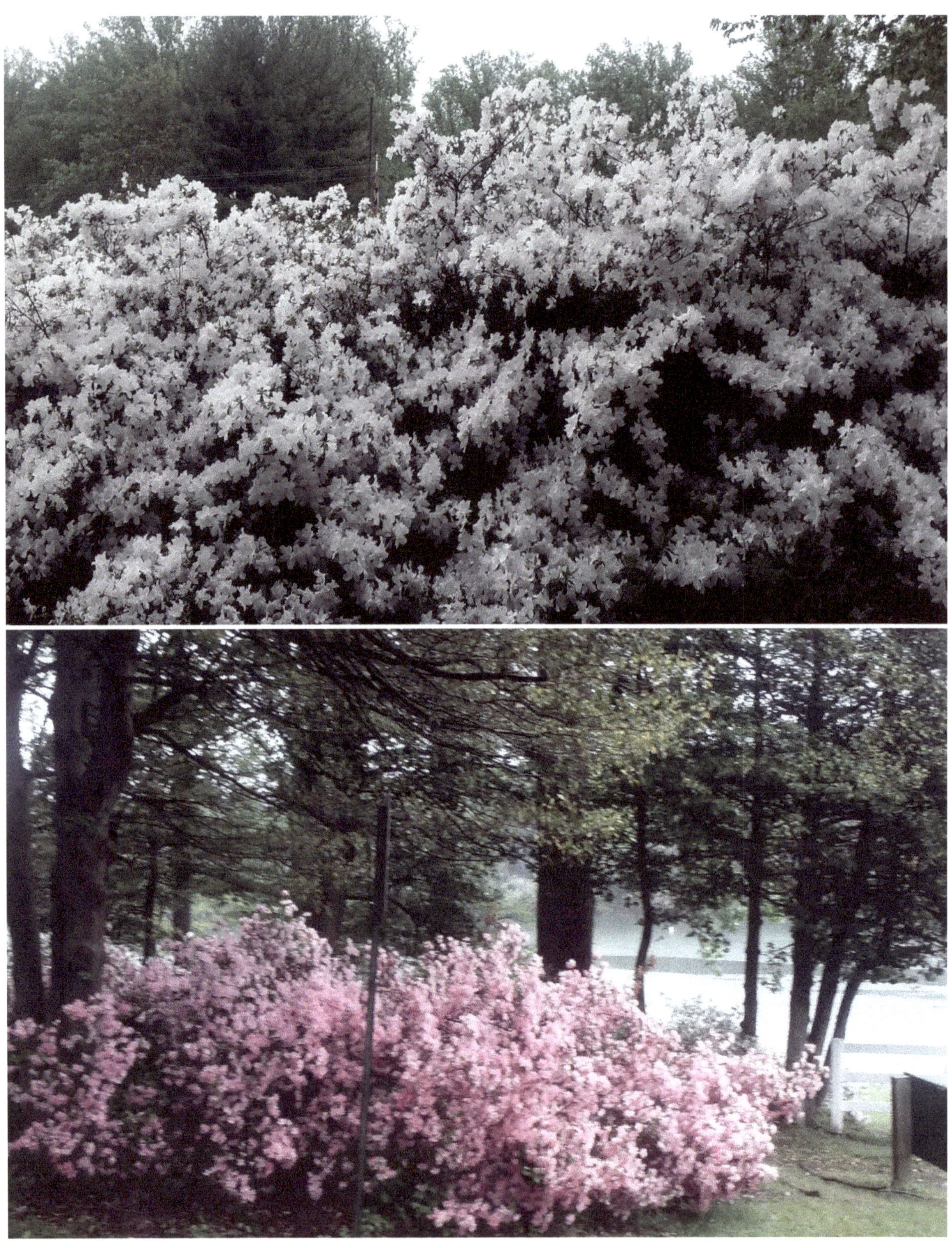

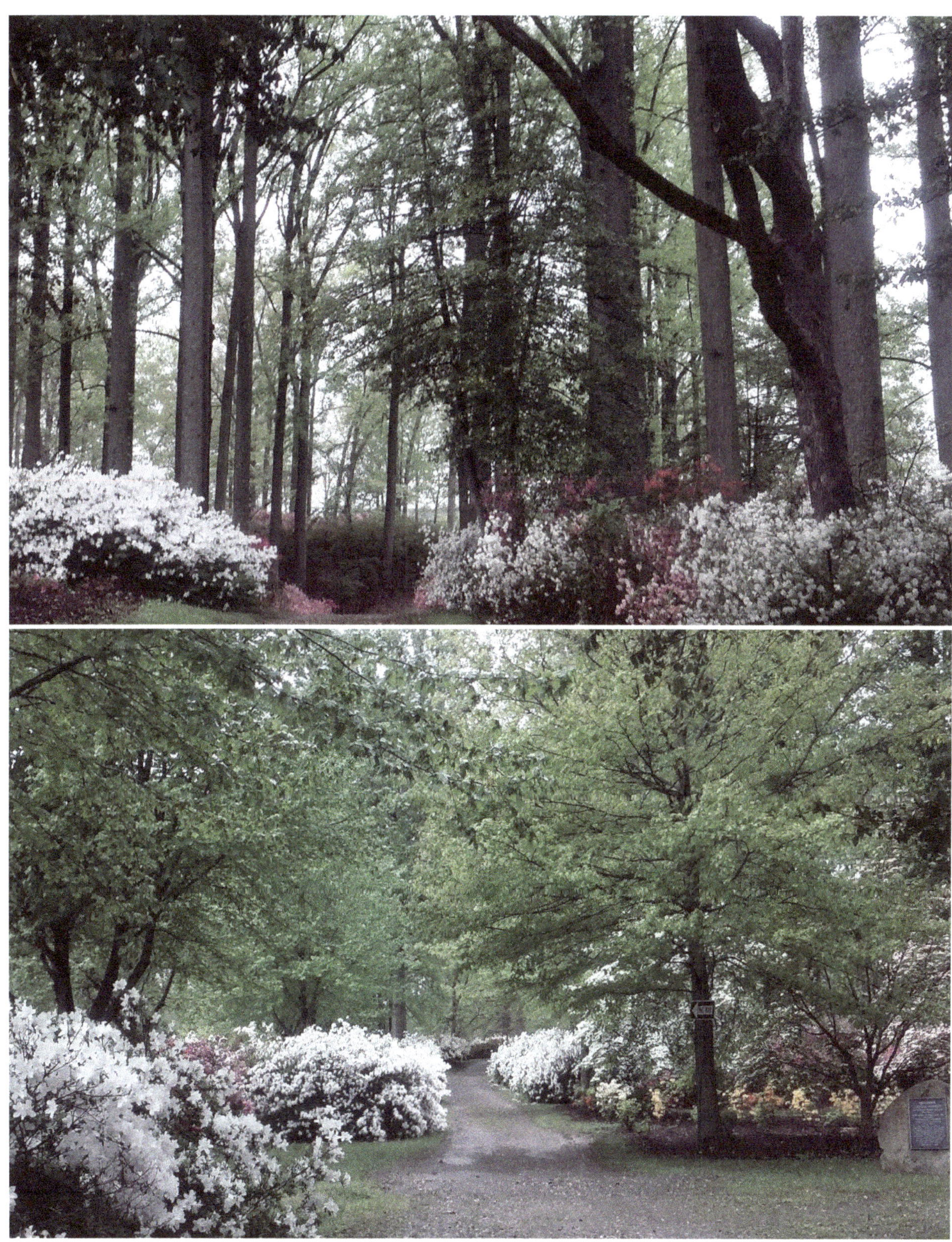

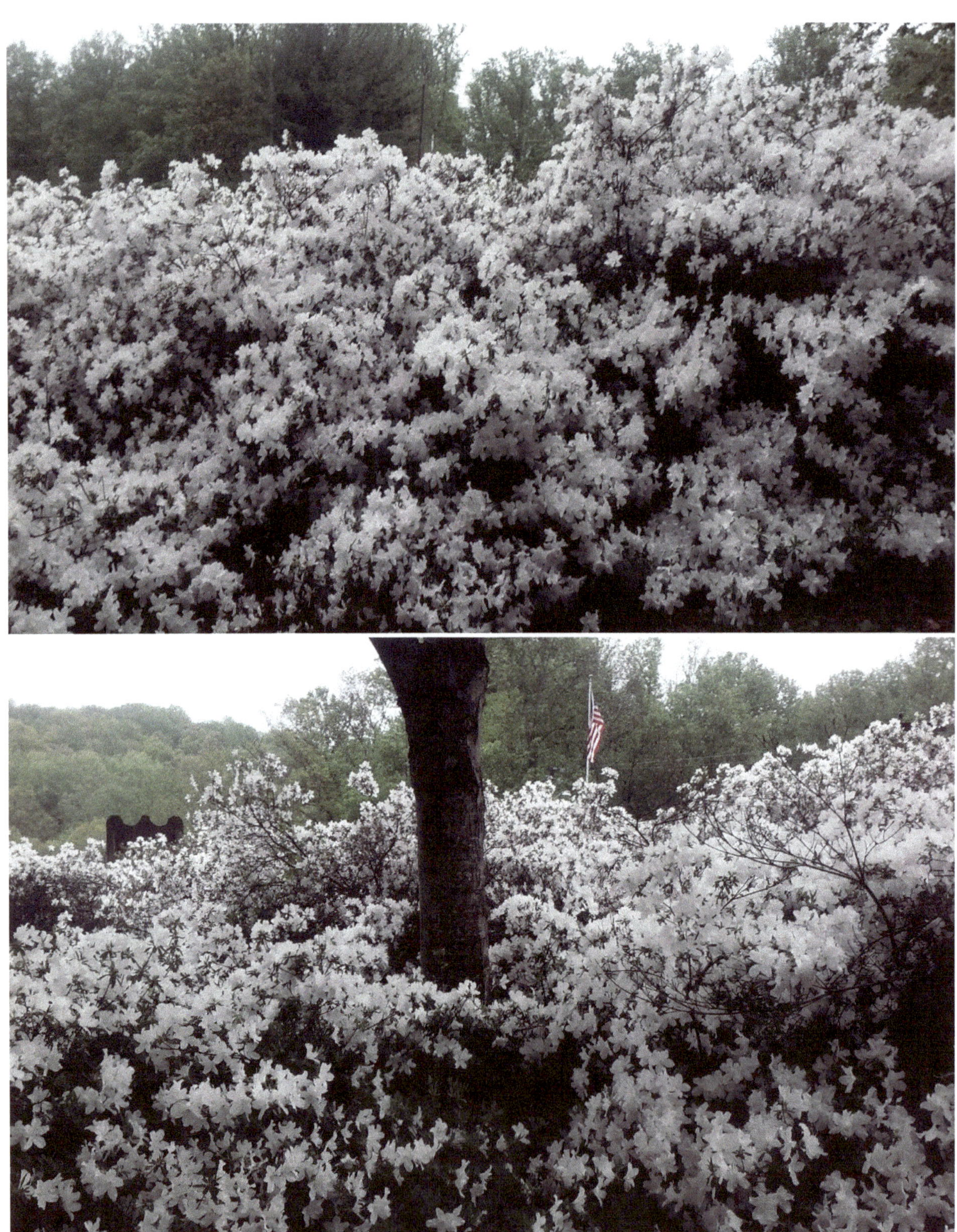

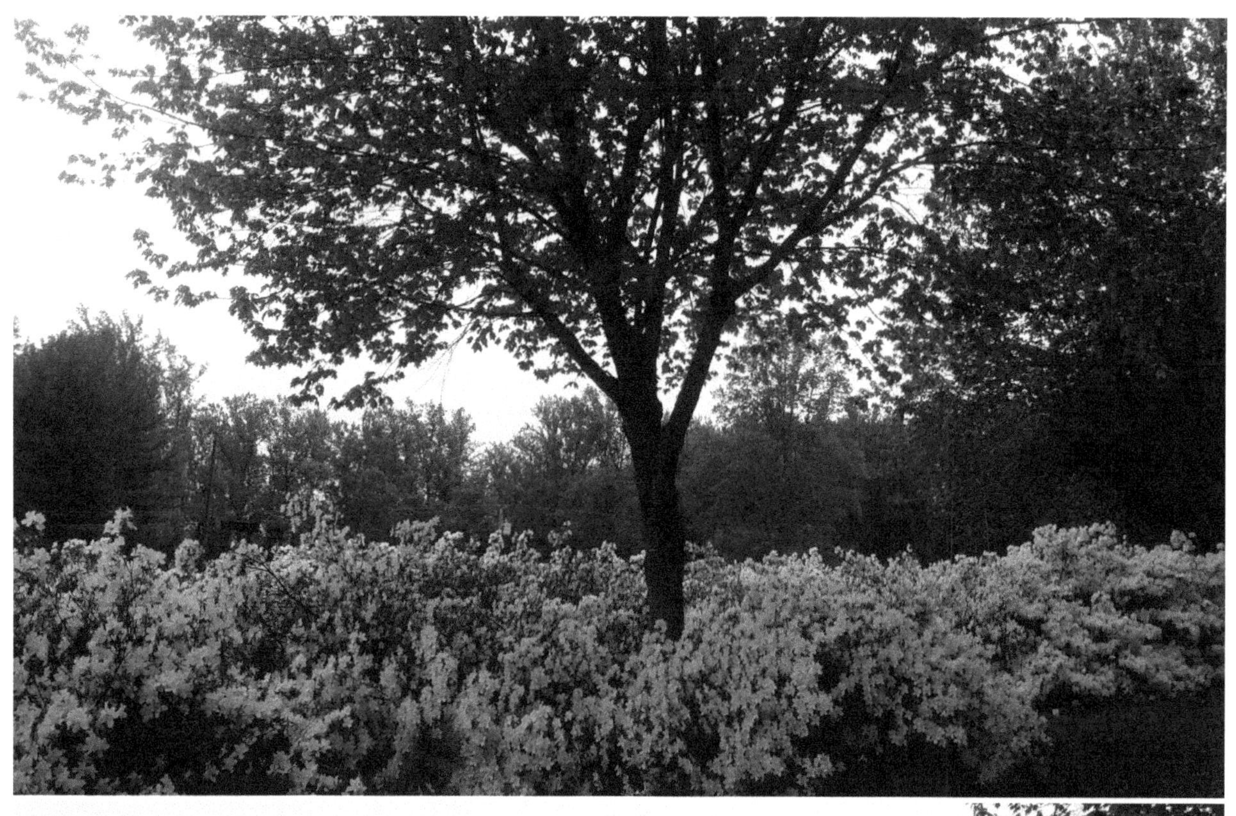

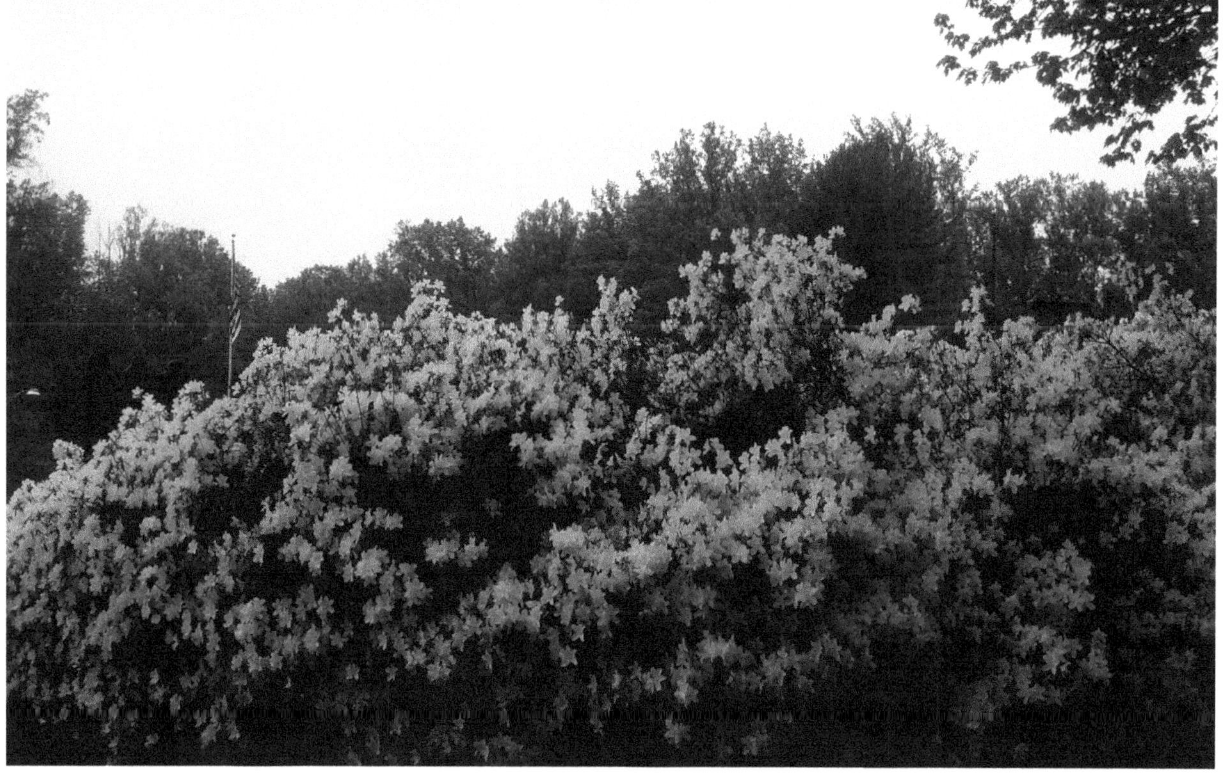

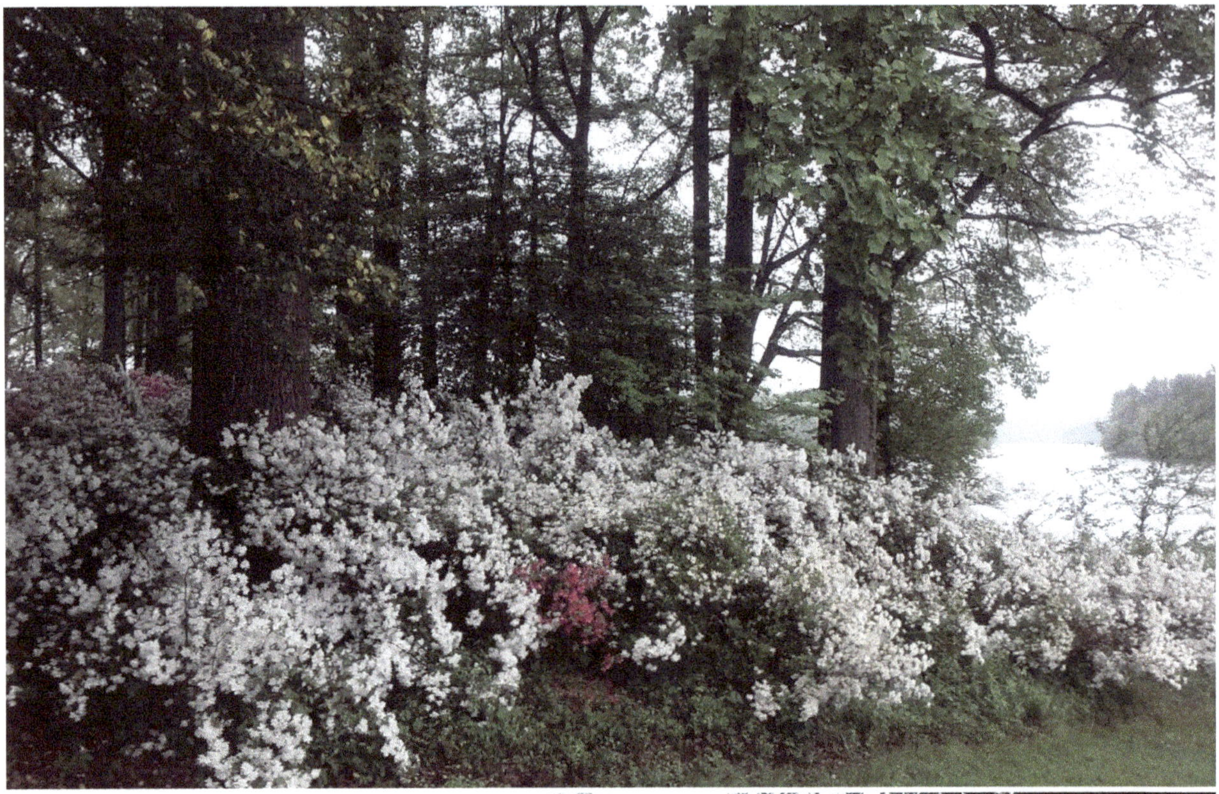

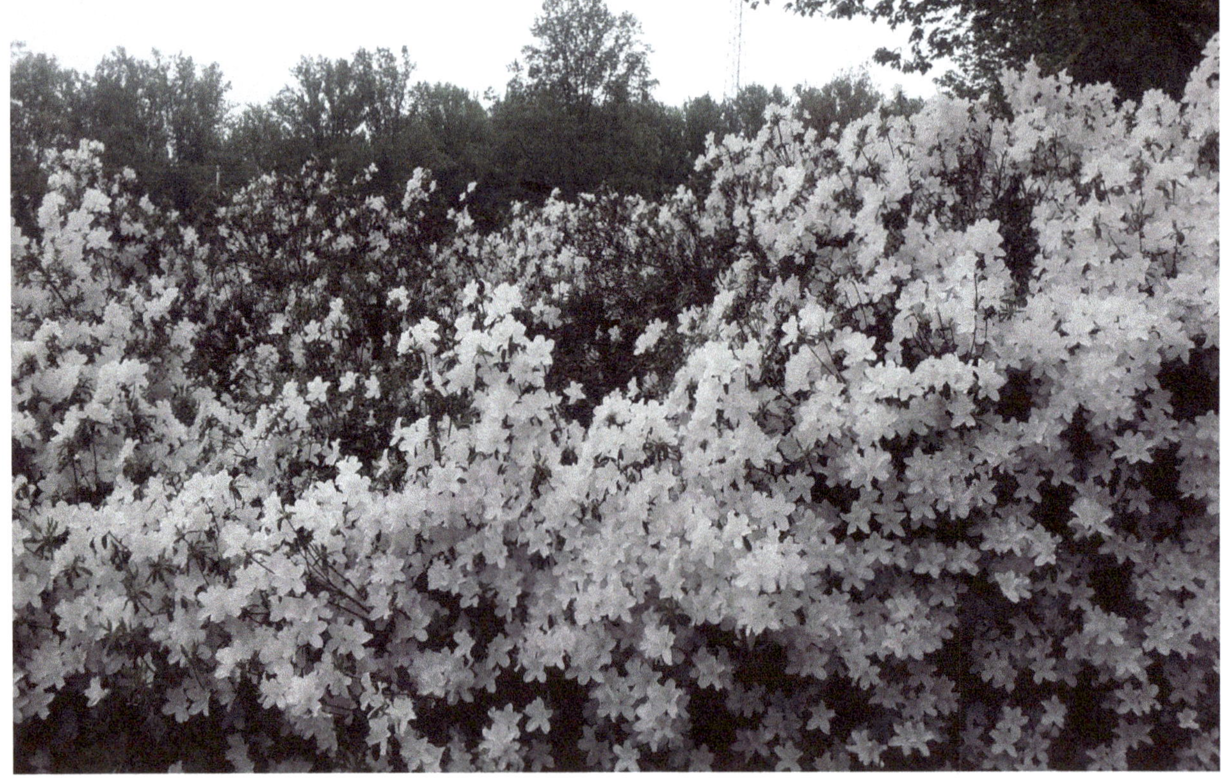

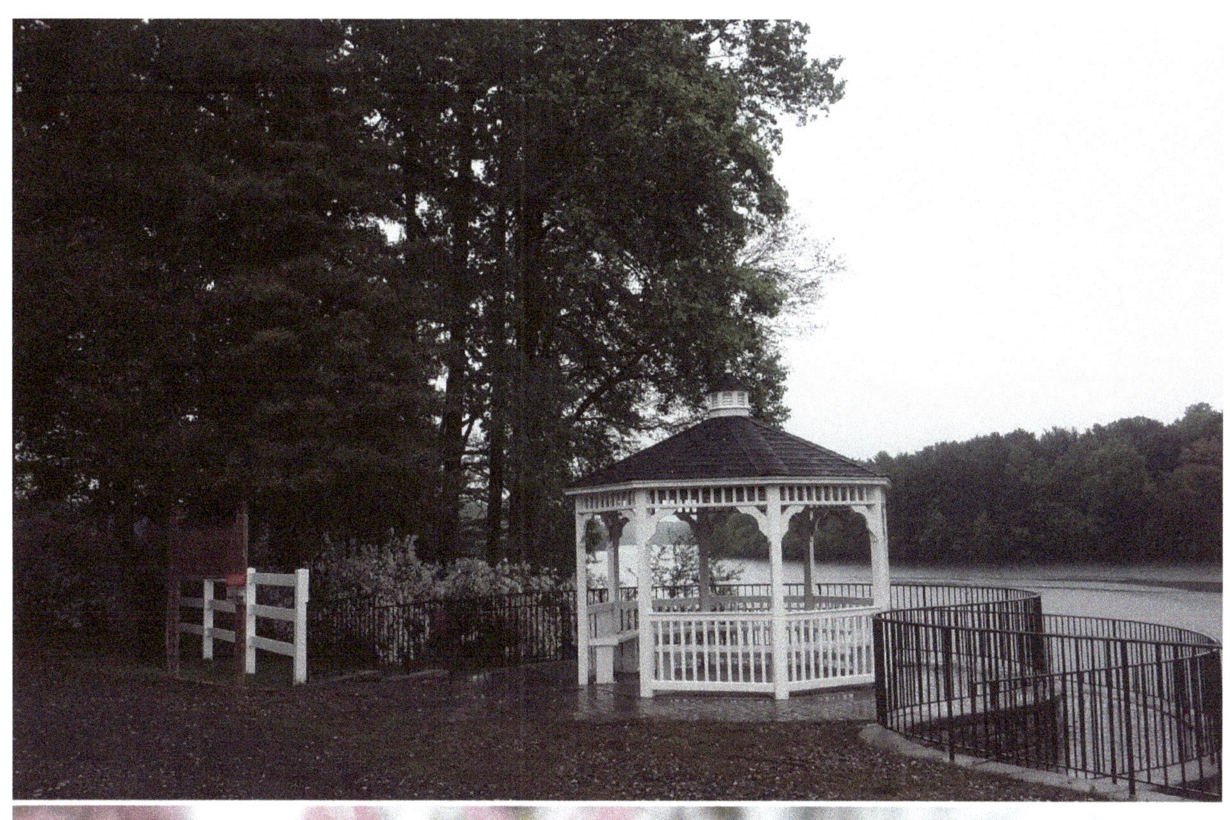

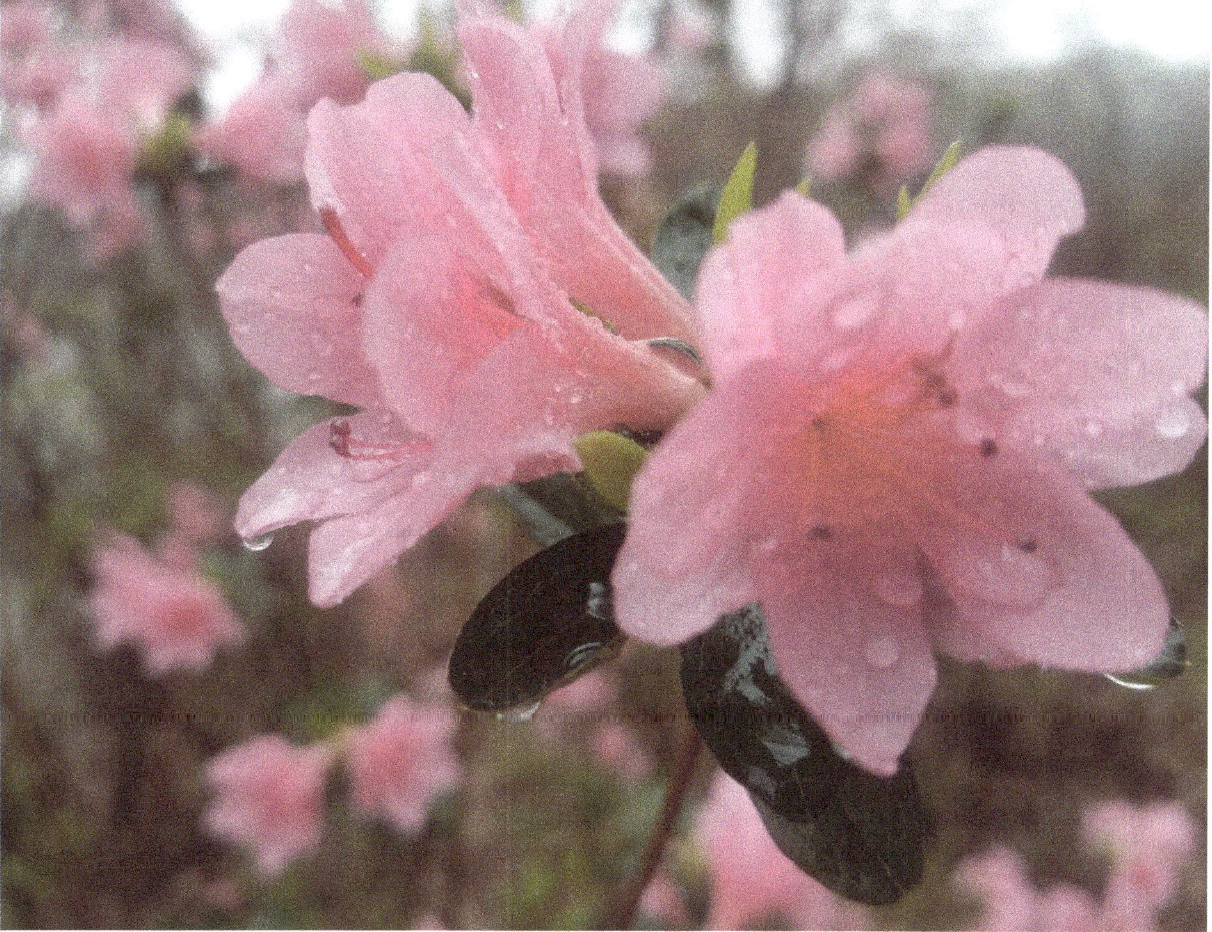

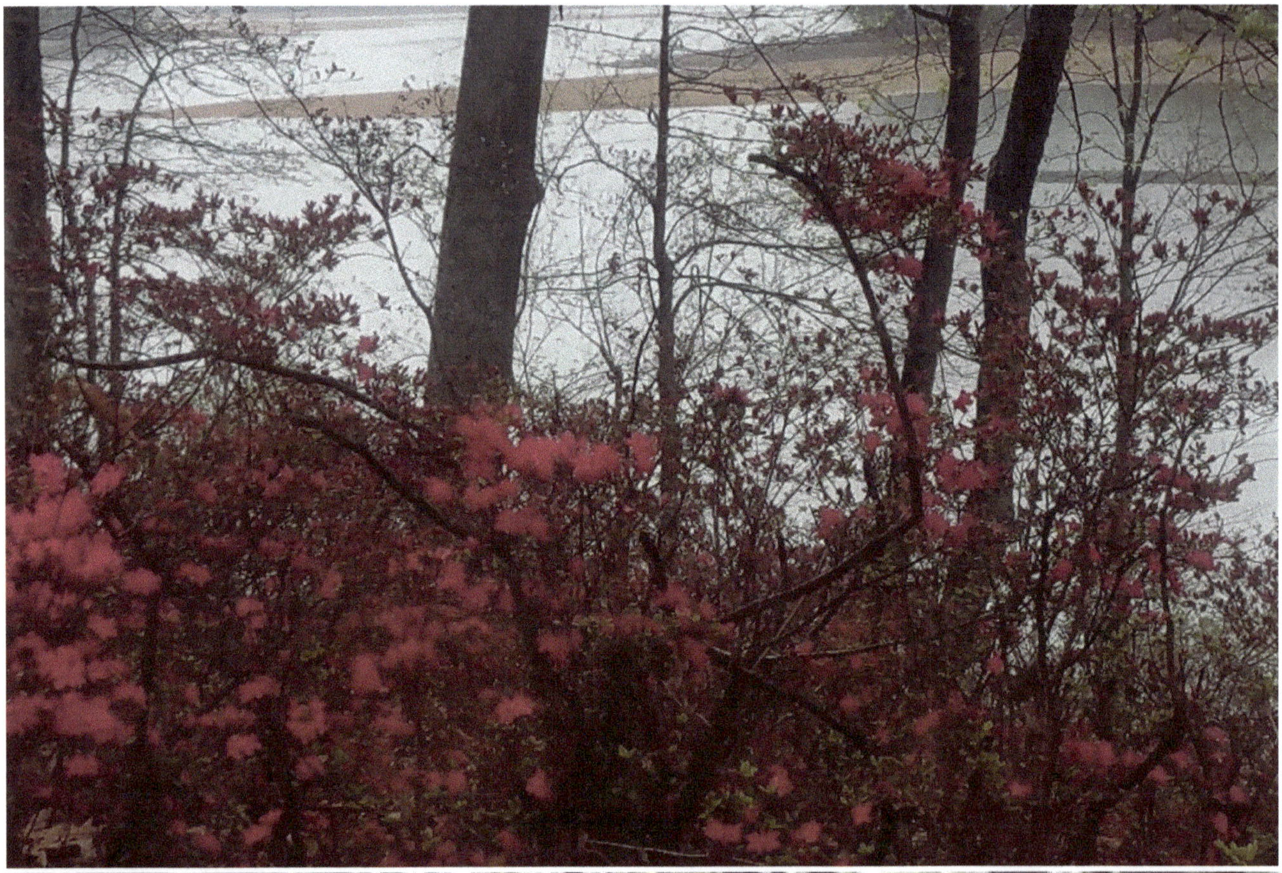

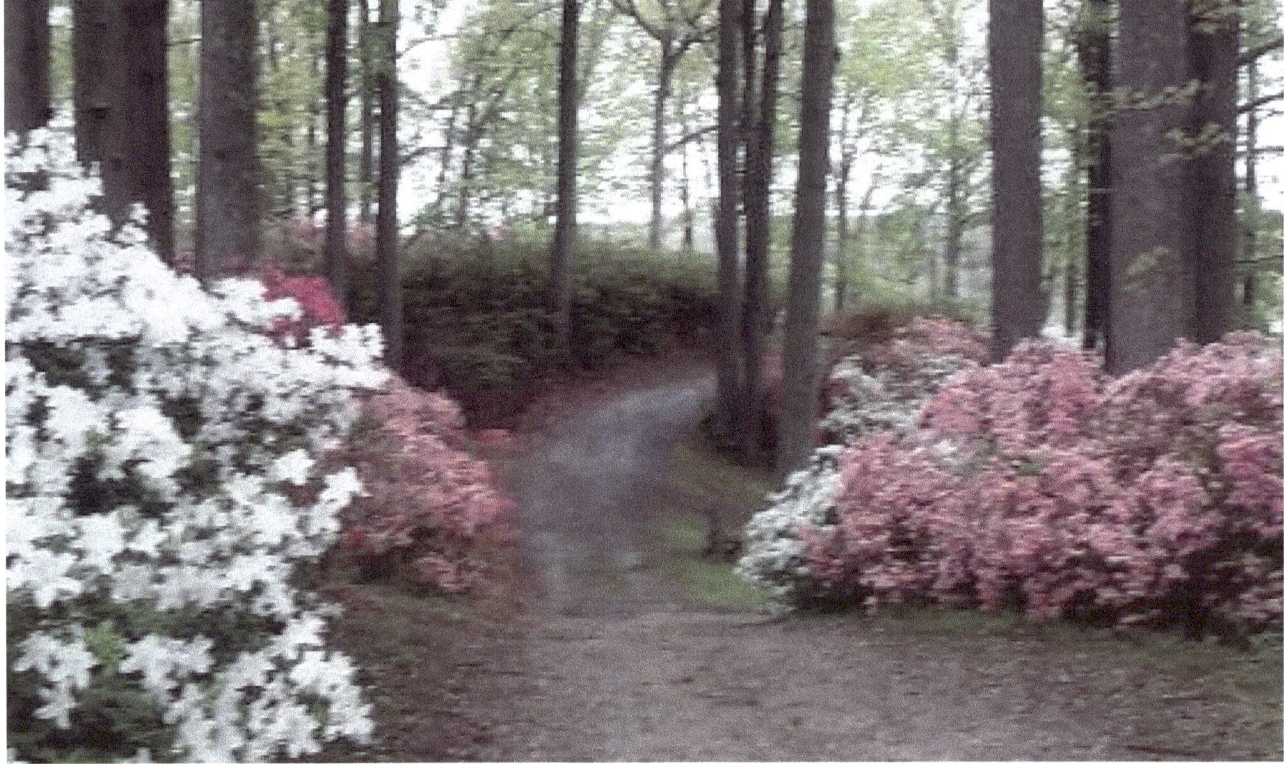

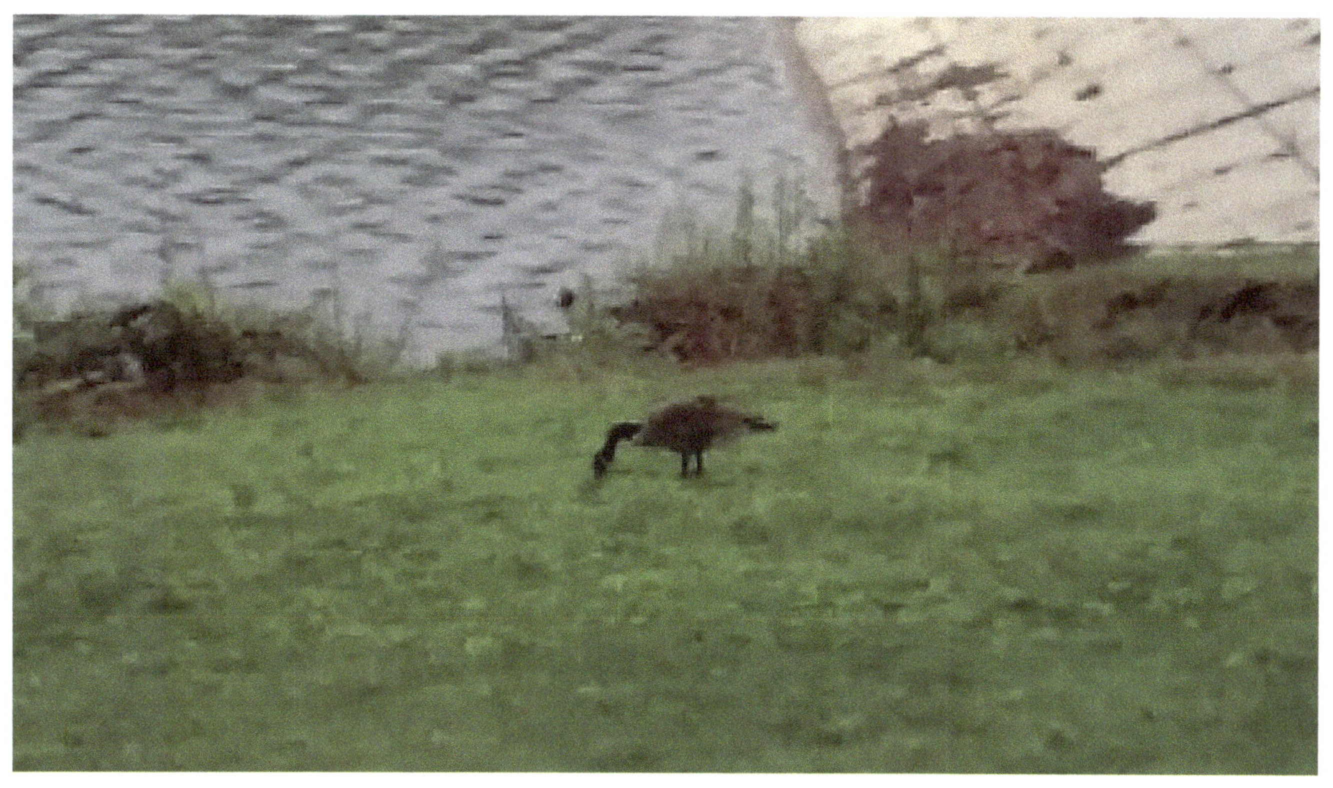

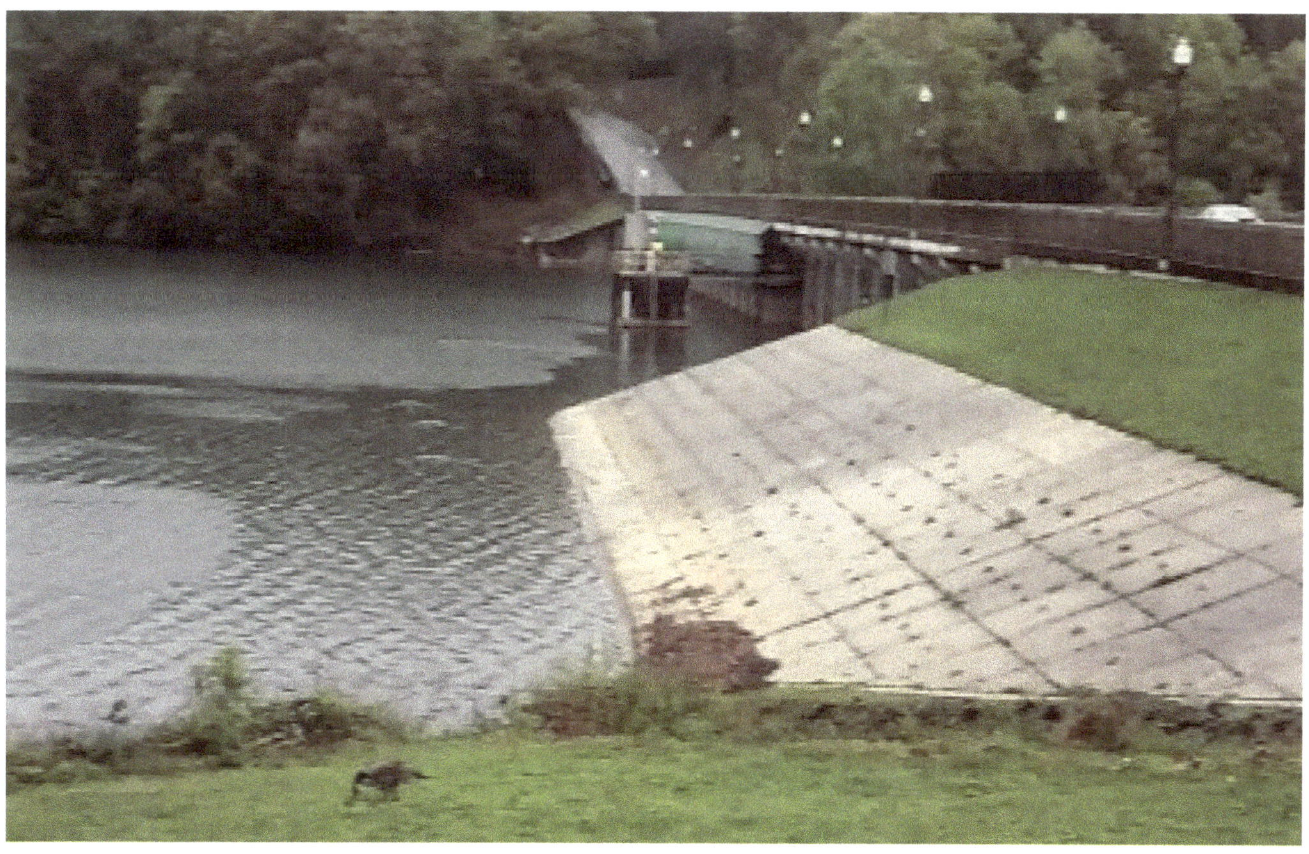

About the Photographer

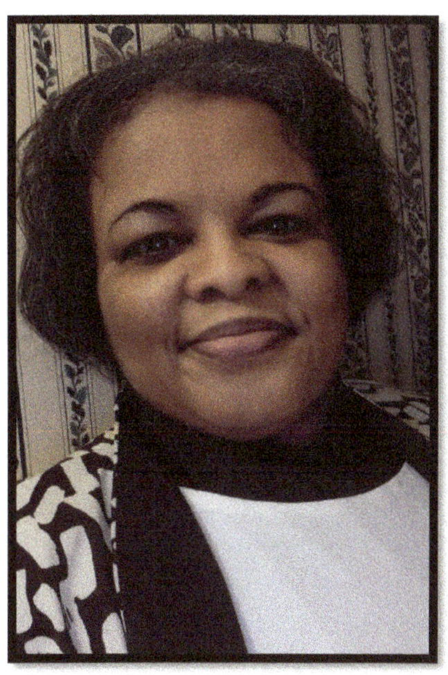

Wynette McKenzie has been an avid photographer since she was a young girl. She studied photography in New York City and in Maryland while pursuing her higher education degree. She has taken countless photographs in her brilliant lifetime.

www.ingramcontent.com/pod-product-compliance
Lightning Source LLC
Chambersburg PA
CBHW041033050726
47599CB00018B/1946